Business Process Management

Andreas Gadatsch

Business Process Management

Analysis, Modeling, Optimization, and Controlling of Processes

Second Edition 2025

 Springer Vieweg

Andreas Gadatsch
FB Wirtschaftswissenschaften Hochschule
Bonn-Rhein-Sieg
Sankt Augustin, Nordrhein-Westfalen,
Germany

ISBN 978-3-658-49338-7   ISBN 978-3-658-49339-4   (eBook)
https://doi.org/10.1007/978-3-658-49339-4

Preface to the 1st Edition

This textbook was first published in 2001. It is among the first textbooks to address the then-emerging topic of "business process management." It was conceived as a "bridge" between business-administrative and organizational methods (in particular, process visualization and analysis) and their digital implementation (especially ERP systems and workflow management). This concept remains relevant today, although the range and depth of methods and tools have since increased.

In addition to methodological foundations for process documentation and analysis, the book offers numerous practical examples and exercises, as well as a continuous small case study at the end that explains the "process life cycle," particularly for students. While the book cannot replace hands-on experience, it is also widely used by practitioners, as evidenced by the many emails the author has received.

The eleventh edition has been improved in several areas, not least based on feedback provided to the author, and adapted to the requirements of digital transformation. A related trend is the increased use of data science methods in process management. Of particular importance are recent research efforts that have been integrated under the heading of "exploratory process management." The chapter on process modeling has been thoroughly updated and now includes more recent methods such as the Business Model Canvas. The use of artificial intelligence is playing an increasingly significant role in process management, which is why these aspects are also addressed. At the request of the student readership, sample solutions have been added to the review questions and exercises.

The quick test at the beginning of the book can be used by readers to conduct an initial analysis of their own situation. The corresponding file can be requested from the author. This also applies, of course, to the figures. An email to andreas.gadatsch@h-brs.de is sufficient.

Even after so many years, a completely error-free book is unlikely. The author is grateful for any corrections and constructive suggestions for improvement.

Sankt Augustin, March 2025   Andreas Gadatsch

Contents

List of Figures

List of Tables

Introduction to Business Process Management

1

Process management is transforming the world of work

Abstract

This introductory chapter first explains the concept and historical development of business process management. It then defines and distinguishes several fundamental terms such as "function," "business process," "process," "end-to-end process," and "workflow." The chapter concludes with review questions and an exercise.

1.1 Definition of Terms

Why do we actually need business process management? This question is not only asked by business administration students, but also by experienced practitioners. If you follow the discussion in practice, the question often arises: "Process management—why do we need it?"

A look at history provides some insight. Since the early 19th century, the world of work has been shaped by the preceding industrial revolution and characterized by a high degree of division of labor. An important role in this was played by so-called *Taylorism*, named after the American Frederick W. Taylor. Complex tasks were broken down into simple, repeatable activities, thereby increasing efficiency. Employees were trained and specialized for their specific individual tasks.

Business process management (BPM), or simply *process management*, was developed in the early 1990s, among other things, to address the negative consequences of division of labor and poor coordination.

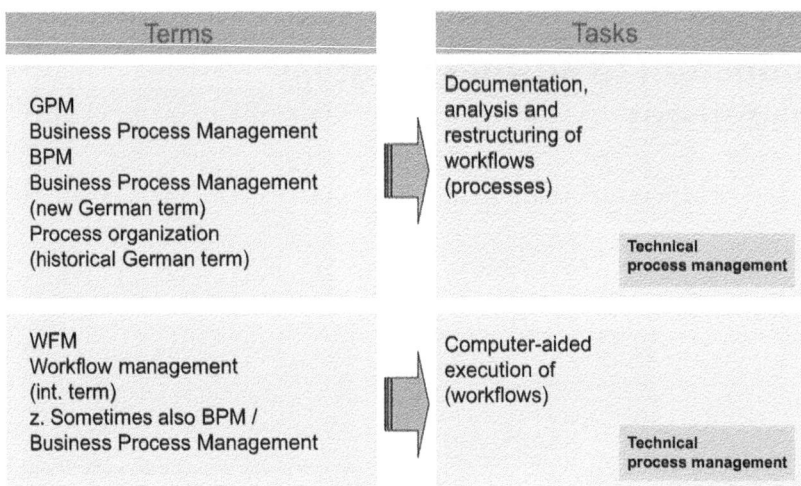

Fig. 1.1 Definition of terms in process management

Business process management deals with the documentation, analysis, and restructuring of workflows (processes). In German-language literature, the term "Ablauforganisation" (workflow organization) was commonly used for a long time. The documentation of processes is also referred to as "business process modeling." Internationally, the term "Business Process Management (BPM)" is standard.

It is important to distinguish this from the term "workflow management (WFM)," which refers to the computer-supported execution of workflows (so-called "workflows"). This is also known as "technical workflow modeling." In international usage, the terms "business process management" and "workflow management" are often not differentiated, and both are usually referred to as "Business Process Management (BPM)." Figure 1.1 provides an overview of these terms.

1.2   Historical Development

The development of process management can be roughly divided into four phases (see Table 1.1).

I. Phase: Division of Labor (Taylorism)
The early phase of process management began with Taylorism, named after Frederick Winslow Taylor (1856–1915). He consistently separated planning and execution activities and broke work down into manageable units.

This organizational structure became established in many companies in the 19th century and assigned a central role to departments (see Sua-Ngam-Iam and Kühl 2021, p. 46). In this phase, according to the prevailing business administration paradigm,

Table 1.1 Development phases of process management

I. Phase	From 1900	Division of labor into functions (Taylorism)
II. Phase	Approx. 1970–1980	Sequencing of functions (action-oriented data processing)
III. Phase	Approx. 1990 to 2015	Process orientation: creation of processes as overarching structural elements (exploitative process management)
IV. Phase	After 2015	Digitalization: processes become digital, development of innovations and new business models (explorative process management)

organizational structure (the structure of a company) and workflow organization (the sequence of activities) were considered separately.

This was first clearly articulated in the literature in the works of Nordsiek and Hennig around 1930 (Gaitanides 2007, p. 7). The thesis published by Nordsiek in 1931 is considered one of the first works in Germany to explicitly address business process modeling (Mendling 2021, p. 1).

The organizational structure defines the disciplinary hierarchy (who reports to whom?) and assigns tasks (who is responsible for which subtask?). This clarifies responsibility for sections of value creation (functions). The workflow organization serves to break down work into small individual steps and ultimately to assign them to elements of the organizational structure, i.e., divisions, departments, groups, and individuals. The advantage of this organizational concept, which made sense at the time, was that it supported industrial mass production through the efficient use of resources (machines, employees, etc.).

However, a disadvantage was the fragmentation of the entire workflow into many segments (functions). Individuals had no view of the entire process, only of their own area of responsibility. This led to a narrow perspective and ultimately little interest in what happened before or after their own activity. In extreme cases, the results of one department's work were simply "thrown over the fence" to the next department, without checking whether the results were needed (see Sua-Ngam-Iam and Kühl 2021, p. 47). This laid the foundation for a long period of departmental thinking and individualism, which continue to hinder collaboration in companies to this day.

II. Phase: Action-Oriented Data Processing (Precursor to Process Management)

It was only with the further development of "Electronic Data Processing (EDP)" that, after many decades, movement returned to the traditional organizational separation of workflows and organizational structure.

In the 1980s, the concept of action-oriented data processing (AODP) was developed as a precursor to process management, aiming to better leverage the capabilities of EDP for controlling collaborative workflows (see Berthold 1983 and Hofmann 1988). The core idea was to control processes at the level of elementary work steps (see Berthold 1983, p. 20).

This was achieved through databases jointly used by the individual EDP components. So-called "action databases" contained information from application programs (e.g., minimum stock level for item no. 4711 has fallen below 10 units) and forwarded this to the respective processor in the form of action messages (e.g., message to dispatcher: "Initiate procurement order for item no. 4711"). Messages were delivered to employees via rudimentary electronic mail systems. The action database functioned as an inbox for the employee, who could view and process the workload and its priorities stored there. Trigger databases also received structured information from programs (events) and, in turn, forwarded these to programs, thereby initiating program runs. A trigger describes an action to be performed and the event that triggers the action (see Scheer 1994, p. 72).

The objectives of AODP were to shorten processing times for work objects, reduce paperwork, and improve resource utilization. In the following years, AODP was successfully implemented in large companies for procurement, customer order management, master data, and bill of materials management (see Berthold 1983, p. 25). Both employee acceptance of the concept and the degree of goal achievement were positive. Nevertheless, the concept did not prevail, as the performance of information technology at the time was insufficient for handling larger data volumes. The underlying idea was only later successfully realized as "workflow management" (see Mertens 2006, p. 28).

III. Phase: Process Orientation (Exploitative Process Management)

At the beginning of the 1990s, a "process management wave" swept through corporate practice, triggered by numerous publications from renowned researchers and practitioners. Well-known names included, in the USA, the authors Hammer and Champy (see Hammer 1990 and Hammer and Champy 1994), in Germany, Scheer (see Scheer 1990), and in Switzerland, Österle (see Österle 1995). They sparked intense debate, as the core ideas of these concepts were contrary to prevailing corporate practices at the time. In particular, they called for the reintegration of disconnected functions into an overarching end-to-end process, as well as the separation of process responsibility from organizational structure. In addition, there was intensive use of the now significantly more powerful information technology as an "integration tool." Many executives and managing directors used the new technologies to break up entrenched structures within companies and "forced" organizational change by deploying process-oriented application software. The business standard software system "SAP R/2" and later its successor "SAP R/3" from SAP AG, Walldorf, particularly benefited from this development worldwide. Until then, the modeling (structured description) of processes had received little methodological support, but was now facilitated by comprehensive, scientifically grounded concepts such as the "Architecture of Integrated Information Systems (ARIS)" by Scheer (see Scheer 1991) and the first generations of powerful modeling tools for personal computers (e.g., "ARIS Toolset" from IDS Scheer, Saarbrücken, or "Bonapart" from UBIS GmbH, Berlin), which had previously been developed as prototypes at German chairs of business informatics (ARIS Toolset at Prof. Scheer, Saarbrücken; Bonapart at Prof. Krallmann, Berlin). Since the focus of this phase was primarily on improving existing business models and their processes, recent research literature also refers to this as "exploitative business process management" (see, e.g., Gross et al. 2019 or Grisold et al. 2019).

IV. Phase: Digitalization (Explorative Process Management)

From around 2015, the beginning of the "digitalization wave" can be observed. "Information technology" is being elevated and is now regarded as an enabler of "digitalization" (see Winkelhake 2021). New concepts in information management such as *cloud computing, big data, and Industry 4.0* are influencing process management in various ways. This has led to the emergence of the term "explorative process management," which is characterized by the forward-looking development of new business models and the search for and implementation of innovations (see Griesold et al. 2021).

In addition to organizational coordination (who does what?), technical coordination is now added (which processes are supported by which "apps"?). Application areas for cloud computing include, for example, the modeling and execution of processes, which had previously been carried out primarily with internally operated software. Typical application areas for big data include real-time analysis of machine data with interventions in the maintenance process in case of irregularities, or "active buyer management" through real-time analysis of sales and prediction of current customer behavior ("We know what the customer will buy tomorrow"). New business models based on big data technologies are increasingly leading to previously unachievable, digitized business processes (see Gadatsch 2014). In academia, the relationship between digitalization and process management was only studied more intensively around 2019 and 2020 (see the comprehensive study by Allweyer 2020).

1.3   Classification of Selected Topics and Methods

Process management has now become a multifaceted term that is interpreted in various ways. Due to numerous publications and practical experiences, different perspectives and variants have emerged. Before delving into individual aspects in detail, an attempt will first be made to broadly classify the key topics and associated methods of process management. The explanation of the terms will follow in subsequent chapters.

Figure 1.2 illustrates three possible levels of process management: strategic, business, and technical process management.

Strategic Process Management

Strategic process management can also be referred to as business model management. It encompasses the analysis and design of business models and their structures. Business models form the foundation of a company or organization; they describe the corporate

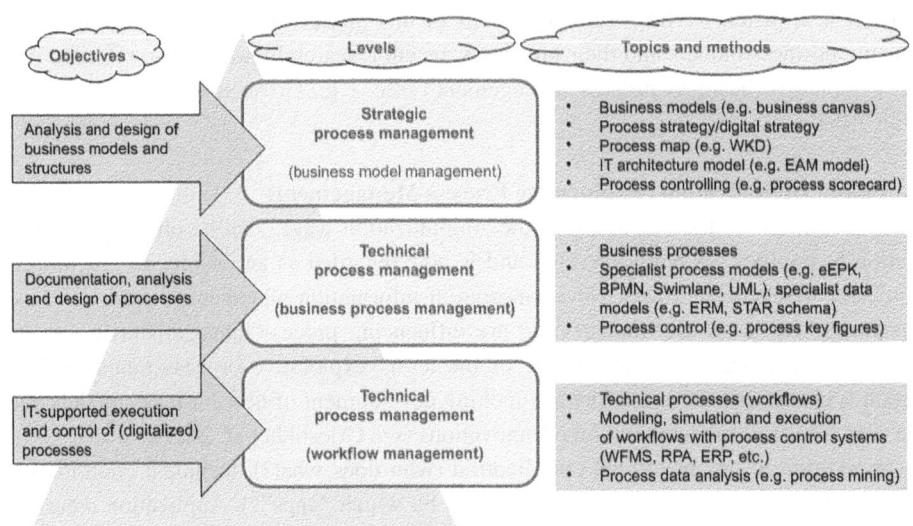

Fig. 1.2 Overview of selected topics and methods

purpose, pricing and sales policy, marketing model, and the manner in which value is created (see Reinhart 2017, pp. 7–8). Business models can be described using the Business Canvas method (see Hansen et al. 2018).

In addition, decisions regarding the fundamental structure of processes are required, which are defined in the process strategy. The process strategy is increasingly formulated as a digital strategy, since manual processes are becoming largely irrelevant. Typical methods of strategic process management include the process map (or value chain diagrams), IT architecture models (e.g., Enterprise Architecture Management/EAM), as well as the Process Scorecard for process controlling.

Business Process Management

Business process management, also referred to as operational process management, focuses from a business perspective on the documentation, analysis, and design of processes. For this purpose, business process models are created using specialized modeling languages (e.g., eEPK, BPMN, Swimlane, or UML). Depending on the level of detail, data models may also be developed, for example using the Entity-Relationship Model (ERM) for ERP systems or the STAR schema for data warehouse systems. Key performance indicators are typically used for operational process control.

Technical Process Management

The first two levels in Fig. 1.2 pertain to the business perspective on processes. Technical process management is responsible for implementing IT support for the execution and control of processes. It is also referred to as workflow management, as workflows represent executable digital processes. At this level, detailed technical modeling, simulation, and execution of workflows are carried out using process control systems (workflow management systems/WFMS, enterprise resource planning systems/ERP, and robotic process automation systems/RPA). The analysis of actually executed processes is performed using process mining tools, which identify the real process flow from the systems' log data.

When considering practical implementation options, it becomes apparent that the objectives, content, and methods of process management can take on many different forms. Possible differences can be found in the organizational level (strategic, business, technical), the time focus (future, present, past), the scope of impact (central, local, fragmented), the area of activity (design, analysis, control, or implementation), and the organizational structure (line, staff, matrix, pure process organization). The morphological box in Fig. 1.3 can be used to visualize the possible "process management variants."

The illustration in Figure 1.3 highlights two variants that are quite typical in corporate practice. The first variant (blue line), "Company-wide process management with networking across all divisions," focuses on the future orientation of a corporation or large enterprise and addresses strategic/design-related issues. It is often found within a matrix organization (see blue line), where process management serves as an additional leadership role alongside the traditional line organization.

We will discuss this in detail later (see Chap. 3). The second common variant (see green line) is a "Decentralized optimization project with a limited scope." These are pro-

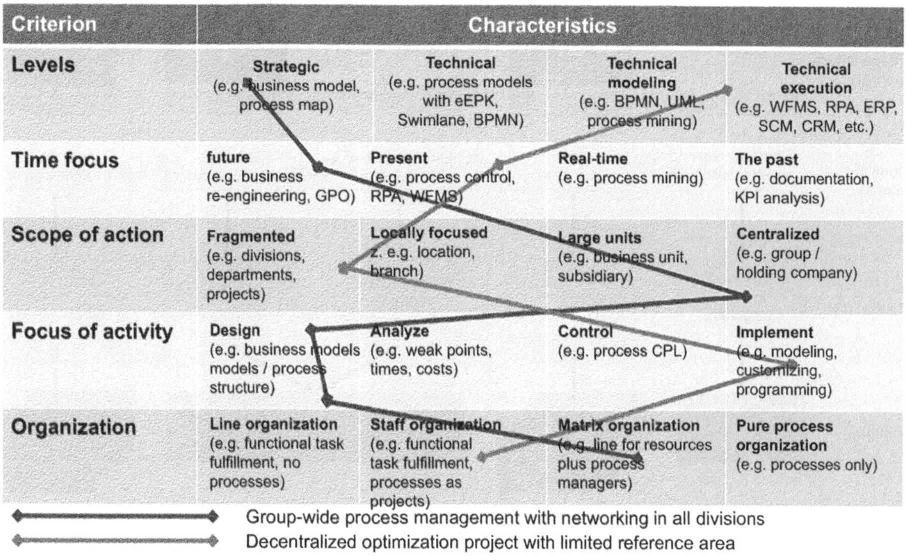

Criterion	Characteristics			
Levels	Strategic (e.g. business model, process map)	Technical (e.g. process models with eEPK, Swimlane, BPMN)	Technical modeling (e.g. BPMN, UML, process mining)	Technical execution (e.g. WFMS, RPA, ERP, SCM, CRM, etc.)
Time focus	future (e.g. business re-engineering, GPO)	Present (e.g. process control, RPA, WFMS)	Real-time (e.g. process mining)	The past (e.g. documentation, KPI analysis)
Scope of action	Fragmented (e.g. divisions, departments, projects)	Locally focused z. e.g. location, branch)	Large units (e.g. business unit, subsidiary)	Centralized (e.g. group / holding company)
Focus of activity	Design (e.g. business models / process structure)	Analyze (e.g. weak points, times, costs)	Control (e.g. process CPL)	Implement (e.g. modeling, customizing, programming)
Organization	Line organization (e.g. functional task fulfillment, no processes)	Staff organization (e.g. functional task fulfillment, processes as projects)	Matrix organization (e.g. line for resources plus process managers)	Pure process organization (e.g. processes only)

◆——————————◆ Group-wide process management with networking in all divisions
◆——————————◆ Decentralized optimization project with limited reference area

Fig. 1.3 Process management variants—Morphological box

jects that are often carried out to implement tools for a specific area of the company. They are frequently initiated and driven by staff units.

1.4 Processes

1.4.1 Characteristics

Fundamental Characteristics

Numerous definitions and synonyms for the term "business process," or simply "process," have now been published, such as enterprise process, value creation process, core process, key process, main process, process chain, organizational process, among others (see Schmelzer and Sesselmann 2013, p. 55).

To begin with, the following key characteristics of a process can be identified: A process supports a business-related objective aligned with the strategy of the company or organization, consists of several individual steps, occurs regularly, is often carried out collaboratively by multiple people, departments, divisions, or even companies, generally requires support from one or more software systems and, if necessary, additional resources (e.g., telephone, copier, transport vehicle, machines, equipment), processes information (input), and leads to a result (output) desired by the company. The overall context of processes and their collaborative nature is illustrated in Fig. 1.4.

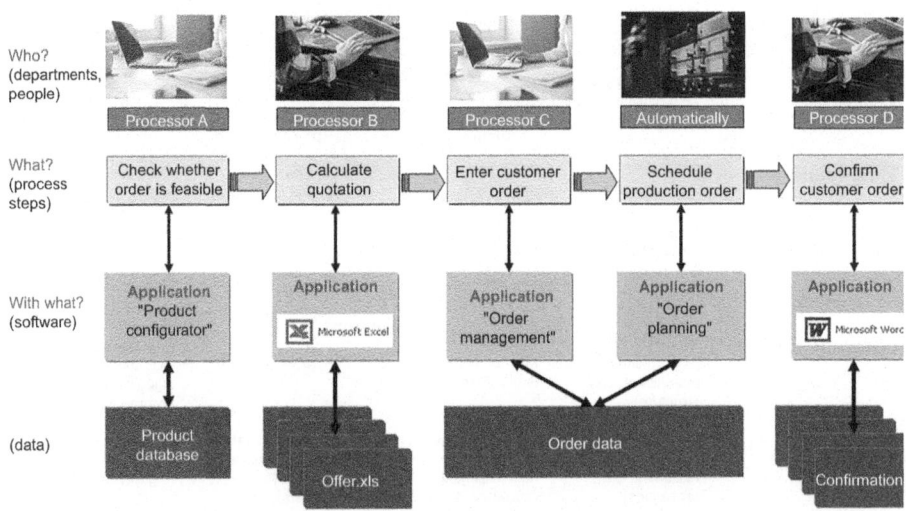

Fig. 1.4 Division of labor in processes—Schematic representation

Typical Processes

The variety of processes in practice is vast. Typical processes include:

- Handling customer inquiries and preparing quotations in an industrial company,
- Creating a production plan in an engine factory,
- Examining and treating patients in a medical practice,
- Conducting courses and examinations at universities,
- Producing baked goods in a bakery,
- Preparing the annual profit and loss statement as well as the balance sheet (annual financial statement),
- Purchasing, storing, and selling goods in a supermarket.

A process differs from a one-time project in that it is repeated multiple times. For example, the implementation of a logistics system for a company or the celebration of a company's 50th anniversary are projects, not processes.

1.4.2   Process Definitions

Hilmer has presented an extensive scientific study on the systematization of the process concept and identified 75 characteristics of processes (see Hilmer 2016, p. 267). He analyzed 101 sources for this purpose (see Hilmer 2016, pp. 268 ff.), indicating a lively academic discussion. The definitions selected here, without claiming to be exhaustive, provide insight into the years-long debate surrounding the concept of business processes.

Business Process according to Hammer and Champy

Hammer and Champy define the *business process* as a set of activities that require one or more different inputs and produce an outcome of value for the customer (Hammer and Champy 1994). As an example, they cite the development of a new product. A business process is managed by a process owner, who should be a member of the senior management team.

Business Process according to Scheer and Jost

Scheer and Jost understand a *business process* as the model-based description of the functions to be performed in a company, including their content-related and temporal dependencies (see Scheer and Jost 1996). Functions are understood as individual tasks and activities that are linked by triggering or resulting events. Scheer equates the term business process with the terms process chain and operation chain (see Scheer 1990), thereby emphasizing the cross-functional nature of the business process, which spans multiple functional steps.

Business Process according to Österle

According to Österle, a *business process* is a sequence of tasks that may be distributed across several organizational units and whose execution is supported by information technology applications (see Österle 1995). A process is both a producer and consumer of services and pursues objectives set by process management. As a specific form of workflow organization, the business process concretizes the business strategy and links it to the information system. Therefore, the business process can be seen as a link between corporate strategy and system development or the supporting information systems.

Berkau

The engineering sciences began formalizing processes and systematically documenting them many years earlier, in order to ensure consistent quality in repetitive tasks performed by different individuals.

Processes can therefore be divided into technical processes and business (commercial) processes (see Fig. 1.5) (see Berkau 2020, p. 27). Technical processes (e.g., milling a cylinder head, assembling an engine) are formally described by bills of materials and work plans (discrete manufacturing) or recipes (process manufacturing). Business processes refer to commercial activities, such as processing customer orders or hiring an employee. They are documented using flowcharts or business process models and are colloquially referred to as "office processes."

For the following discussion, the definition of business process according to Gehring (1998) will be used as a basis:

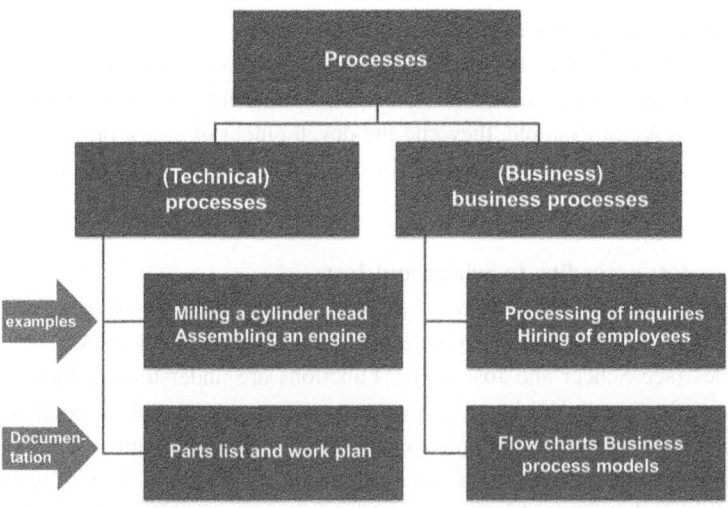

Fig. 1.5 Process variants according to Berkau (2020)

Gehring

A business process is a goal-oriented, temporally and logically ordered sequence of tasks that can be performed collaboratively by several organizations or organizational units using information and communication technologies. It serves to deliver services in accordance with predefined process objectives derived from corporate strategy. A business process can be formally described at different levels of detail and from multiple perspectives. The maximum level of detail is reached when the specified tasks can each be performed in one go by an employee without changing their workstation (see Gehring 1998).

1.4.3 Process Hierarchization

Processes can be considered at different levels of abstraction. Especially in very large companies, it is important to identify these levels and use them for further work. The hierarchization of business processes is carried out step by step according to the "top-down principle." Figure 1.6 illustrates the principle of hierarchization, starting from the business process, through business process steps, down to elementary business process steps that do not require a change of operator to complete the task (see Fig. 1.6).

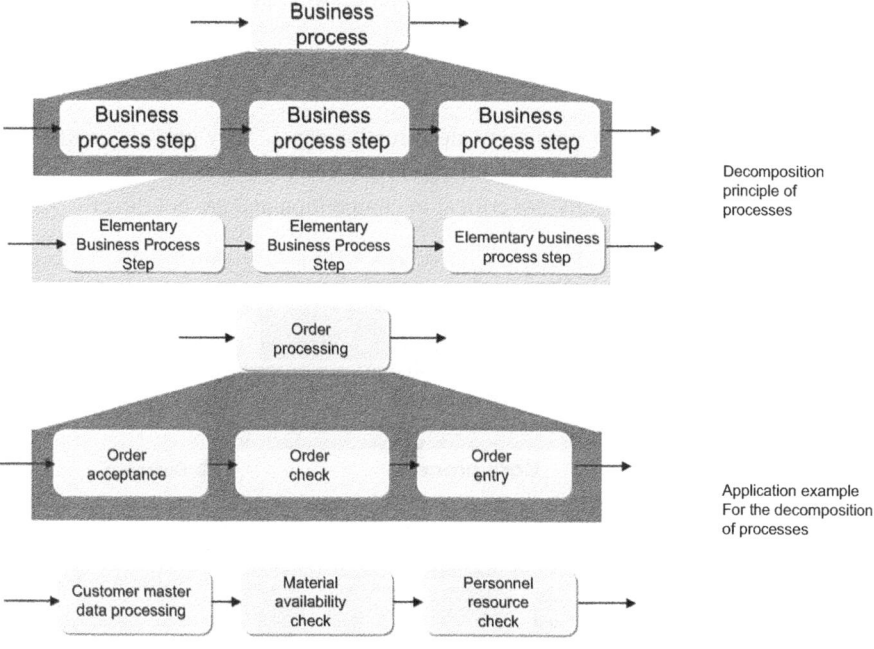

Fig. 1.6 Process hierarchization

1.4.4   Categories of Processes

An important way to categorize business processes is by distinguishing them based
on their proximity to a company's core business (see, e.g., Seidlmeier 2002, pp. 2 f.).
According to this approach, processes can be differentiated into "management processes" (also referred to as "governance processes"), "core processes" (also "primary
processes"), and "support processes" (alternatively "cross-sectional processes") (see
Fig. 1.7).

Management Process
Management processes actively regulate the interaction of all business processes (e.g.,
strategy development, corporate planning). They provide the overarching framework for
value-creating and support processes, ensuring a goal-oriented structure.

The distinction from support processes (see below) is not always clear-cut. The central question, therefore, is whether a process influences the structure or even the existence of other processes.

Core Process
Core processes are business processes with a high value-creation share. They define the
essence of the company, are typically critical to competition, and represent the value-creation processes from the initial customer request to the delivery or service as perceived
by the customer. Typical examples include order processing, product development, production, distribution, and service.

Support Process
Support processes have little or no direct value-creation share. They provide cross-functional services for other processes, without which the company's value creation would
not be possible. They are generally not critical to competition and are not directly visible

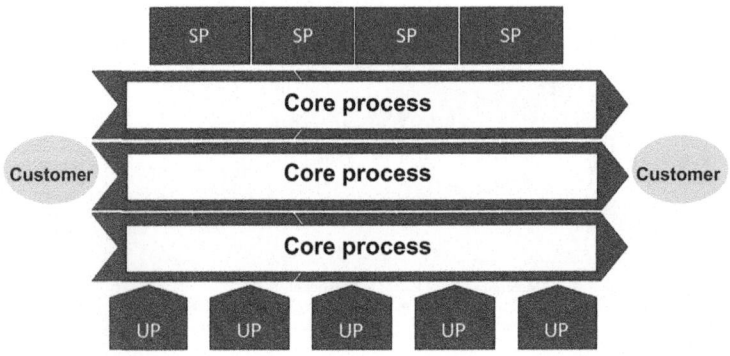

Fig. 1.7 Process categories

to the customer. Examples include financial accounting, cost accounting, reporting, or human resources management.

Figure 1.8 shows an example of process categorization for a fictional automotive business. At the top of the diagram, four management processes are depicted: strategy development, controlling, product planning, and personnel management. Below, the two core processes ("car purchase" and "service") are shown in detail, with the main business process steps presented sequentially. At the bottom, the support processes marketing, accounting, customer catering, information technology, and administration are listed. All support processes are not directly assigned to a single process, but are either generally effective for the entire company (e.g., information technology, administration) or for several processes (e.g., customer catering for "car purchase customers" and "service customers").

1.4.5 Documentation Relevance of Processes

Documentation Hierarchy
The introduction of process management in a company requires regulations to document and communicate the complex content involved. In practice, a process management manual or a modeling manual is often used, which contains important information for employees as well as external personnel.

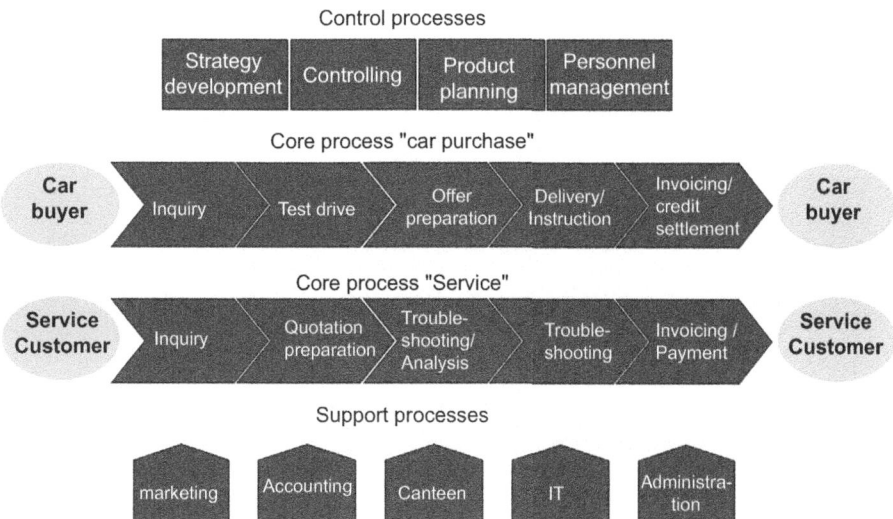

Fig. 1.8 Process categories in an automotive business

The typical regulations are illustrated in a documentation hierarchy in Fig. 1.9. The process management manual describes fundamental questions of process management, such as the role concept (e.g., process owners, modelers), the processes of process management (e.g., the procedure for process modeling and updating, implementation of optimization projects), and specific responsibilities within the company.

The modeling manual defines the modeling rules, describes the modeling methods and naming conventions to be used, in order to coordinate collaboration between different departments. In addition, it documents modeling examples and "best practices," i.e., the experiences of third parties.

The process documentation includes documents on the company's business model (Business Canvas), a process overview (process map), and, for the most important processes, detailed process models (event-driven process chains, Business Process Model and Notation, etc.).

There are also specific organizational supplements, such as work and inspection instructions, checklists and forms, as well as specifications for number ranges (e.g., for invoices, orders) or codes (e.g., country codes, location codes).

Documentation Relevance
Not all processes in a company need to be documented in the same level of detail. Especially in medium-sized and large companies, a prioritized selection must be made.

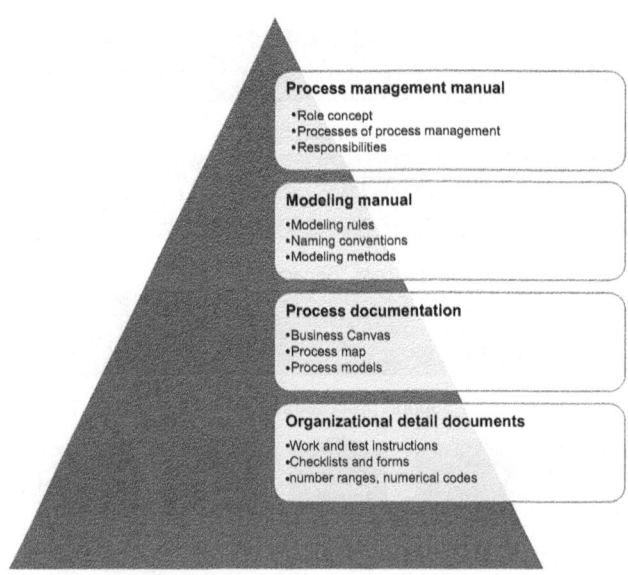

Fig. 1.9 Documentation hierarchy

Processes differ in terms of the variability of process requirements and the volume to be processed (see Fig. 1.10) and can be considered in varying levels of detail.

Many processes are based on strict rules that must be followed exactly, but vary in the volume to be processed. These include rule-based standard processes (e.g., preparation of the monthly balance sheet and profit and loss statement) and rule-based mass processes with high volumes (e.g., sales and shipping of products, handling of complaints or incidents). These processes must be documented in detail and also included in the process management manual. A variety of methods are available for documentation, which are described in detail in this book (e.g., process map, EPC, BPMN). Creative processes (e.g., development of a business model) and agile processes (e.g., software development) have higher variability in process requirements and do not follow strict rules as closely. For these, it is not necessary to describe every step in detail, but rather to provide a sketch. Methods for this are also available and will be explained in this book (e.g., Business Model Canvas, value chains).

1.5   Workflows

1.5.1   Key Terms in Information Processing

The increasing digitalization is leading to more and more processes being executed with computer support. In this context, the term "workflow" plays a central role. Workflows

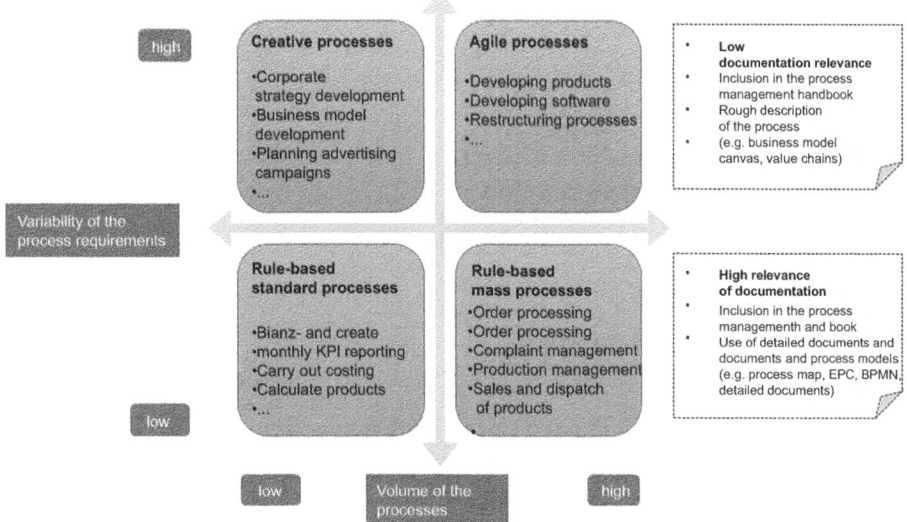

Fig. 1.10 Documentation relevance of processes

are processes that are controlled on the basis of models and algorithms. They therefore require at least partial automation of the process and its execution with the help of software systems.

Before examining the concept of workflow in more detail, some selected terms in the context of hardware, software, and business processes should be clarified (see Fig. 1.11). The lowest level of IT support consists of hardware (e.g., computers, printers) and other technical equipment (e.g., readers, scanners), which is referred to as the hardware system. Together with the software system, which consists of application software (e.g., email, accounting) and system software (e.g., operating system), the hardware system forms the "application system." If the application system is supplemented by organizational components (people and business processes), it is referred to as an "information system."

1.5.2   Workflow Definitions

The digitalization of processes is currently a topic of intense discussion. Workflows are business processes executed digitally and controlled by a software system based on rules. The first definitions of workflows date back quite some time:

- Galler and Scheer view the workflow as a technical refinement of the business process (see Galler and Scheer 1995). The degree of refinement is determined by the potential for automation. The workflow must be usable as input and as a set of rules for control by a software system specialized in process management (workflow management system).

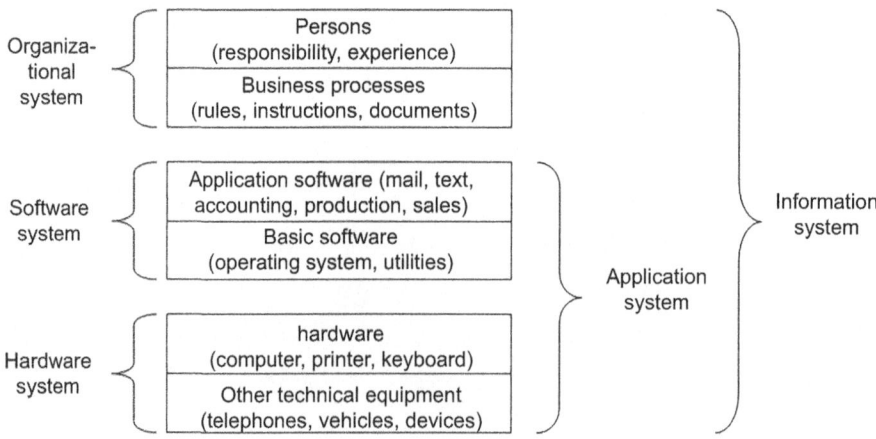

Fig. 1.11   Key IT terms (cf. Herzwurm and Pietsch 2009, modified)

- Similarly, Österle (1995) describes the workflow as a refined business process. Starting from a process design at the macro level and its successive decomposition into subprocesses, the micro level is reached when tasks are specified in such detail that they can be implemented by process participants as work instructions. Based on the chain of tasks, a manager can control the workflow. The workflow thus represents the detailed form of the micro process. Instead of a manager, the computer now takes over process control.

1.5.3 Distinguishing Business Process and Workflow

Business processes and workflows both describe work procedures, but at different levels of detail. From a business perspective, business processes describe who performs which activity. The workflow is a refinement of the business process from an information technology perspective (see Fig. 1.12).

A clear distinction is not always possible due to the shared subject matter, and this often leads to the terms being used interchangeably, even though they pursue different objectives. There are, however, some key differences, which are summarized in Fig. 1.13:

Business Process The business process describes "what" needs to be done to implement the specified business strategy. The workflow describes "how" this is to be accomplished. The business process belongs to the professional-conceptual level, while the workflow is assigned to the operational level. The required level of detail for a business process is reached when it describes the work steps that can be performed by an employee in one go at a workstation. Thus, the business process is a business management concept.

Workflow The workflow level is reached when the level of detail is such that the executing employee can understand it as a concrete work instruction, and the description

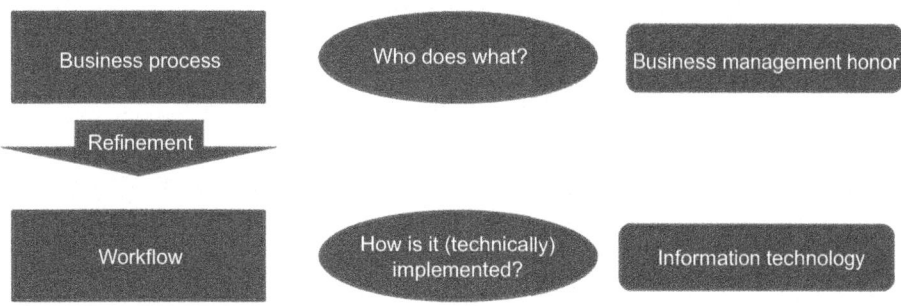

Fig. 1.12 Business Process and Workflow

	Business process	Workflow
Goal	Analysis and design of workflows in terms of given (strategic) goals	Specification of the technical execution of workflows
Design level	Conceptual level with connection to business strategy	Operational level with connection to supporting technology
Level of detail	Work steps that can be executed in one go by one employee at one workstation	Specification of work steps in terms of work procedures and human and technological resources

Fig. 1.13 Business Process versus Workflow

of software-controlled tasks is specified in such detail that they can be executed by an application system. A clear distinguishing feature is whether execution is carried out by a human task performer (employee) or a computer program. The workflow is therefore a more technical term with a strong connection to computer science.

▶ **Workflow Definition** A workflow is a formally described business process that is fully or partially automated. It includes the temporal, functional, and resource-related specifications required for the automatic control of the workflow at the operational level. The work steps to be initiated may be intended for execution by employees or by application programs. It is important to distinguish between the workflow as a type or schema of a partially or fully automated workflow and a workflow instance, which refers to a specific execution of the workflow (see Gehring 1998).

In a workflow, the computer controls the process
Current trends in digitalization are causing the distinction between business processes and workflows to become increasingly blurred, as hardly any processes can be imagined without the support of software systems, and active process control by computers is rapidly increasing. In a workflow, the computer controls the sequence of activities, whereas in a business process, control is exercised by humans.

1.5.4 Workflow Types

Workflows can be distinguished based on the degree of structure in the underlying processes and the level of computer support provided for those processes.

Workflows by Process Structurability

The **general workflow**, also referred to as a production or transaction workflow, involves well-structured work procedures within organizations, such as travel expense accounting. General workflows are characterized by their repetitive nature and by work steps that can be defined in detail in advance. They can be highly automated or supported by information processing systems.

The **case-based workflow**, also known as a flexible workflow, describes work procedures that cannot be fully standardized. An example is the processing of loan applications in banks. The transition from case-based to general workflow is gradual. Compared to general workflows, case-based workflows offer greater flexibility for users. Individual steps can be skipped or modified (e.g., omitting certain verification steps during loan processing or skipping an assessment center when hiring an employee).

Ad hoc workflows are unstructured process steps whose sequence cannot be determined in advance. In ad hoc workflows, the user of a workflow instance independently selects the next person responsible (Scheer 1998, p. 90). Ad hoc workflows cannot be modeled (e.g., a working group developing an advertising campaign). Another example is the processing of investment applications in large corporations. This is often only roughly pre-structured, for example with respect to signature regulations, and allows a high degree of freedom regarding participants and process flow. Depending on the type of investment, different contacts and preparatory work may be required before the application is approved.

Workflows by Degree of Computer Support

Workflows can be classified according to the degree of computer support. The **manual workflow** is carried out entirely by a human operator (e.g., checking the responsibility for an incoming inquiry). In this case, only process flow control is possible, i.e., verifying whether all steps have been completed in the correct order. The **semi-automated workflow** is performed by a human operator with the support of an information processing program (e.g., entering master data for a new customer). The **automated workflow** is executed by a program without human intervention (e.g., printing an invoice after delivery has been completed). In semi-automated and automated workflows, both process flow control and execution control are possible, meaning it can be ensured, for example, that a specific transaction has actually been carried out.

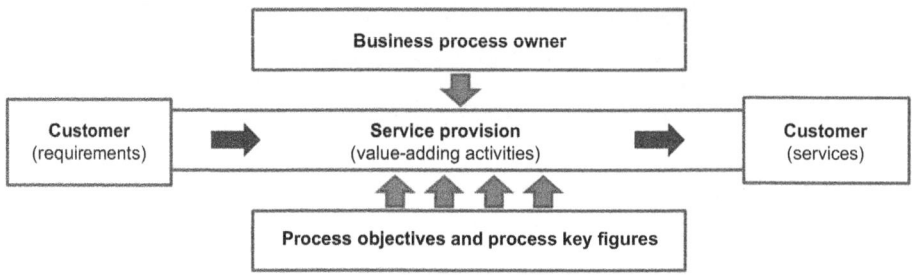

Fig. 1.14 Diagram of an end-to-end process (Schmelzer and Sesselmann 2013, p. 53)

1.6   End-to-End Processes

Process management, developed in the 1990s, focused on improving customer satisfaction. Processes serve directly (core process) or indirectly (support process, management process) to fulfill the needs, expectations, or requirements of customers. Processes are managed by a process owner, who defines the objectives and key performance indicators for process control in line with the company's strategy.

An **end-to-end process** is a customer-focused process. The term "customer" can be interpreted broadly. "Customer" may refer to an external business customer who, for example, places an order, or to an "internal process customer" who uses the output of another process. For instance, in the process "employee management," the process "hiring new employees" may request the service of issuing an employment contract for a selected candidate.

The end-to-end process begins with initiation by the (process) customer and ends with the fulfillment of the customer's needs. Core processes of a company should be organized as end-to-end processes (see the diagram in Fig. 1.14). In the case of external customers, these are referred to as "customer-to-customer processes."

▶   *Note* An end-to-end process starts with a customer need and ends with the
       delivery of a product or service to the customer.

An example of the end-to-end process "quotation processing," described in Table 1.2, is shown in Fig. 1.15.

1.7   Function versus Process

The organizational structure of a company serves to represent the hierarchy vertically. Each position (employee, manager) performs individual functions as part of the division of labor within the company. The function "check inventory" is carried out in materi-

Table 1.2 End-to-end process: Quotation processing

Key customer requirements	Promptly prepared quotation with realistic and appropriate delivery dates and competitive prices
Main activities in service delivery	Receiving the inquiry, clarifying details, clarifying quotation contents (products, dates, prices, additional services, resource check, involving suppliers if necessary), preparing and sending the quotation, monitoring the quotation
Possible process objectives	High-quality quotation with realistic delivery dates and binding prices
Possible key performance indicators for control	Processing time Order rate (number of orders/quotations)

Example of an end-to-end process description

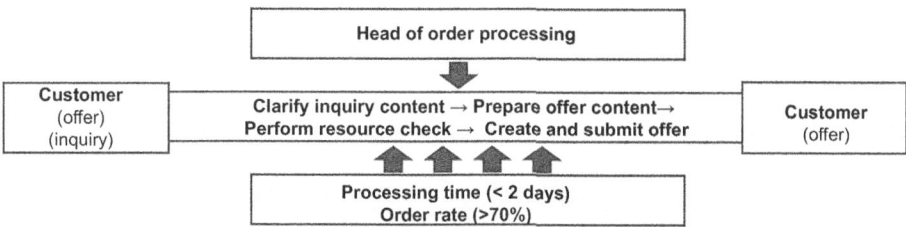

Fig. 1.15 End-to-end process (example based on Schmelzer and Sesselmann 2013, p. 53)

als planning, while the function "enter customer order" is performed in sales. The overall process ("processing customer orders") is not visible, and there is a lack of overall responsibility across all involved departments.

A process is created by meaningfully linking individual functions, such as "enter order," "check inventory," under unified management by the process owner (e.g., "processing customer orders" in Fig. 1.16), to form a coherent whole.

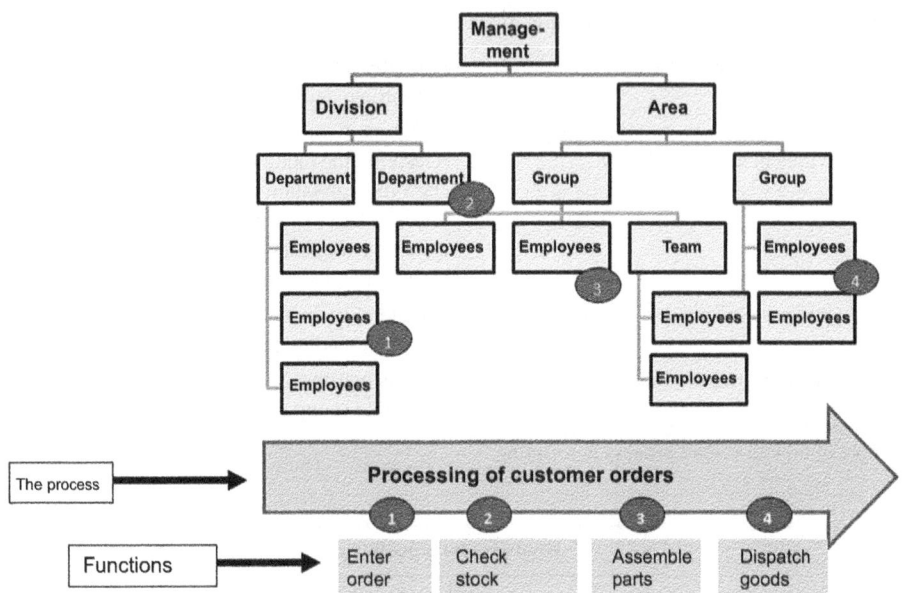

Fig. 1.16 Process versus Function

1.8   Maturity Model for Process Management—Self-Assessment

The following "quick test" is intended for practitioners. It can be used for a self-assessment of a company or public authority. This provides readers with a simple tool to roughly evaluate which areas of the organization still have development potential and where active intervention may be necessary.

A total of eight questions are to be answered on a scale from 1 to 5; intermediate values are permitted. The result can be presented as a radar chart and compared with other organizations.

Process Management Quick Test—Questionnaire

Question 1: Experience with Process Management

1 = Process management is largely unknown and there is no experience with it.
2 = Process management is known (e.g., from training or studies) but has not yet been introduced in the company.
3 = Initial activities have been started to introduce process management, such as a preliminary or pilot project, but there are no regular activities yet.

4 = Processes are partially formally documented, e.g., process map, some detailed processes (swimlane, eEPC, BPMN, UML, etc.); responsibility for processes is not yet or only partially defined and communicated.

5 = Responsibility for processes (e.g., appointment of process owners) is established for all processes in the company.

Question 2: Strategic Process Management

1 = No process strategy exists or processes are not part of the corporate strategy.

2 = A process map is in progress, process strategy is planned.

3 = Process map is known and communicated, process strategy is formulated.

4 = Process strategy is managed using a process scorecard with corresponding goals and measures.

5 = Measures to implement the process strategy have been initiated or already started and are managed through process controlling.

Question 3: Professional Process Management

1 = Processes are not documented or only in exceptional cases or in a fragmented manner.

2 = Individual processes are documented, initial approaches for process optimization have been developed.

3 = Key processes (e.g., core processes) have been analyzed and optimization concepts developed.

4 = Processes are stored in an IT tool and described with additional elements (e.g., process profile). The content is communicated, and selected optimization processes are running regularly.

5 = The process management control cycle is established (strategy, professional modeling, redesign/restructuring of processes, implementation, use, and monitoring).

Question 4: Technical Process Management

1 = Not known, not available.

2 = Workflow tool or ERP/RPA system with workflow functions is under evaluation.

3 = Workflow tool has been selected and initial processes for digitalization have been chosen.

4 = Selected processes have been implemented with the workflow tool.

5 = All key processes (e.g., core processes) are managed by the workflow tool.

Question 5: Process Organization

1 = Functionally structured line organization, e.g., departments such as purchasing, warehouse, production, sales, shipping for all products or processes.

2 = Staff unit within a functional line organization.

3 = Staff unit with project organization.

4 = Matrix organization with functional responsibility and additional process responsibility (process manager).

5 = Purely process-oriented structure of organizational units, possibly with shared service centers for cross-functional tasks.

Question 6: Process Modeling

1 = No documentation of processes available.

2 = Processes are represented using simple flowcharts, e.g., with MS Visio or similar graphics programs.

3 = Processes are documented using modeling tools, e.g., BIC Design, ARIS, Signavio.

4 = Processes are analyzed using modeling tools.

5 = Processes are dynamically evaluated using the simulation functions of modeling tools with regard to time, cost, quantity, or similar criteria.

Question 7 Process Automation

1 = Processes are controlled entirely manually (e.g., routing slips, verbal instructions).

2 = Processes are digitally supported, but control is provided by static aids (e.g., routing slips) or individuals (e.g., handing over the case to the next person).

3 = Processes are partially rule-based and controlled by systems (e.g., purchase requests are forwarded to different recipients depending on value).

4 = Processes are partially executed and controlled by rule-based management tools (e.g., workflow management systems, ERP systems, RPA tools).

5 = Processes are predominantly executed and monitored by management tools.

Question 8 Process Controlling

1 = No process metrics available.

2 = Metrics defined for individual processes.

3 = Metrics are available for key processes, but there is no metrics system (e.g., process scorecard).

4 = A metrics system (e.g., process scorecard) centrally provides metrics for key processes (e.g., via data warehouse).

5 = The metrics system is used for both operational and strategic process management.

Figure 1.17 presents an anonymized practical example from participating institutions. If you are interested in conducting a self-assessment using this model, you can request a blank table (Microsoft Excel) by emailing andreas.gadatsch@h-brs.de.

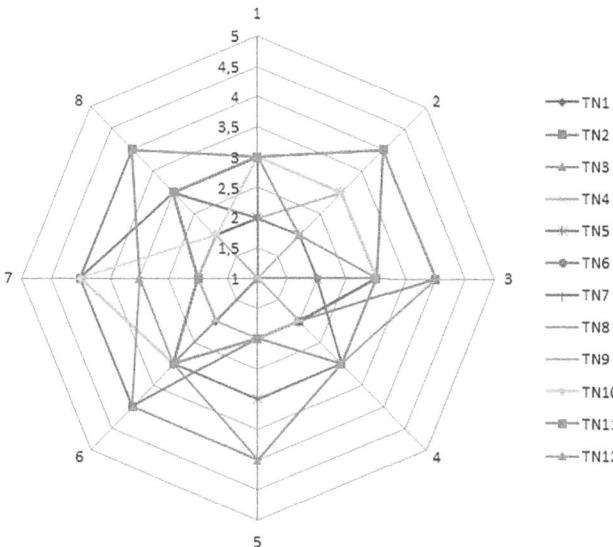

Fig. 1.17 Quick Test Process Management Results

Readers who have completed the previously described quick test will likely identify deficiencies within their organizations, which is not uncommon. Even in academia, there are still open questions, as demonstrated by a contribution authored by over 40 renowned scholars entitled "The biggest business process management problems to solve before we die" (Iris et al. 2023, p. 1), which, among other things, lists the following unresolved issues:

- **Data-driven value creation in business process management:** The vast flood of data has significantly changed the way companies are managed. These changes require adaptations in business processes.
- **Expansive business process management:** Despite significant efforts by companies to advance business process management, only fragments are often visible. Frequently, only individual processes are in focus, not the overall picture.
- **Automated process improvement:** Although there are major efforts to improve processes as automatically as possible, process improvement remains predominantly a manual and demanding task that is time-consuming, labor-intensive, and prone to errors.
- **Lack of objectivity in process descriptions:** Process descriptions in the form of process models are the basis for many business process management activities such as process (re)design, documentation, analysis, and automation. Often, consistent granularity and objectivity cannot be ensured with existing methods.

1.9   Review Questions and Exercises

1.9.1   Review Questions and Answers

Questions
1. Distinguish **business process management** from workflow management.
2. Describe the key **characteristics of processes.**
3. Differentiate between a business process and a workflow.
4. Distinguish a **project** from a business process.
5. Explain different **categories of business processes** and provide an example from an industry of your choice for each category.
6. Explain the difference between a business **function** and a **business process** using an example of your choice.

Answers
1. **Business process management** focuses on the design of processes within an organization, addressing the objectives and content of a workflow (process). Workflow management, on the other hand, is a tool for digitizing processes, dealing with the technical implementation (use of software).
2. The key **characteristics of a process** are: defined start and end, repeatability, division of labor, processing of information, and, if applicable, potential for automation (in which case it is referred to as a "workflow").
3. A **workflow** is a digitized business process, i.e., a computer program controls the process based on formalized rules, which are, for example, stored in the form of a process model.
4. A **project**, in contrast to a business process, is carried out only once.
5. Common **categories of business processes** are management processes (e.g., managing a car dealership), core processes (e.g., selling new vehicles), and support processes (e.g., marketing for vehicles).
6. A function (e.g., creating a customer order) is part of a business process (e.g., selling vehicles).

1.9.2   Exercise "End-to-End Process"

Task
Identify an "end-to-end process" of your choice and create a process diagram that includes the following information: process name, key customer requirements, main activities involved in service delivery, possible process objectives, and potential key performance indicators for management.

Sample Solution

- *Process name:* Sale of new vehicles at a car dealership
- *Key customer requirements:* Competent advice, flexible pricing, smooth and timely processing, delivery of a high-quality product
- *Activities:* Customer consultation, conducting test drives, recording special requests, order entry, customer support, vehicle handover, handling complaints, payment processing
- *Process objectives:* Sale of vehicles with the highest possible contribution margin per time period, ensuring high customer satisfaction
- *Key performance indicators:* Number of vehicles sold per time unit, customer satisfaction, contribution margin per vehicle, lead time from order entry to delivery

References

Allweyer, T.: Prozessmanagement für die Digitale Transformation. Untersuchung aktueller Ansätze des Geschäftsprozessmanagements als Enabler für die digitale Unternehmenstransformation. Forschungsbericht. Hochschule Kaiserslautern (2020)

Berkau, C.: Instrumente der Datenverarbeitung für das effiziente Prozesscontrolling. Kostenrechnungspraxis, Sonderheft **2**(1998), 27–32 (2020)

Berthold, H.J.: Aktionsdatenbanken in einem kommunikationsorientierten EDV-System. In: Informatik-Spektrum, **6**, 20–26 (1983)

Gadatsch, A.: Big data: chance für das Informationsmanagement. In: Keuper, F., Schmidt, D. (eds.) „Smart (Big) Data Management", pp. 41–58. Berlin (2014)

Gaitanides, M.: Prozessorganisation: Entwicklung, Ansätze und Programme des Managements von Geschäftsprozessen, 2. edn. München (2007)

Galler, J., Scheer, A.-W.: Workflow-Projekte: Vom Geschäftsprozessmodell zur unternehmensspezifischen Workflow-Anwendung. Inf. Manage. **1**, 20–27 (1995)

Gehring, H.: Betriebliche Anwendungssysteme, Kurseinheit 2. Fern-Universität Hagen, Hagen, Prozessorientierte Gestaltung von Informationssystemen (1998)

Griesold, T., vom Brocke, J., Gross, S., Mendling, J., Röglinger, M., Stelzl, K.: Digital innovation and business process management: opportunities and challenges as perceived by practitioners. In: Communication of the Asscociation for Information Systems, April (2021)

Grisold, T., Gross, S., Röglinger, M., Stelzl, K., vom Brocke, J.: Exploring explorative bpm—setting the ground for future research. Proceedings of conference on business process management (BPM 2019) (2019)

Gross, S., Malinova Mandelburger, M., Mendling, J.: Navigating through the maze of business process change methods. Proceedings of the 52nd hawaii international conference on system sciences (HICSS-52), pp. 6270–6279 (2019)

Hammer, M.: Reengineering work: don't automate, obliterate. Harvard Bus. Rev. **68**(4), 104–112 (1990)

Hammer, M., Champy, J.: Business Reengineering, 2. edn. Frankfurt, New York (1994)

Hansen, H.-R., Mendling, J., Neumann, G.: Wirtschaftsinformatik, 12. edn. Berlin (2018)

Herzwurm, W., Pietsch, W.: Management von IT-Produkten, Heidelberg (2009)

Hilmer, C.: Prozessmanagement in indirekten Bereichen, Wiesbaden (2016)

Hofmann, J.: Aktionsorientierte Datenbanken im Fertigungsbereich, Reihe Betriebs- und Wirtschaftsinformatik 27, Berlin (1988)

Iris, B., et al.: The biggest business process management problems to solve before we die. In: Science Direct, Computers in Industry, **146**, 103837. https://www.sciencedirect.com/science/article/pii/S0166361522002330 (2023). Accessed 9 Sept 2023

Mendling, J.: Business process modeling in the 1920s and 1930s as reflected in Fritz Nordsieck's PhD Thesis. In: Enterprise modelling and information systems architectures, **16** (2021)

Mertens, P.: Moden und Nachhaltigkeit in der Wirtschaftsinformatik, Arbeitspapier Nr. 1/2006, Universität Erlangen-Nürnberg, Bereich Wirtschaftsinformatik I (2006)

Österle, H.: Business Engineering. Prozess- und Systementwicklung, Band 1, Entwurfstechniken, Berlin (1995)

Reinhart, G.: Handbuch Industrie 4.0. Geschäftsmodelle, Prozesse, Technik. München, Hanser (2017)

Scheer, A.-W.: Architektur integrierter Informationssysteme—Grundlagen der Unternehmensmodellierung, Berlin (1991)

Scheer, A.-W.: ARIS—Vom Geschäftsprozess zum Anwendungssystem, 3. edn. Berlin (1998)

Scheer, A.-W.: EDV-orientierte Betriebswirtschaftslehre, 4. edn. Berlin (1990)

Scheer, A.-W.: Wirtschaftsinformatik—Referenzmodelle für industrielle Geschäftsprozesse, 4. edn. Berlin (1994)

Scheer, A.-W., Jost, W.: Geschäftsprozessmodellierung innerhalb einer Unternehmensarchitektur. In: Vossen, G., Becker, J. (eds.) Geschäftsprozessmodellierung und Workflowmanagement, Modelle, Methoden, Werkzeuge, Bonn, pp. 29–46 (1996)

Schmelzer, H.J., Sesselmann., W.: Geschäftsprozessmanagement in der Praxis, 8. edn. Hanser, München (2013)

Seidlmeier, H.: Prozessmodellierung mit ARIS®. Eine beispielorientierte Einführung für Studium und Praxis, Braunschweig und Wiesbaden (2002)

Sua-Ngam-Iam, P., Kühl, S.: Das Wuchern der Formalstruktur. J. Psychol. **29**(1), 39–71 (2021). https://doi.org/10.30820/0942-2285-2021-1-39

Winkelhake, U.: Information technology as an enabler of digitisation. In: The Digital Transformation of the Automotive Industry. Springer, Cham (2021). https://doi.org/10.1007/978-3-030-83826-3_8

Concepts of Process Management

2

Process management requires the use of methods

Abstract

This chapter first presents an integrated concept for business process and workflow management. The concept is described in terms of its elements (levels, phases, and perspectives). Standardized optimization concepts for business processes are then discussed, along with an introduction to several well-known management concepts that pursue objectives similar to those of process management. The chapter concludes with a section on reference models for process management, as well as questions and an exercise.

2.1 Integrated Business Process and Workflow Management

Business processes and workflows are closely interconnected and cannot be developed independently of each other. Therefore, process management must be represented holistically within an integrated concept. The framework of the concept for integrated business process and workflow management, as shown in Fig. 2.1, encompasses, on multiple levels, the development and control of corporate strategy (strategic level), process management in the narrower sense (business-conceptual level), technically oriented workflow management (operational level), as well as the application system and organizational design tasks linked to process management (see Gehring and Gadatsch 1999, p. 70). The concept serves to align with corporate strategy, to organize processes, to implement them

© The Author(s), under exclusive license to Springer Fachmedien Wiesbaden GmbH, part of Springer Nature 2026
A. Gadatsch, *Business Process Management*,
https://doi.org/10.1007/978-3-658-49339-4_2

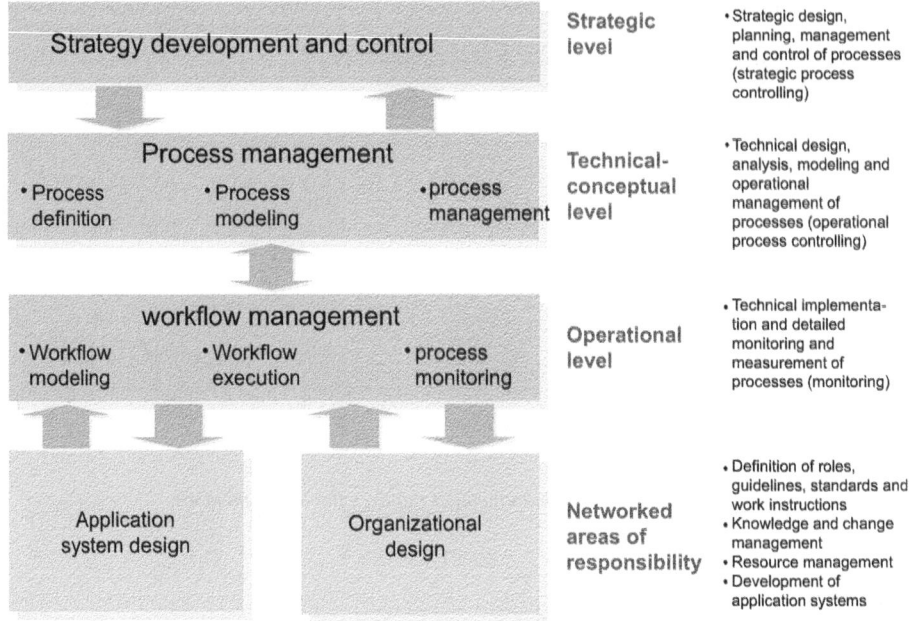

Fig. 2.1 Integrated business process and workflow management – Concept

technically using appropriate communication and information systems, and to support both strategic and operational process controlling.

Strategic Level (Strategy Development and Control)
At the strategic level, a company's business areas are considered, including the critical success factors that are effective in this context. Here, the company's core processes are identified, planned, and implemented using appropriate measures. Strategic process controlling monitors and manages the implementation and achievement of objectives through the initiated measures, using strategic key performance indicators, and initiates corrective actions if deviations from target values become too great.

At the underlying business-conceptual level, processes are derived as part of process management. Here, process management provides the link to corporate planning at the strategic level, while workflow management, from the perspective of the next lower level—operational execution—incorporates application system and organizational design.

Business-Conceptual Level (Process Management in the Narrow Sense)
Process management encompasses the phases of process delimitation, process modeling, and process management throughout the process lifecycle:

- Process delimitation describes the emergence of processes. Based on business areas and strategically oriented specifications such as product range, critical success factors, etc., process candidates for each business area must be derived and evaluated in a step-by-step approach. Finally, the processes to be modeled and implemented are selected.
- Process modeling involves representing segments of reality from a business area in a business process from a business-conceptual perspective. Depending on a company's strategic objectives, this may involve, for example, a complete redesign of workflows or further automation of existing processes. For instance, the BMW Group develops specific business strategies in tool and plant engineering that explicitly take into account increased environmental requirements regarding CO_2 emission limits, as well as the associated reduction in consumption and safety requirements. These are then reflected in revised business processes adapted to these requirements (see Brunner et al. 2002, pp. 312 f.).
- The process management phase relates to process execution. Its goal is to align processes with specified metrics for process success, known as process control variables. These control variables are to be derived, if necessary in several steps, from the critical success factors of the respective business areas. Depending on the extent of identified performance deficits, weaknesses in project execution, etc., re-modeling or a renewed process modeling cycle may be required.

Operational Level (Workflow Management)

Workflow management is divided into the phases of workflow modeling, workflow execution, and workflow monitoring. Workflow modeling follows business process modeling. Here, the modeled business process is extended by specifications necessary for automated process execution under the control of a workflow management system. This is followed by the workflow execution phase, which includes the creation of process objects and the progression of these objects through the designated processing stations under the control of a workflow management system. Subsequent workflow monitoring serves to continuously monitor process behavior. Comparing process control variables with the corresponding actual process values at the workflow level provides information on whether a process is already properly configured or whether corrective interventions are required.

Due to their support function for business process management, workflow management systems are increasingly referred to as BPM systems (Business Process Management Systems) or process management systems (PMS) (Dadam et al. 2011, p. 364).

Interconnected Task Areas (Application System and Organizational Design)

Organizational design complements process management as a general support function by defining roles, policies, standards, and specific work instructions for employees. In addition, it provides methods for knowledge and change management and manages the administration of personnel and other resources.

Application system design provides process-oriented information systems. These can be developed individually for the company or implemented as standard software adapted for use within the organization.

2.2   Structural Elements

2.2.1   Perspectives of the Process Cube

The structure of process management can be divided into three perspectives (levels, phases, and views) (see the "Process Cube" in Fig. 2.2). The abstraction levels include strategy, processes, and workflow (see Sect. 2.2.2). The phases comprise business modeling, technical modeling, and the deployment and monitoring of ongoing activities (see Sect. 2.2.3). Modeling can be structured according to the views of organization, function, data, software, and process (see Sect. 2.2.4).

Application of the Process Cube
Using the structural elements of the process cube, a process-oriented concept for starting a business can be described. The cube serves as a framework for structuring this

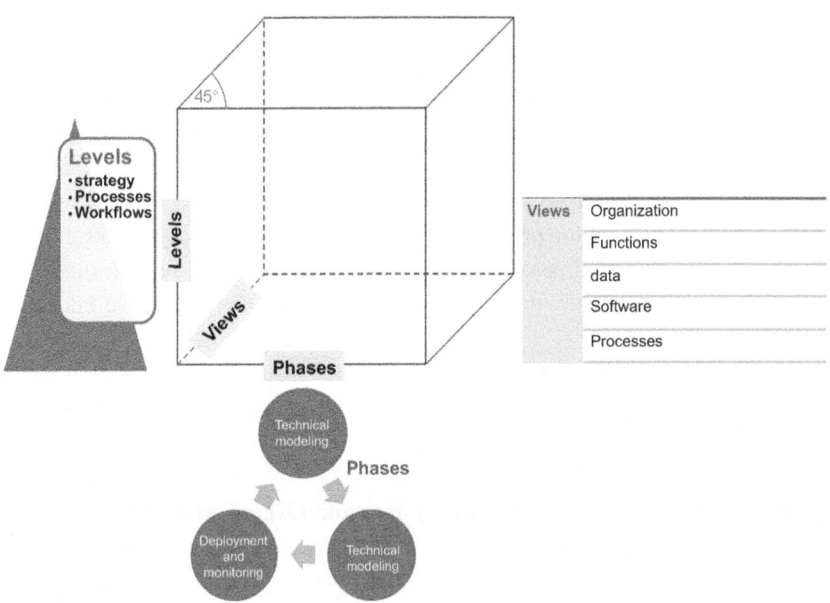

Fig. 2.2 GPM Cube

approach. The following are examples of aspects that should be considered, for instance, when founding an "online car dealership."

- Abstraction Levels
  - *Strategy:* An online car dealership needs to differentiate itself from competitors. It competes with manufacturer-owned dealerships, independent local car dealers, and specialized EU importers. The advantage of the online dealership is the complete handling of the car purchase—from consultation and selection to delivery and handover—via digital media, thus particularly appealing to younger and media-savvy buyers.
  - *Processes:* All customer-facing processes should be digitized and accessible via any internet-enabled device (PC, tablet, smartphone). Paper-based processes should be avoided except where legally required.
  - *Workflow:* Numerous processes in the online car dealership should be implemented as workflows, meaning they are managed by a software system. Examples include: capturing customer data, recording insurance information, searching the vehicle inventory, requesting vehicle information, selecting a vehicle, reserving a vehicle, registering and insuring the vehicle for the customer, scheduling test drives, online consultations with staff, ordering, arranging handover appointments, and handling cancellations or withdrawals from purchases.
- Phases
  - *Business Modeling:* First, management, core, and support processes must be described at the business level. The models should be visible to relevant employees (e.g., online sales consultants) on the intranet and later serve as a reference.
  - *Technical Modeling:* The implementation of the processes at the workflow level is outsourced to an external software company for development. It is important to ensure that general IT standards and the specific requirements of the automotive industry are addressed to enable integration with the data networks of car manufacturers.
  - *Deployment and Monitoring:* After programming and testing, the applications should be put into operation. For process monitoring, customer reactions (e.g., model comparisons, session abandonment) should be tracked in real time.
- Views
  - *Organization:* Internal departments (accounting, administration, marketing, IT), external departments (sales/consulting; service)
  - *Function:* Master data entry, vehicle data entry, price data entry, etc.
  - *Data:* Vehicle data, price data (own prices, competitor prices), customer data, customer behavior, statistics (sales, inventory duration, average prices), etc.
  - *Software:* Internal software for accounting, administration, payroll, online portal with all customer-oriented functions, customer app for operational handling of consultation and purchase as well as customer retention

- *Process:* Management processes (corporate planning, marketing strategy, controlling); core processes (providing vehicle information, handling the purchase process, processing complaints, delivering vehicles, etc.), support processes (accounting, inventory management, human resources, IT services, etc.)

2.2.2   Layers

The distinction between business processes and workflows leads to a differentiation according to abstraction and modeling layers (cf. Gehring 1998). Due to the differing objectives and complexity of these terms, it is advisable to establish modeling perspectives and structure them into phases, in order to focus on the specific questions under investigation in practical work. The business analysis and modeling of processes aims to determine which tasks are to be performed by which organizational units. The technical analysis and modeling specifies how the process is to be executed in detail with the help of software systems. For modeling purposes, two layers are therefore established: the layer of business-conceptual process modeling and the operational layer of workflow modeling derived from it (cf. Fig. 2.3).

▶   In practice, the distinction between abstraction layers is also referred to as "business modeling" and "technical modeling." "Round-trip modeling" refers to a holistic approach in which a business model is successively refined into an executable model. This is possible, for example, with the modeling language BPMN (cf. Sect. 5.8).

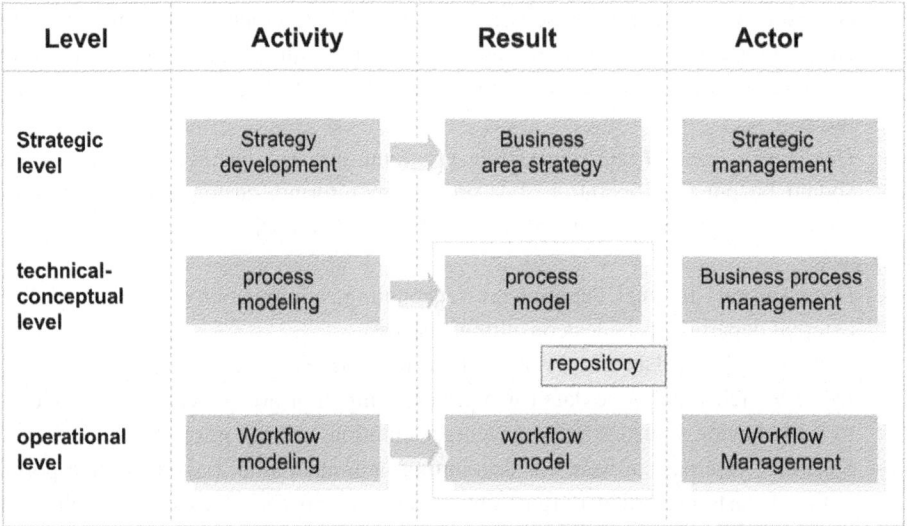

Fig. 2.3 Layer concept (Gehring 1998)

Repository (Model Database)

In addition to the relationships presented in the framework concept, the results of design and modeling activities are added. These are permanently stored in the form of models (process model, workflow model, and supplementary information). The repository serves as a dictionary used to describe the modeling components and the relationships between them. It records business processes as well as connections between business processes and workflows. Interfaces to the modeling environment are also described. The latter primarily consists of the respective business field strategy, the supporting information systems, and the organizational units involved.

▷   Processes and workflows must be documented permanently in order to be used within the organization. Ideally, workflows are derived from processes, i.e., refined. When using modeling tools, it is therefore advisable to use a unified repository for processes and workflows. In the context of using modern software tools that, for example, generate executable workflow models using the modeling language BPMN 2.0 (see Sect. 5.8), the repository is a necessary prerequisite for process execution.

2.2.3   Phases

Process management is organized collaboratively in projects (cf. Sect. 3.3). For this purpose, phase or life cycle models are used to structure the complex activities, especially in the context of modeling tasks. Modeling can be performed in a single stage or in two stages.

In single-stage modeling, the workflow model is created directly without requiring a preceding business process model. In the two-stage approach, a workflow model is derived from a previously created business process model. The two-stage workflow modeling approach acknowledges the fact that business processes and workflows serve different purposes, even if a clear distinction is not always possible in every individual case. In practice, the two-stage approach is often preferred, since, in addition to the different purposes of the models, there are only a few software tools that support the single-stage approach in such a way that the requirements of all involved user groups are fully met. Figure 2.4 shows a two-stage workflow life cycle that includes three partially interlinked sub-cycles.

Sub-cycle (1)

Sub-cycle (1) comprises business process modeling, analysis, and restructuring, as well as business strategy development, and can be assigned to the strategic or business-conceptual layer of the integrated overall concept. The starting point for sub-cycle (1) is the collection and modeling of the as-is business process models. These are then subjected

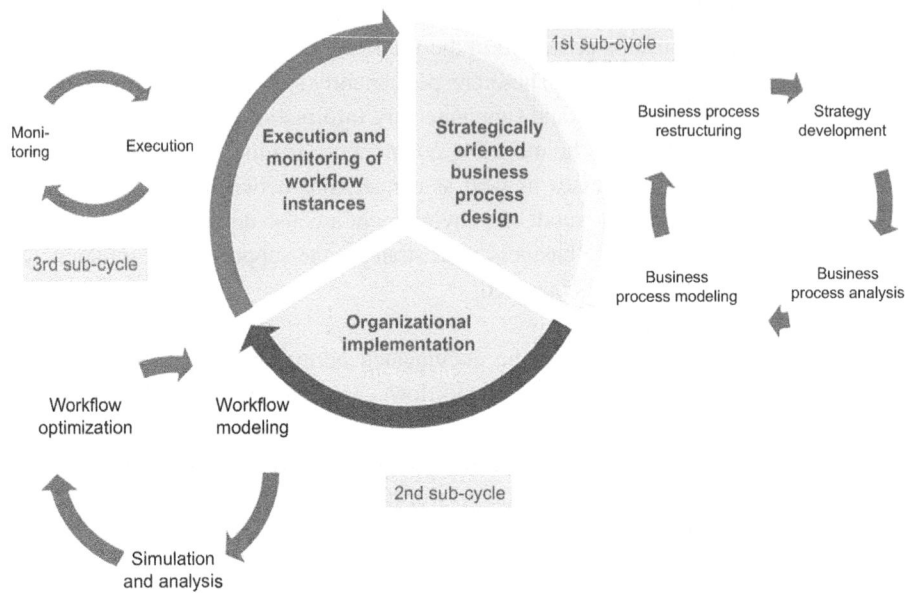

Fig. 2.4 Business process and workflow life cycle model

to business process analysis with regard to their contribution to achieving the business process objectives derived from the business strategy. In this process, unproductive or redundant business processes and organizational structures are identified. Business process analysis can also have feedback effects on the initially specified business strategy of the company, which in turn influences the subsequent design and restructuring of business processes. The newly designed and, with respect to the strategic objectives, restructured business processes are formally described as target business process models. A subsequent analysis of the target business process models can lead to further restructuring cycles until the design of the business processes is consistent with the specified or, if necessary, adjusted business objectives.

Sub-cycle (2)

With the completion of sub-cycle (1), the business-conceptual design of the business processes is finished. In the subsequent sub-cycle (2), the business process models are refined down to the operational workflow level. The intended level of detail should, on the one hand, allow for automatic execution and, on the other, enable simulation-based analysis of workflows. The workflow optimization that follows the analysis completes the second, potentially iterative, sub-cycle.

Subcycle (3)

The execution of workflows and their ongoing monitoring mark the beginning of sub-cycle (3), which also belongs to the operational level. Depending on the degree of deviation between the monitored process results and the expected outcomes, feedback is provided to subcycle (1) or (2). Minor deviations lead to incremental changes in the form of a renewed iteration of subcycle (2), i.e., optimizations of the workflow models. Major deviations from reference values indicate modeling deficiencies and may necessi-tate re-modeling or a return to subcycle (1). Thresholds that trigger monitoring activities for workflow instances must be defined as tolerance ranges for process control variables during business process modeling. In cases of significant deviations, the results of work-flow monitoring can also impact the company's business strategy.

Phase models are important in practice. Companies therefore develop customized pro-cedural models tailored to their needs. Figure 2.5 provides an example of the life-cycle model used by EON, which includes all relevant process steps for integrated business process and workflow management (see von Büdingen and Schlaf 2011, p. 83).

A distinctive feature of the EON model in Fig. 2.5 is the integration of a process step "Process Controlling" to emphasize the importance of these tasks. Process controlling (see also in detail Chapter 4) should, however, be understood as a control loop, as illus-trated in Fig. 2.6. Starting from the corporate strategy, a process strategy is derived. This is then specified with target values and measures. These are later compared with the actual values from the implemented measures, which are evaluated as part of a variance analysis. The controlling life cycle thus overlays the process management life cycle as a higher-level meta-control loop.

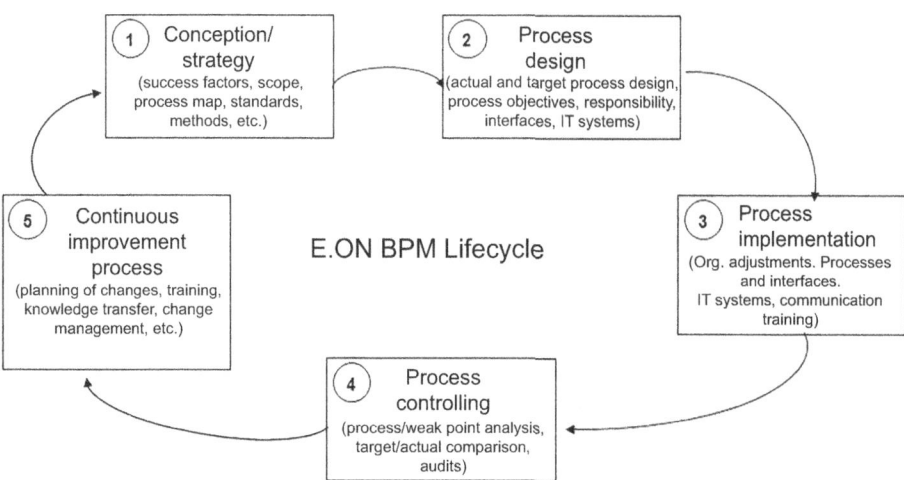

Fig. 2.5 Life-cycle model of EON for business process and workflow management

Fig. 2.6 Controlling control loop

View concepts of business process modeling						
Becker	**Ferstl/Sinz**	**Gadatsch**	**Gehring**	**Österle**	**Scheer**	**Weske**
Organization view	Performance view	Process view	Organizational view	Organization view	Organization view	Function Modeling
Business object	Control view	Organizational structure view	Function view	Functions view	Functional view	Information Modeling
Process	Process view	Activity structure view	Data view	Data	Data view	Modeling Organization
Resource		Application structure view		[Personnel]	Control view	Modeling
		Information structure view		[...]	Performance view	IT Landscape Modeling

Fig. 2.7 View Concepts

Summary: The Role of Phase Models in Process Management

Phase models represent the chronological sequence of process management. Since process management is a continuously repeating life cycle, circular diagrams are commonly used to describe the essential steps in carrying out process management activities. In practice, these models are often adapted to company-specific requirements.

2.2.4 Views

In process modeling, it is not practical to represent all modeling-relevant aspects in a single depiction, as this would result in a loss of clarity. To reduce the complexity of representations and improve transparency, it is advisable to apply a view-based concept (cf. Sinz 1996), which organizes the aspects to be considered in a meaningful way. Figure 2.7 provides an overview of the views used in selected concepts for process management (extended presentation based on Gehring 1998).

Becker et al

The approach by Becker (cf. Becker et al. 2007, 2008) aims to provide an overview of the process landscape and to support measures for the reorganization of the business processes under consideration. To support these objectives, four views are proposed: organizational view (Who performs an activity?), business object view (What is processed/produced?), process view (How is something executed?), and resource view (With what is something executed?). These views are realized in four model types: business object model, organizational model, process module, and resource model.

Gadatsch

With regard to the requirements of workflow modeling, Gadatsch distinguishes a central process view and four supplementary structural views (cf. Gadatsch 2000, pp. 179 f.). The process view describes the modeling objects involved in a process from a process-oriented perspective. The structural views describe the structure of the modeling objects that are brought together in the process view.

Gehring

In defining views, Gehring is guided by the classical core elements of process modeling: the process itself, organizational structures, and data (cf. Gehring 1998).

Österle

Österle does not refer to views in his concept, but rather to design dimensions (cf. Österle 1995). He identifies organization, data, functions, and personnel as dimensions of business engineering, but does not include the personnel dimension in the concept. There is no separately designated "dynamic" dimension. However, dynamic aspects are taken into account in the representation of processes using task chain diagrams.

Scheer

Scheer distinguishes five views. The primarily static descriptive objects of business processes are represented in the organizational, data, function, and service views. The dynamic aspects are consolidated in the control view (cf. Scheer 1998a, b).

Weske

Weske differentiates between the modeling domains of function modeling, information modeling, organization modeling, and IT landscape modeling (cf. Weske 2007, p. 77). In doing so, he acknowledges the particular importance of information technology.

The concepts of Gadatsch, Gehring, Scheer, Österle, and Weske, briefly outlined above, each consider the process or function as the central element, which transforms input data into output data with the help of organizational units.

In contrast, the object-oriented concept of Ferstl and Sinz (cf. Sinz 1996) regards the process as a whole and dispenses with detailed views for representing data and organizational units.

2.3   From Functional Thinking to Process Thinking

The traditional functional organization of companies (see Fig. 2.8) is strictly hierarchical. At the top of the organization is the management, e.g., the executive board or managing director of the company. Below that are areas differentiated according to professional criteria. These are structured according to business functions (e.g., purchasing, sales, warehousing, production, human resources, finance).

Processes are not the focus of a functional organization. They run across the entire organization, without necessarily being defined, described, or even known. Often, employees have no concept of what a process is; they identify with "their" task. However, in practice, several organizational units are usually involved in executing processes,

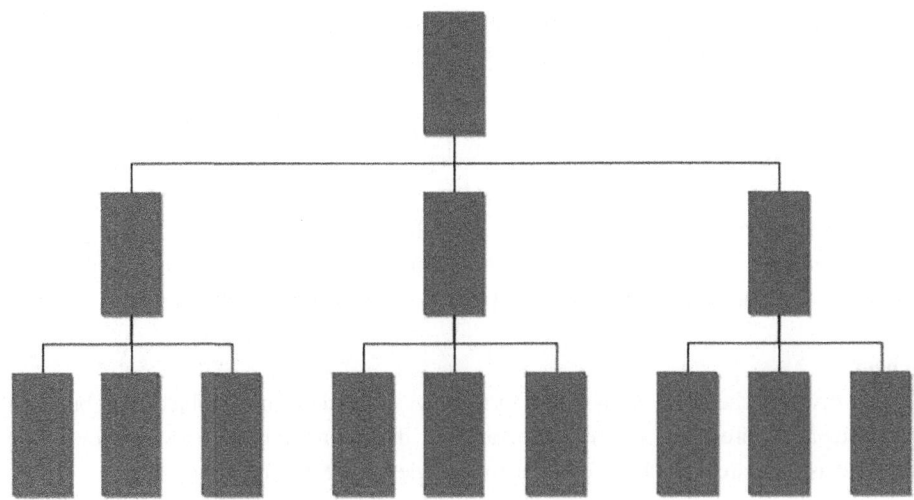

Fig. 2.8 Functional organization (schematic)

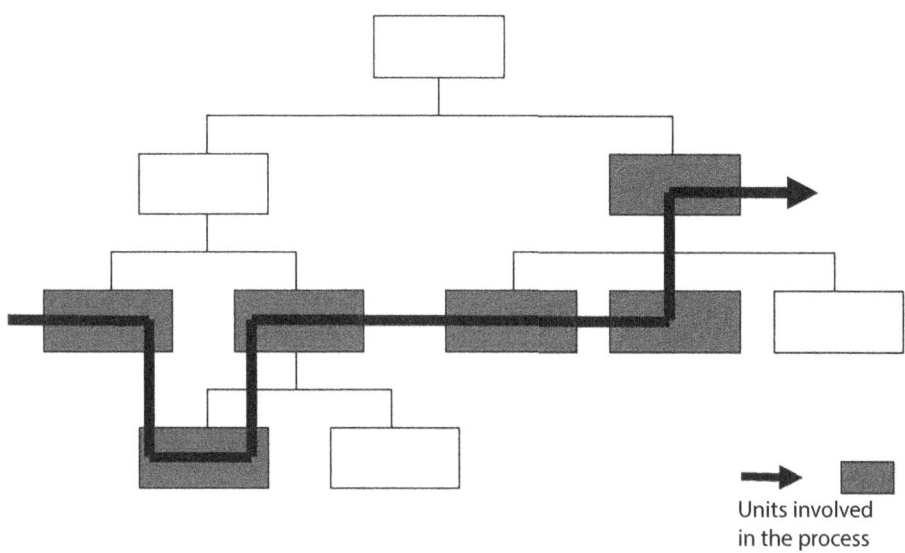

Units involved
in the process

Fig. 2.9 Process flow in functionally structured organizations (Dillerup and Stoi 2012)

even if these are not formally defined. In fact, the processes already exist, but they are not formally manifested.

At the interfaces between the organizational units involved in a process, handovers occur where the process is repeatedly interrupted by the transfer of object information (e.g., order data) (see Fig. 2.9). There is also a risk of media discontinuities when existing data is re-entered or transformed. Ultimately, there is a lack of process control across organizational units, since each unit is only responsible for its own "process segment." As a result, the processes, though not formally defined but existing in reality, "find their way" through the company's functional organization.

Summary: Functional Thinking versus Process Thinking

Many companies are organized by functions (e.g., purchasing, manufacturing, sales, accounting, cost accounting), meaning there are numerous organizational units (divisions, departments, etc.) that are divided according to groups of activities (functions). However, in such organizations, processes usually pass through several of these organizational units, i.e., they are "cross-departmental." Functional thinking focuses on the tasks of one's own area, department, etc., while process-oriented thinking encompasses the entire process chain, potentially spanning multiple departments or divisions.

Chimney Effect

In small organizations, a functional structure poses no problem because employees know each other, are familiar with how processes interact, and can communicate directly to

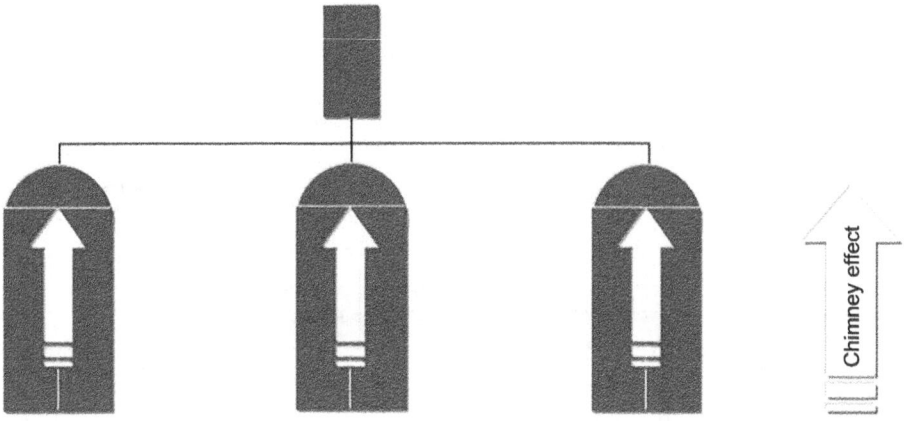

Fig. 2.10 Chimney effect (Osterloh and Frost 2003, p. 29)

coordinate and resolve conflicts. In growing organizations, however, many areas tend to focus only on their own responsibilities. The overall picture is lost. The areas become silos: large, thick, and windowless (Osterloh and Frost 2003, p. 28 f.). They see only what happens within their own boundaries. The functional thinking of traditional organizations leads to internal blockages and to "information silos," where internal communication between departments takes place only via reporting systems, memos, and notes. This results in the "chimney effect," as cross-departmental problems, due to a lack of horizontal communication, are escalated to top management "like smoke rising in a chimney" (see Fig. 2.10, based on Osterloh and Frost 2003, p. 29).

In a function-oriented organization, goals are set for the heads of functional areas and are sometimes linked to compensation. For example, the logistics manager may be tasked with keeping inventory levels as low as possible to reduce capital costs. The sales manager, on the other hand, aims to sell as many units as possible, which would be easier with high inventory levels than with low ones.

In a process-oriented organization, the focus is on process goals and the resulting outcomes. These generally do not coincide with the departmental or divisional goals and results of the classic functional organization (see Fig. 2.11).

Example: Classification of Invoice Verification in the Procurement Process

A typical example of the different perspectives of process and functional thinking is the procurement of goods and services. When designing procurement workflows, the question regularly arises as to which area the subtask of "invoice verification" should be assigned: logistics or accounting.

Assigning it to logistics is justified by the fact that invoice verification involves qualitative and quantitative checks. Among other things, logistics aims to deliver the right goods in the right quantity and quality to the recipient at the right time. Accounting, on

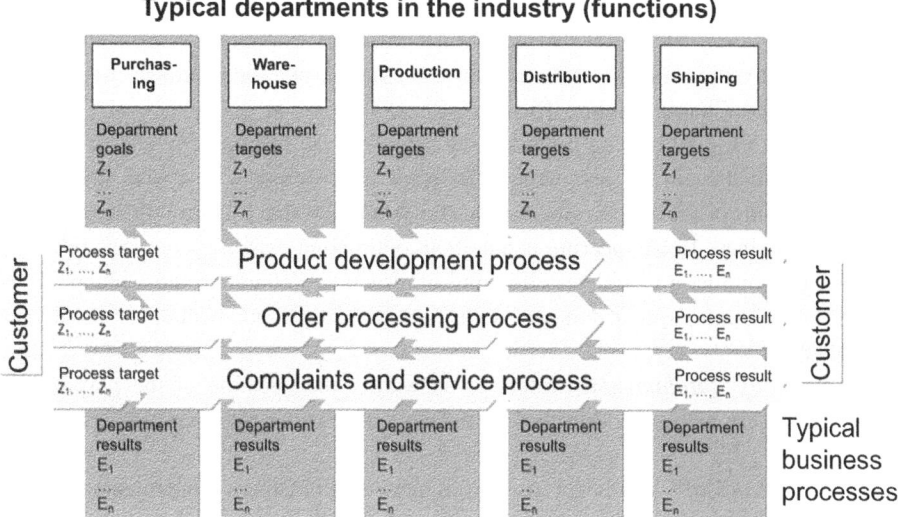

Fig. 2.11 Goals and goal conflicts in functional organizations

the other hand, often claims responsibility for checking account assignments and payment terms. Its goal is, among other things, to prepare proper balance sheets and profit and loss statements.

If the process is split, for example, so that the qualitative and quantitative checks are first carried out in logistics and, after the documents (e.g., delivery note) are passed on, the commercial or financial verification is performed in accounting, delays are almost inevitable due to the change of handler. ◀

2.4   Optimization Concepts

2.4.1   Business Reengineering

The concept of Business Reengineering refers to a management approach for radical corporate restructuring, which gained significant popularity in the early 1990s through the work of Hammer and Champy (see Hammer 1990 and Hammer and Champy 1994). The discussion initially took place primarily in corporate practice, especially within management consulting. Academic research on Business Reengineering followed later. This development led to a series of further advancements of the original concept by Hammer and Champy (Hess and Österle 1995, p. 128). In this context, terms such as "Business Process Reengineering," "Business Engineering," and "Business Redesign" are sometimes used synonymously. These concepts focus primarily on the analysis and restructuring of primary processes with a market and customer orientation, such as sales processes. However, there are also occasional practical examples of such approaches being applied to supporting cross-functional processes, such as accounting.

Hammer and Champy define Business Reengineering as a "radical cure" for the company. By this, they mean a fundamental rethinking of the company and its business processes, with the aim of achieving significant improvements in costs, quality, services, time, and, in particular, customer value (Hammer and Champy 1994, p. 48). In their view, Business Reengineering is not about optimizing existing processes, but about a fresh start—that is, a complete rethinking of structures (Hammer and Champy 1994, p. 12). They summarize their concept with the keywords "fundamental," "radical," and "dramatic."

The keyword *"fundamental"* refers to answering the question of the purpose and necessity of every activity within the company, as well as the way in which it is carried out.

The term *"radical"* stands for the willingness to implement fundamental changes within the company. In other words, it is not about optimizing existing processes (see also Hammer and Champy 1994, p. 12), but about a new beginning—a complete rethinking of structures.

The keyword *"dramatic"* describes the demand for quantum leaps in changes to the company and the efficiency of its workflows. Hammer and Champy assign information technology a pivotal role in fulfilling these tasks (see Hammer and Champy 1994, pp. 113 f.). Their main concern is to exploit the innovative potential of information processing.

In short, Business Reengineering means answering the question: *"How would we proceed if we could start all over again?"* Management is tasked with rethinking how work would be performed and how the organization would be structured if they were to start from scratch (Robbins 2001, p. 33).

The approaches of Business Reengineering have been taken up and further developed by other authors. Terms such as Business Process Reengineering, Business Engineering, and Business Process Redesign are often used interchangeably. In German-speaking countries, the approaches of Scheer and Österle have become particularly well known. Österle defines Business Reengineering comprehensively as a top-down approach, starting with the development of business strategy and extending down to the level of information systems (Österle 1995, p. 24). He uses the term Business Engineering to refer to the redesign of the information-based economy (Österle 1995, p. 14). Figure 2.12 shows Österle's breakdown into the levels of business strategy, process, and information system (Österle 1995, p. 30).

The business strategy defines the global framework for the company, such as corporate structure and business areas. The process level specifies the organizational units and determines the business processes and their outputs. It also defines the main entity types for information processing, such as customer or account. The information system level

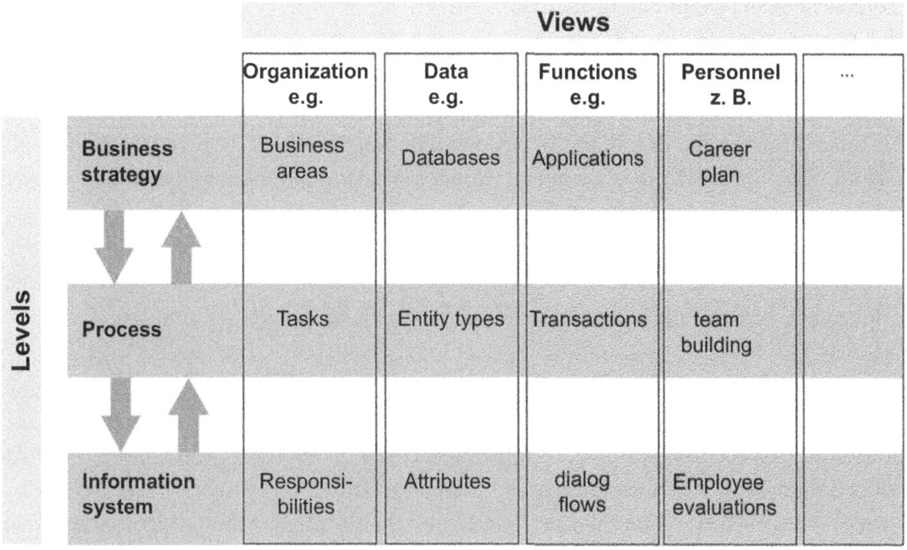

Views					
Levels	**Organization** e.g.	**Data** e.g.	**Functions** e.g.	**Personnel** z. B.	...
Business strategy	Business areas	Databases	Applications	Career plan	
Process	Tasks	Entity types	Transactions	team building	
Information system	Responsibilities	Attributes	dialog flows	Employee evaluations	

Fig. 2.12 Business Engineering according to Österle (1995, p. 30)

provides detailed specifications. The level-based approach is complemented by a perspective concept. For each level, Österle distinguishes the perspectives of organization, data, and function (see Österle 1995, p. 30), and leaves room for the inclusion of additional perspectives, such as personnel, marketing, or legal.

Summary: Business Reengineering
Business Reengineering is a radical concept in process management and is assigned to the strategic level. It involves fundamentally rethinking the organization and its processes in order to achieve rapid improvements in costs, quality, and customer value.

2.4.2   Business Process Optimization

Business reengineering and business process optimization, although the terms are often used interchangeably, are distinct approaches to restructuring a company's business processes.

The objective of business process optimization is to sustainably improve a company's competitiveness by aligning all essential workflows with customer requirements. This primarily means focusing efforts on those business processes that are directly triggered by customer actions (e.g., order placement, invoice payment, complaint).

Practical examples of causes include:

- Media discontinuities in the workflow: Entering data into a PC database that was taken from a printed report generated by the SAP ERP system.
- Change of processor during the workflow: Incoming invoices are received in the mailroom, then forwarded to accounting via internal mail, and after processing, a copy is sent to purchasing for verification.
- Duplicate work: Data is entered twice because responsibilities are not clearly defined.
- Waiting or idle times: Data from the finance department is needed to post a payment document, but the inquiry is unsuccessful due to the employee's absence.

Basic Forms of Process Restructuring

Key objectives of business process optimization are to reduce throughput time and improve process quality. Figure 2.13 illustrates, based on Bleicher (1991, p. 196), fundamental design options. Explanations can be found in Tab. 2.1.

Process restructuring can take various forms. Purely organizational approaches such as "eliminating unnecessary activities," technical measures such as "using a web portal," or hybrid forms can be distinguished (see Tab. 2.1).

In addition to these fundamental methods, the concept of segmentation is frequently used. Here, process variants are identified for which different processes are developed.

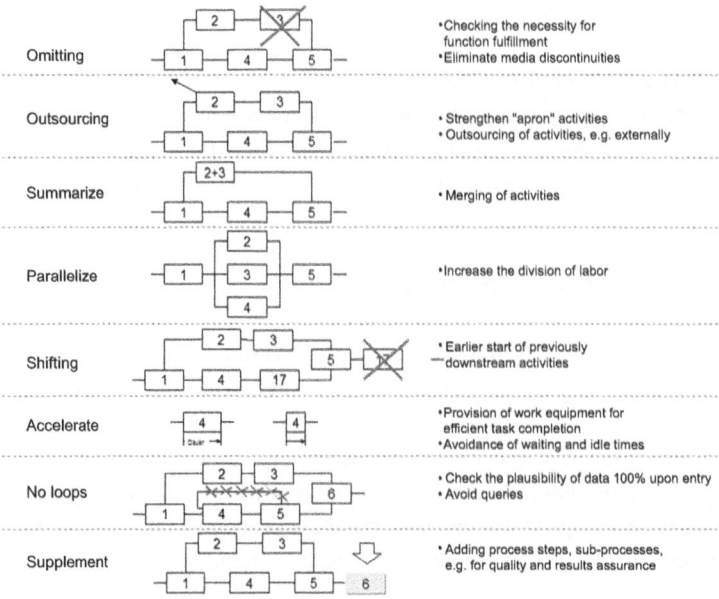

Fig. 2.13 Restructuring approaches according to (Bleicher 1991, modified)

Tab. 2.1 Basic forms of process restructuring according to Bleicher 1991, modified

No.	Concept	Explanation
1	Eliminate	Reviewing the necessity of processes or subprocesses for fulfilling functions, eliminating media discontinuities, and removing unnecessary approval steps
2	Outsource	Assigning subprocesses or entire process chains to external specialized service providers (e.g., bookkeeping and accounting by a tax consultant)
3	Combine	Tasks divided among several people are combined so that one person can complete related subprocesses in full without a handover (e.g., customer consulting and order entry through to the creation of the order confirmation)
4	Parallelize	Increasing division of labor in steps that can be performed in parallel (e.g., exam grading by several examiners for different sections)
5	Relocate	Moving process steps so that tasks are performed earlier, preventing bottlenecks later on (e.g., complete collection of customer information during order entry)
6	Accelerate	Use of time-saving tools (document management system replaces paper documentation), reduction of waiting and idle times by increasing capacity
7	Avoid Loops	Designing processes without loops, i.e., avoiding repetition of subprocesses (e.g., online entry of all customer and order data during order processing, and release of the order only after complete validation of the data)
8	Add	Avoiding downstream processes for "damage control" (e.g., adding a quality control step after assembly to prevent a possible "rework process" or a "recall of defective goods")

Source: Own illustration based on Bleicher 1991

This approach originates from military and disaster medicine: when many casualties need to be treated simultaneously, sequential processing can be fatal. Therefore, priorities must be set. However, the method is also applied in routine cases: after a clinical examination, it is decided whether it is a "standard case" or whether further examinations or treatments are required. Different process variants then follow (see Hellmann and Eble 2010).

2.4.3 Case Study: Restructuring Spare Parts Procurement

The approach to business process optimization will be illustrated using a deliberately exaggerated, yet realistic, fictional example. The organizational structure and the business process prior to optimization are shown in Fig. 2.14.

The subject of the business process under consideration is the procurement of spare parts for a fictional mechanical engineering manufacturer.

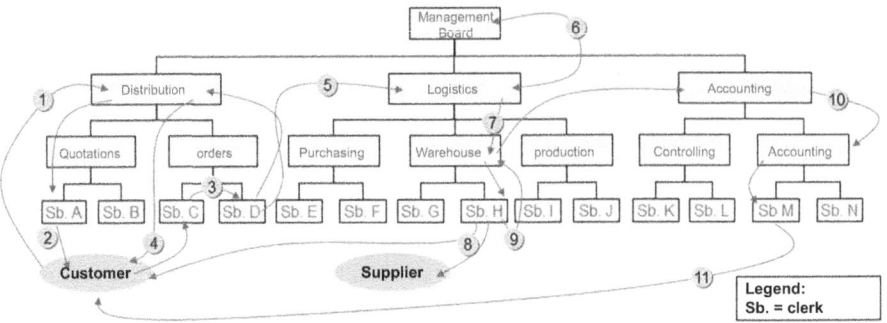

Fig. 2.14 Spare parts procurement before process optimization – prior to optimization

1. The process begins with the sales manager, who personally handles incoming customer inquiries.
2. The quotation is then sent to the customer by clerk A. Before the quotation is sent, it is reviewed by the sales manager. Since the sales manager is not always present, it can happen that a quotation prepared by clerk A remains pending for several days.
3. If the customer places an order, it is manually checked by clerk C and then entered into the order processing system by clerk D.
4. The customer receives an order confirmation after the sales manager has reviewed and approved the order.
5. After the order is entered, it is forwarded to the head of the logistics department. This person personally decides whether a part can be taken from stock, needs to be procured, or even produced.
6. If uncertain, the logistics manager consults with the executive board.
7. The warehouse manager then receives the order to dispatch the material. If the warehouse manager is not present that day, the order is handed over to one of his clerks, e.g., H, on the next working day.
8. This clerk (in this case, H) removes the part from stock, ships it to the customer, and places a reorder for the spare part with the responsible supplier.
9. After shipping, clerk H in the warehouse reports the outgoing transaction to his supervisor. The supervisor checks the document and forwards it to the head of accounting.
10. The head of accounting passes the document to the head of the bookkeeping department, who in turn forwards it to one of his clerks. Since the head of accounting is often assigned to planning tasks by the executive board, documents frequently remain unprocessed for several days.
11. In this case, clerk M prepares the invoice and sends it to the customer.

The main weaknesses of the process are relatively easy to identify:

- Managers make operational decisions up to the executive level,
- too many people are involved, resulting in frequent handovers between clerks,
- there is little direct interaction at the clerk level, as process handovers are often managed by supervisors,
- in the event of absence, there is evidently no substitution policy in place.

From this, several opportunities for improvement can be derived in terms of process optimization, i.e., incremental changes:

- the executive board generally does not participate in operational business process decisions,
- managers intervene in the process only in exceptional cases; the process is consistently managed at the clerk level,
- the customer communicates directly with the (responsible) clerks,
- clerks exchange information directly with each other,
- employees complete an entire processing step themselves.

If these principles are applied to the business process, an optimized version of the process could take the course shown in Fig. 2.15.

The sequence of the revised business process is now as follows:

1. The process begins with the sales clerk, who independently prepares quotations based on customer inquiries.
2. The quotation is then prepared by clerk A and sent to the customer.
3. If the customer places an order, it is checked by clerk C and then entered directly into the order processing system.

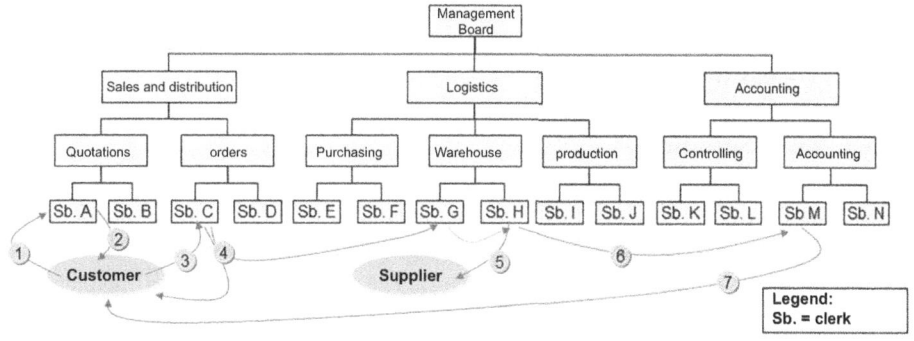

Fig. 2.15 Spare parts procurement after process optimization

4. Clerk C then informs the responsible buyer, warehouse clerk, or production clerk, depending on how the business transaction is to be handled (alternatives are sale from stock, in-house production, or external procurement). At the same time, the customer receives an order confirmation with the specified delivery date.
5. In the case considered here, employee G in the warehouse receives the order to deliver the material to the customer. If he is absent that day, his deputy H takes over the task. H removes the part from stock, ships it to the customer, and places a reorder for the spare part with the responsible supplier.
6. Employee H then informs clerk M in accounting.
7. Clerk M then prepares the invoice based on the information received and sends it to the customer.

For the operational implementation of reengineering or optimization projects, it is advisable to develop a customized analysis checklist with approaches for process optimization (Riekhof 1997, p. 15):

- Can duplicate work or unnecessary administration be eliminated?
- Can process elements be simplified and standardized?
- Can process elements be automated?
- Can the sequence of activities be optimized?
- Can process elements be designed to be error-proof?
- Can non-value-adding elements be eliminated?
- Can the division of labor between process customers and suppliers be optimized?

Summary of Business Process Optimization
The objective of business process optimization is to achieve sustainable improvement of processes through the gradual implementation of coordinated measures. This typically involves a thorough as-is analysis of the current situation, followed by optimization and IT-supported implementation.

2.4.4 Case Study: Process Optimization in Incoming Invoice Processing

2.4.4.1 Initial Situation
The example is based on a real case that has been slightly simplified. In a medium-sized engineering firm, the processing of incoming supplier invoices is largely paper-based. IT support is limited to posting in the accounting system and the use of online banking. Document storage is paper-based (file folders!). The volume is about 250 invoices per month, with minor fluctuations.

The process, shown in Fig. 2.16 as a swimlane or simple BPMN diagram, consists of two areas of activity: invoice receipt processing and archiving, which are outlined below.

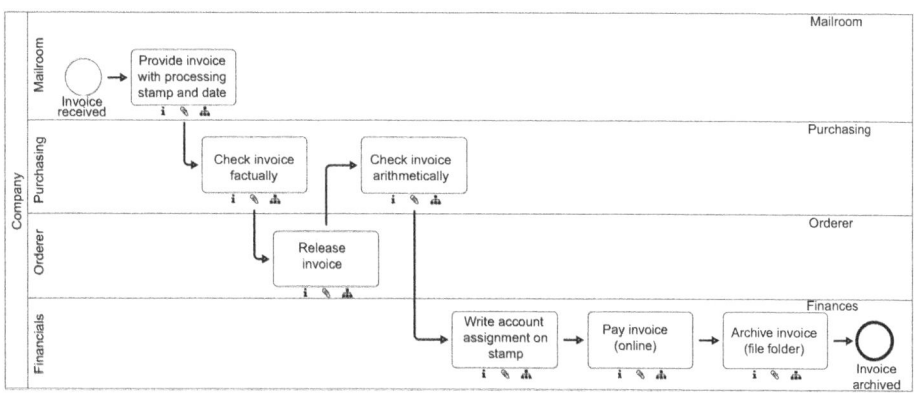

Fig. 2.16 As-is process for incoming invoice processing

- Receipt: Manual processing of incoming paper invoices; for email receipts, invoices are printed (usually PDF files); in some cases, invoices are also retrieved from online portals of very large suppliers
- Archiving: Printing multiple copies and filing them chronologically and alphabetically by business area and supplier.

A brief analysis revealed numerous weaknesses, such as many interfaces between process steps. The ERP system used in the company is only integrated late in the process (starting from invoice posting). The paper-based work of employees does not allow for mobile working and leads to many processing errors.

2.4.4.2 Problem Solution

In a workshop following the analysis, the company reviewed the process using the "checklist" presented in Fig. 2.13 and developed the following suggestions for optimization:

- *Omit:* Incoming and processing stamps are eliminated; "stamping" is performed automatically by scanning software, which also eliminates the need to make manual "photocopies" for other departments
- *Outsource:* In the long term, a cloud solution for the ERP system and the document management system (DMS) is being considered
- *Consolidate:* The steps "content check," "accuracy check," as well as "approval" and "account assignment" with "payment" are partially consolidated.
- *Parallelize:* Content and accuracy checks are performed in parallel (at least for complex invoices)
- *Relocate:* Archiving is performed directly after scanning by the DMS, with ongoing updates to the archive

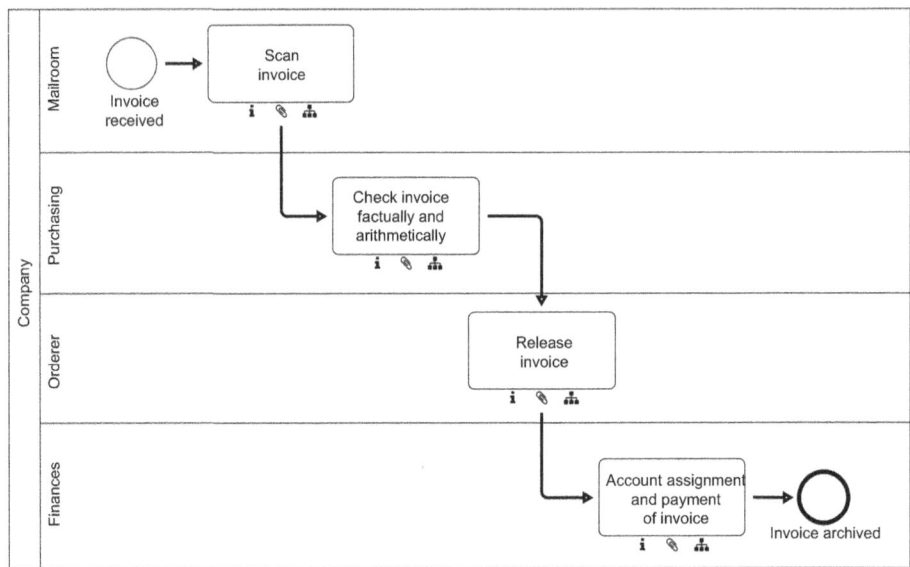

Fig. 2.17 Target process for incoming invoice processing

- *No loops:* Only validated data is transferred to the system
- *Add:* Evaluations and analyses of existing invoices are provided for quality control, to reduce errors and improve processing quality

The resulting target process is shown in Fig. 2.17.

2.4.5 Case Study: Process Optimization of Order Processing in IT Services

2.4.5.1 Initial Situation
The process concerns the handling of purchase requisitions in the IT service department of a mechanical engineering company. It is depicted as both the current and target process in Fig. 2.18 as a simplified process model using the ARIS-Express modeling tool and the simplified eEPK notation (see Sect. 5.7).

The process has evolved over many years and exhibits several weaknesses:

- Internal IT user orders (purchase requisitions, or "BANF") are submitted as "free text" without a material number, resulting in frequent, time-consuming clarifications between IT procurement and IT users.
- If items are unavailable, a manual entry is made in the so-called "delivery database," an "Excel spreadsheet."

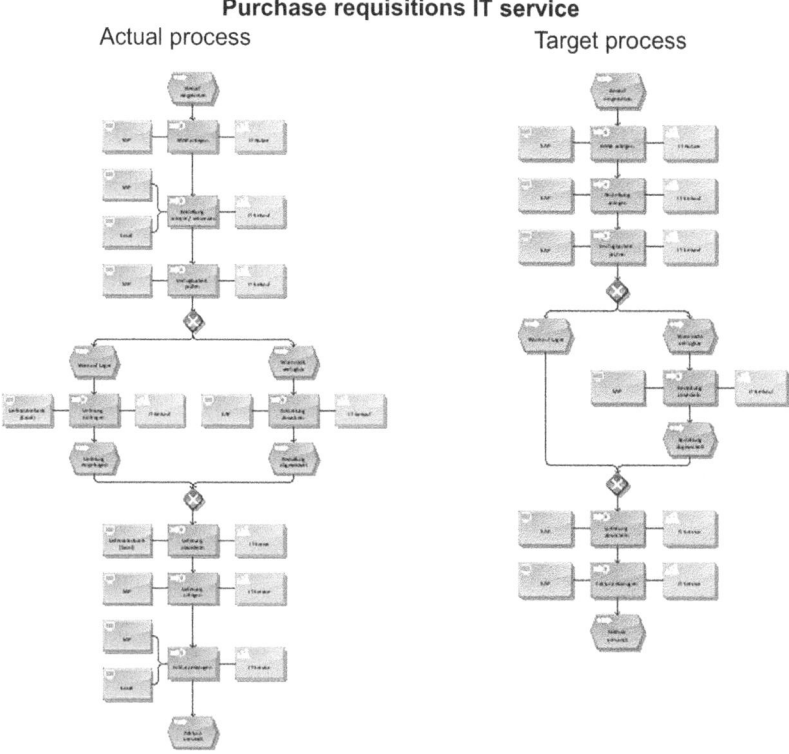

Fig. 2.18   Current and Target Process: Purchase Requisitions in IT Services

- IT users do not receive an order confirmation from IT services for their submitted orders.
- There is no up-to-date order status available, neither for IT users nor for IT services.
- Due to the partially manual processing, only collective invoices are generated.

Overall, the process is characterized by multiple media discontinuities, i.e., information that is available electronically in the SAP system is copied out and sent by email, as well as the aforementioned "Excel spreadsheet."

2.4.5.2 Solution
The process was optimized. The chosen solution was to integrate the entire process into SAP as an automated workflow. IT users now use the material number from the very beginning of the process. For this purpose, a search function in the SAP system was provided. All process-related data is recorded in the SAP system. IT users receive an automated order confirmation. The order status is available at any time (for both IT users and IT procurement). The process no longer contains any media discontinuities; all data is

centrally available. Due to integrated data management, invoices can be generated for each individual order.

2.4.6 Case Study: Optimization of Applicant Management

2.4.6.1 Initial Situation

This case study concerns a large multinational corporation. The company aims to fill open positions as quickly as possible with suitable candidates. In the past, there have been repeated cases where filling vacant positions took several months and suboptimal hiring decisions were made. The Chief Human Resources Officer therefore commissions a process improvement team to analyze the personnel recruitment process and propose optimization measures.

2.4.6.2 Solution

The team first examines the time required to fill positions, measured from the decision "Position can be filled" to the event "Employment contract signed" (see Fig. 2.19).

   The time to fill positions varies greatly depending on the hiring department. The reasons differ. The Organization and Information Technology (Org/IT) department has a high demand for skilled workers, which clearly leads to faster hiring. Other departments (e.g., procurement, production, or sales) take more time. Hierarchy level appears to have little influence on the time to hire.

   The situation is different when considering the contact medium with applicants. Traditional media such as newspapers or university job fairs result in average or good

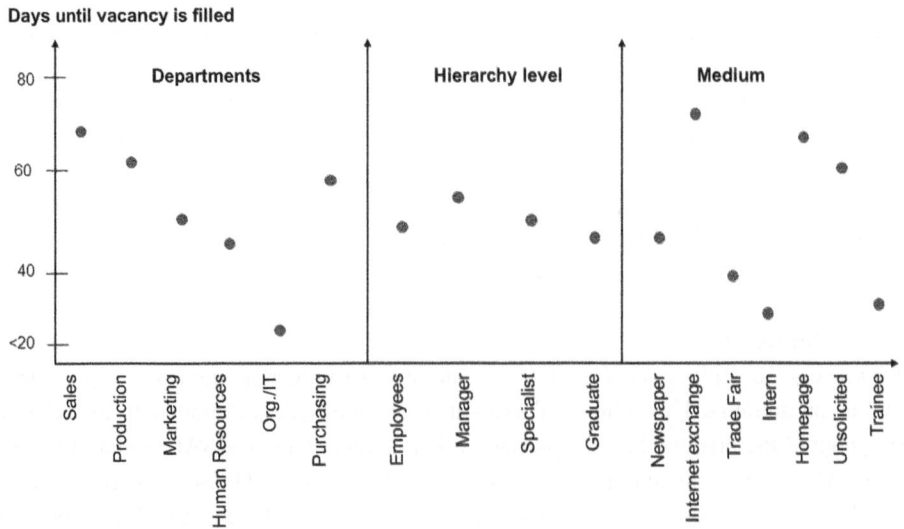

Fig. 2.19 Analysis of Time to Fill Positions

values. However, these solutions are comparatively expensive (especially newspaper ads) or labor-intensive (job fairs require booth staff and are only worthwhile if a sufficiently large number of positions need to be filled). Modern and supposedly "fast" media such as online job boards or the company's own website generate a high number of applications, but these are often of very poor quality (missing/contradictory information, many unsuitable candidates, etc.). This ties up significant resources in the HR department and the hiring departments. Hires based on unsolicited applications are also very time-consuming, as suitable positions are often lacking for good candidates and may need to be created. Relatively short times to fill positions are observed for university interns and participants in trainee programs. Since these individuals are already known to the company, the departments can assess their quality and suitability very well and are highly motivated to expedite hiring.

An analysis of the relationship between the time to fill positions and the quality of the first personnel evaluation by the direct supervisor reveals a concerning picture. The shorter the time to fill, the higher the likelihood of a good evaluation. Apparently, the longer the search for candidates, the greater the risk of compromising on candidate quality just to fill the position.

Proposal for Process Improvement
The analyses lead to the decision to significantly expand the intern pool and intensify the trainee program for university graduates. Online job board postings will be discontinued in the future. Job advertisements in traditional print media will be limited to management and specialist positions, as these cannot be filled from the pool of interns and trainees. Only positions that are simultaneously advertised in print media will be posted on the company website.

2.5   Related Management Concepts

In recent years, numerous management concepts have been developed and implemented in practice that pursue objectives at least partially comparable to those of process management.

These approaches particularly focus on objectives such as customer orientation, efficiency, reduction of interfaces, and simplification of work organization. Concepts in this context include Process Performance Management, Lean Management, Kaizen/Continuous Improvement Process (CIP), and, more recently, agile methods in software development.

2.5.1   Process Performance Management

Process Performance Management (also known as "Business Performance Management," Scheer and Hess 2009, p. 145) has evolved from process management (Oehler

2006, p. 50). The concept encompasses process management and places particular emphasis on the identification and analysis of key performance indicators derived from ongoing processes. Implementation requires powerful Process Performance Management systems, which are used for data collection and analysis. Data warehouse systems serve as the technical foundation for Process Performance Management systems. They handle the formal cleansing, content validation, and aggregation of data. The Process Performance Management system accesses this data to generate key figures and reports (see Schmelzer and Sesselmann 2013). Like process management, Process Performance Management aims to improve the performance of business processes across all areas, with Business Performance Management taking a broader approach by also focusing on the financial sector in addition to processes (Scheer and Hess 2009, p. 145).

2.5.2   Lean Management

A study conducted by the Massachusetts Institute of Technology (MIT) in the early 1990s, which compared Japanese, American, and European automobile manufacturers, led to the development of the Lean Management concept. Initially, the focus was on production, as reflected in the term "Lean Production." Later, the concept was expanded to encompass the entire organization. Lean Management refers to a streamlined approach to corporate management, aiming for high efficiency, speed, and superior quality (see, for example, Schmelzer and Sesselmann 2013).

2.5.3   Kaizen/Continuous Improvement Process (CIP)

Kaizen, a Japanese management philosophy (literally "improvement"), or CIP (Continuous Improvement Process), refers to an ongoing process of improvement involving employee participation. The approach emphasizes strong process orientation, meaning the focus is not on the outcome but on the process of achieving the outcome, as well as on involving employees and leveraging their skills to solve existing problems within processes. The goal is to achieve continuous improvement in process performance through incremental changes (see, for example, Schmelzer and Sesselmann 2013).

2.6   Reference Models

A reference model is a pre-designed model of an "ideal" process that can be used for one's own organization with little or no modification. Typical applications include the analysis and restructuring of business processes, in-house software development, selection of standard software, and documentation of software or standard software by software developers or vendors. Sources for reference models include other comparable companies in the same industry, literature, management consultants, and software providers.

The benefit of using reference models lies in the broader base of experience that can be incorporated into one's own projects and the reduction of modeling effort. Risks primarily involve the loss of competitive advantage due to process standardization. The company loses the opportunity to differentiate itself positively from competitors. In addition, a significant amount of training is required. Ultimately, there is a risk of low employee acceptance, as they are confronted with a model in whose development they were not involved. Research on this topic has already been published under the term "process acceptance theory" (see, for example, Drewes and Nissen 2022).

Types of Reference Models

A distinction is made in particular between global business reference models, software reference models, and enterprise process models (see Schmelzer and Sesselmann 2013): Business reference models are general information models tailored to specific application areas (e.g., functions, industries). They serve as guidance and recommendations for the construction of company-specific models. An example is the "SCOR model" (SCOR = Supply Chain Operations Reference for Supply Chains) (see SCOR 2001).

Software reference models are offered by standard software vendors and describe the processes supported by the standard software. They provide customers with templates that reduce the effort required to implement the standard software. SAP AG from Walldorf, for example, provides extensive model-based descriptions of its software's functionality with the "SAP Solution Map" and the "SAP Business Scenario Map."

Enterprise process models are tailored to the specific situation of a company. They contain guidelines and rules for business units on how their processes should be structured and described. These are often centrally specified by company management as internal regulations. Elements of the models include, among others: guidance on compliance with legal requirements, rules for organizational documentation, specifications for selecting ERP systems, and for customizing standard systems. An example is the "V-Model," a process model for software development in the public sector (IABG n.d., accessed 28.07.2016).

2.7 Explorative Process Management

"Explorative Process Management" is a more recent research approach within process management, taking a forward-looking perspective on innovation and new business models (see Grisold et al. 2019; Gross et al. 2019; and Recker and Mendling 2016).

The concept is based on the realization that the focus of previous methods in process management has been primarily retrospective, dealing mainly with the improvement (optimization) of existing processes. For this reason, it is also referred to as "Exploitative

Process Management" (see Grisold et al. 2019). Typical questions addressed by traditional "Exploitative Process Management" include:

- How can we reduce the number of process variants?
- How can we reduce process cycle times?
- How can we avoid idle times in the process?
- How can we reduce process costs?
- How can we ensure that "process rules" or "compliance rules" are followed?

The approach is therefore "inside-out," following the principle: "How can I use my current processes, in an improved form, to meet customer needs?" In explorative process management, the focus is on innovation to secure the "profit of tomorrow's company." The approach is "outside-in" (see Grisold et al. 2019), working in an opportunity-driven manner—such as by leveraging new market trends—to develop ideas for new, mostly digital, business models.

Figure 2.20 compares the two exploitative BPM concepts, business reengineering and business process optimization, with the explorative approach. While both business reengineering and business process optimization focus on optimizing the existing business model and further developing processes, the explorative approach develops the business model itself and provides the necessary processes for it. The disruptive impact is therefore particularly high with the explorative approach, whereas business process optimization only brings about minor changes.

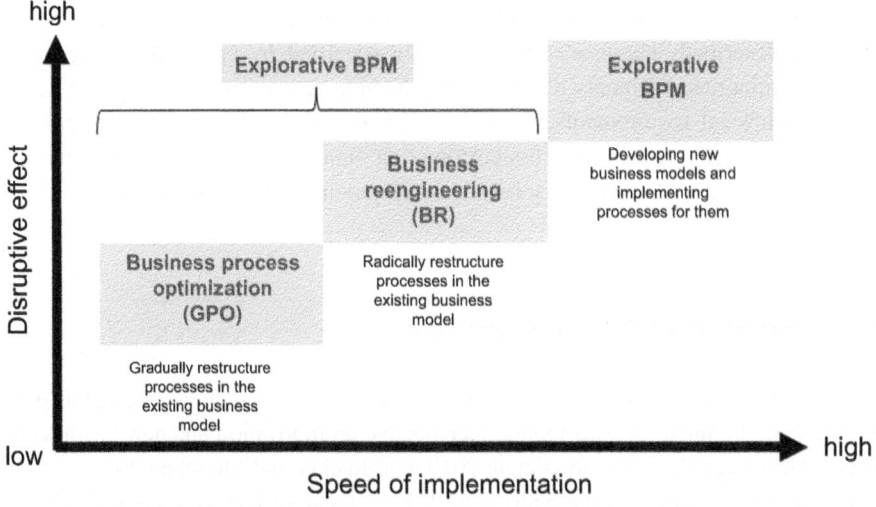

Fig. 2.20 Classification of different BPM concepts

Ideally, both concepts are combined. "Explorative Process Management" secures the strategic environment and thus long-term competitiveness through the introduction of innovations. "Exploitative" process management ensures the efficient and economic implementation of these concepts (vom Brocke et al. 2019).

2.8   Review Questions and Answers

Questions
1. Explain the concept of **holistic business process and workflow management.**
2. Why is **two-stage process modeling** (1. business process, 2. workflow) often preferred in practice?
3. Describe the essential steps of a **process management life cycle model.**
4. Why are **views** created in the context of process management?
5. Explain under what conditions the **"chimney effect"** occurs in organizations.
6. Compare the optimization concepts of **business reengineering and business process optimization.**
7. Distinguish **"explorative process management"** from **"exploitative process management."**

Answers
1. **Holistic business process and workflow management** considers the strategic and functional design of processes and their technical implementation within a unified modeling approach, which is represented in three levels of abstraction.
2. Many companies initially start with the pure documentation of processes from a business perspective in order to implement a process management concept. The technical execution of processes (digitalization) is generally not implemented for all processes. Therefore, a **two-stage approach** often appears more practical to companies.
3. A **life cycle model** of process management includes the design, technical implementation, and execution of processes.
4. **Views** in process management represent different details that are not needed in every situation or by every person. However, they are necessary overall to manage processes in a goal-oriented manner.
5. The **"chimney effect"** occurs when, in the context of cross-departmental processes, communication takes place vertically through the management hierarchy.
6. **Business reengineering** is a radical management concept for restructuring companies. It starts from scratch without regard for existing structures. **Business process optimization** seeks to build on a given situation and further develop it in a goal-oriented manner.
7. **"Explorative process management"** designs new business models and the processes required for them. **"Exploitative process management"** optimizes processes within existing business models, but does not change the business models themselves, only the necessary processes.

References

Becker, J., Algermissen, L., Pfeiffer, D., Räckers, M.: Bausteinbasierte Modellierung von Prozess-landschaften mit der PICTURE-Methode am Beispiel der Universitätsverwaltung Münster. In: Wirtschaftsinformatik, **49**(4), 267–279 (2007)

Becker, J., Bergener, P., Kleist, S., Pfeiffer, D., Räckers, M.: Business process model-based evaluation of ict investments in public administrations. In: 16th European Conference on Information Systems, Proceedings (CD-ROM), Galway (2008)

Bleicher, K.: Organisation, 2. edn. Wiesbaden (1991)

Brunner, H., Hartel, M., Georges, T.: Szenariotechnik zur Entwicklung von Geschäftsstrategien am Beispiel des Werkzeug- und Anlagenbaus der BMW Group. In: Zeitschrift für Organisation, **71**(5), 312–317 (2002)

Dadam, P., Reichert, M., Rinderle-Ma, S.: Prozessmanagementsysteme, Nur ein wenig Flexibilität wird nicht reichen. In: Informatik Spektrum, **34**(4), 365–376 (2011)

Dillerup, R., Stoi, R.: Unternehmensführung, 2. edn. München (2012)

Drewes, L., Nissen, V.: Akzeptierte Geschäftsprozesse gestalten und implementieren. HMD **59**, 572–587 (2022). https://doi.org/10.1365/s40702-022-00856-x

Gadatsch, A.: Entwicklung eines Konzeptes zur Modellierung und Evaluation von Workflows, Dissertation, FernUniversität Hagen, 1999, Frankfurt (2000)

Gehring, H., Gadatsch, A.: Ein Rahmenkonzept für die Prozessmodellierung, in: Information Management & Consulting, **4**, 69–74 (1999)

Gehring, H.: Betriebliche Anwendungssysteme, Kurseinheit 2. FernUniversität Hagen, Hagen, Prozessorientierte Gestaltung von Informationssystemen (1998)

Graf von Büdingen, G., Schlaf, S.: BPM-Methoden und Tools als Basis für wirtschaftliche und compliancegerechte Abläufe im E.ON-Energie-Konzern. In: Komus, A. (Eds.) BPM Best Practice, Berlin, (2011)

Grisold, T., Gross, S., Röglinger, M., Stelzl, K., vom Brocke, J.: Exploring explorative BPM – setting the ground for future research. Proceedings of Conference on Business Process Management (BPM 2019) (2019)

Gross, S., Malinova Mandelburger, M., Mendling, J.: Navigating through the maze of business process change methods. Proceedings of the 52nd Hawaii International Conference on System Sciences (HICSS-52), pp. 6270–6279 (2019)

Hammer, M.: Reengineering work: don't automate, obliterate. Harvard Bus. Rev. **68**(4), 104–112 (1990)

Hammer, M., Champy, J.: (1994): Business Reengineering, 2. edn. Frankfurt, New York (1994)

Hellmann, W., Eble, S. (Eds.): Ambulante und sektorenübergreifende Behandlungspfade, Berlin (2010)

Hess, T., Österle, H.: Methoden des Business Process Redesign: Aktueller Stand und Entwicklungsperspektiven. In: Handbuch der modernen Datenverarbeitung, **183**, 120–136 (1995)

IABG (Eds.): V-Modell. http://www.v-modell.iabg.de (o. J.). Accessed 28. Juli 2016

vom Brocke, J., Grisold, T., Gross, S., Röglinger, M., Stelzl, K.: BPM tutorial 2019. Exploring Explorative Business Process Management, Slideshare (2019). Accessed 28 Juli 2020

Oehler, K.: Corporate performance management. Mit Business Intelligence Werkzeugen, München (2006)

Österle, H.: Business engineering. Prozess- und Systementwicklung, Band 1, Entwurfstechniken, Berlin, (1995)

Osterloh, M., Frost, J.: Prozessmanagement als Kernkompetenz, 4. edn. Wiesbaden (2003)

Recker and Mendling: The state of the art of business process management research as published in the BPM conference. Bus. Inf. Syst. Eng. **58**(1), 55–72 (2016)

Riekhof, H.-Ch.: Die Idee des Geschäftsprozesses: Basis der lernenden Organisation. In: Riekhof, H.-Ch. (Hrsg.) Beschleunigung von Geschäftsprozessen. Wettbewerbsvorteile durch Lernfähigkeit, Mit Fallstudien von Bosch – Phoenix – Siemens – Volkswagen – Würth, Stuttgart, pp. 7–28 (1997)

Robbins, S.P.: Organisation der Unternehmung, 9. edn. München (2001)

Scheer, A.-W.: ARIS – Modellierungsmethoden, Metamodelle, Anwendungen, 3. edn. Berlin (1998a)

Scheer, A.-W.: ARIS – Vom Geschäftsprozess zum Anwendungssystem, 3. edn. Berlin (1998b)

Scheer, A.-W., Heß, H.: Business process/performance management im rahmen eines ganzheitlichen controlling-ansatzes. Controll. Z. erfolgsorient. Unternehmenssteuerung, 21(3), 145–151 (2009)

Schmelzer, H.J., Sesselmann., W.: Geschäftsprozessmanagement in der Praxis, 8. edn. München (2013)

SCOR: Supply chain operations reference model, supply chain council. http://www.supply-Chain.org (2001). Accessed 28 Apr 2001

Sinz, E.J.: Ansätze zur fachlichen Modellierung betrieblicher Informationssysteme – Entwicklung, aktueller Stand und Trends, In: Heilmann, H., Heinrich, L.J., Roithmayr, R. (Eds.) Inf. Eng. pp. 127. München, Wien (1996)

Weske, M.: Business process management, concepts, languages, architectures. Berlin (2007)

Organization and Implementation of Business Process Management

3

Process management is continuous project work

Abstract

The introduction of process management is a classic change project that affects the entire organization at all levels and in every area. Many stakeholders, ranging from top management ("Chief Process Officer") and middle management ("Process Manager") down to individual employees, the "Process Experts," must be involved. Changing and optimizing processes primarily means "changing people" and motivating them towards process-oriented collaboration.

This chapter describes approaches to process-oriented organization within companies and the optimization of processes. In addition, it introduces the various roles and stakeholders, which must be developed to varying degrees depending on the size of the company. Special emphasis is placed on project organization, which is particularly important when project management concepts are being introduced for the first time. The chapter concludes with review questions and an exercise.

3.1 Process-Oriented Organizational Structures

3.1.1 Design Approaches

The implementation of process-oriented organizational structures (in short: process organization) has not yet become established in practice, even though it is considered a traditional method in business administration under the term "workflow organization."

© The Author(s), under exclusive license to Springer Fachmedien Wiesbaden GmbH, part of Springer Nature 2026
A. Gadatsch, *Business Process Management*,
https://doi.org/10.1007/978-3-658-49339-4_3

A scientific study on business process management yielded a sobering result: "For over 80% of participants, improving quality and increasing transparency are the most important objectives for process management in companies. However, these goals are achieved by less than 50% of these companies." (Gadatsch et al. 2016).

Incidentally, the "optimal" organizational structure for process management is just as difficult to realize as the design of "digitalization organizations" in public management, whether as a "super digital ministry" with extensive powers or as a networked system of decentralized "digitalization officers" in federal ministries or "state governments" (see Mertens 2021 for a detailed discussion).

Classical Line Organization

In many companies, classical functional structures still dominate the organizational structure. A simplified example is shown in Fig. 3.1. (It depicts a company that produces engines, brakes, and transmissions.) The company is functionally divided into various departments (sales, purchasing, production, etc.), each responsible for specific tasks (functions). The process flow for the core processes (production and sales of engines, transmissions, and brakes), on the other hand, runs horizontally, but without any dedicated unit responsible for these processes. In other words, there is no process control. The processes are divided into separate, independent sections by the various departments.

Due to the lack of process control within the framework of the functional line organization, concepts for process-oriented organization were developed. The organizational

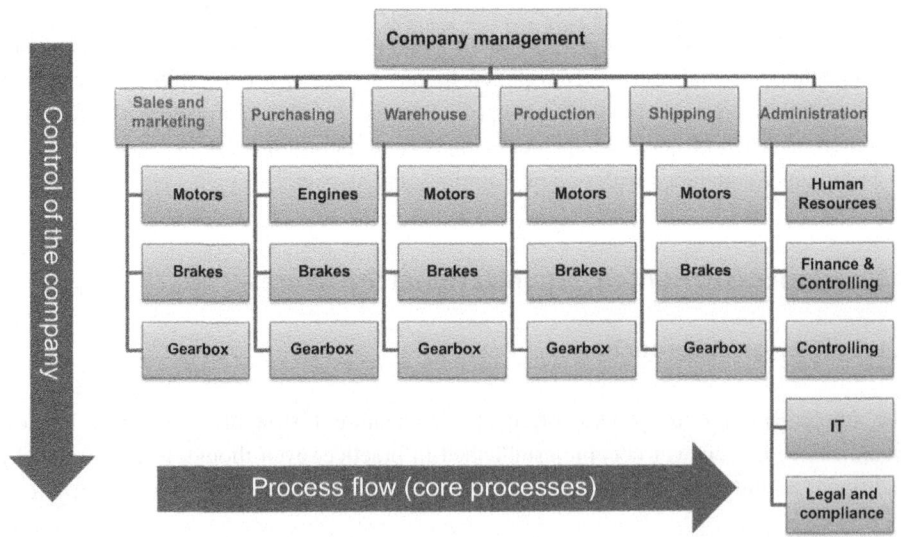

Fig. 3.1 Forms of Process Organization—Classical Line Organization

design of process management has a significant impact on a company's success. Process management can be established as a classical process organization, as a staff unit within a functional organization, or as a matrix organization (see Fig. 3.2).

In a **pure process organization**, activities are arranged to align as closely as possible with customer requirements in the sense of an end-to-end process. The goal is to sequence the steps so that the process can be executed smoothly. In this context, processes must be organized in a way that avoids overlaps (e.g., retail business, business customer operations, mail order).

Figure 3.3 shows the example from Fig. 3.1 as a pure process organization. For each core process (e.g., engine production and sales), there is a dedicated unit, the "Chief Process Officer" for the respective process. All necessary resources (budget, personnel, machinery, raw materials, buildings, etc.) required for the process are assigned to this unit.

Cross-functional activities (e.g., shared purchasing, sales) must be coordinated, as there is no functional responsibility. In practice, these are also referred to as "shared services." The process owners assume entrepreneurial responsibility for their process. The processes themselves become the "departments" of the process organization.

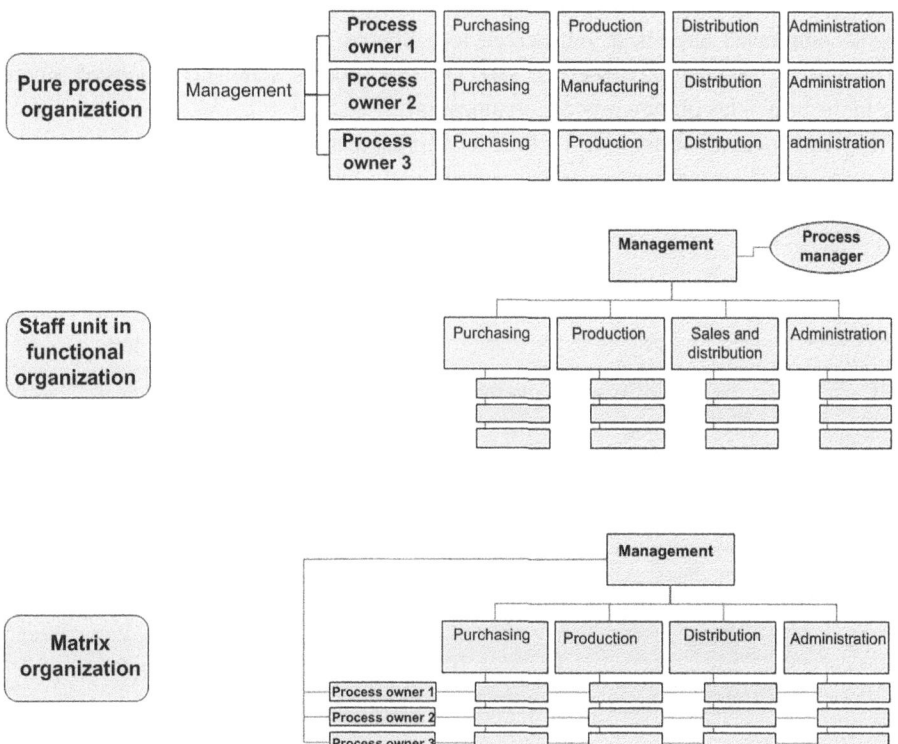

Fig. 3.2 Basic Design Approaches to Process Organization

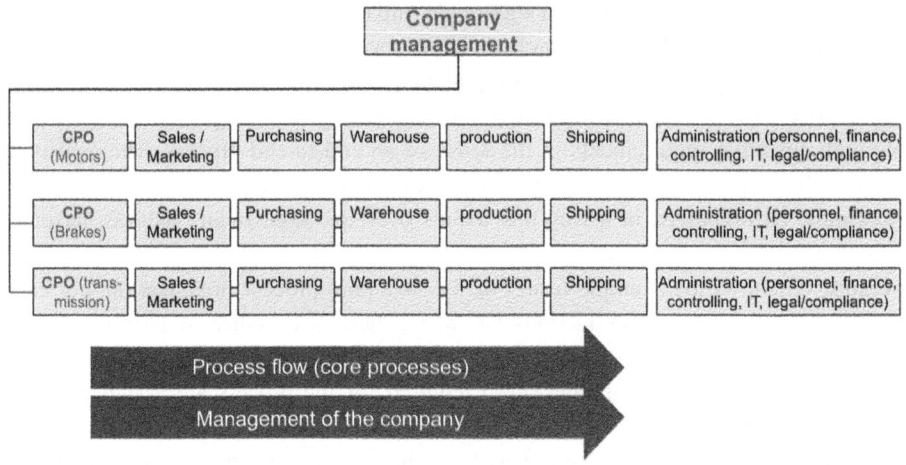

Fig. 3.3 Forms of Process Organization—Pure Process Organization

For this purpose, the example of the pure process organization from Fig. 3.3 has been slightly modified: the process steps for Human Resources, Finance, Controlling, IT, and Legal/Compliance have been outsourced to a Shared Service Center, i.e., a unit with cross-process responsibility (see Fig. 3.4). The core processes are still structured according to the principles of pure process organization.

The **staff organization** within a functional organization coordinates processes within the company. However, the functional organization (divisions, departments, groups, etc.)

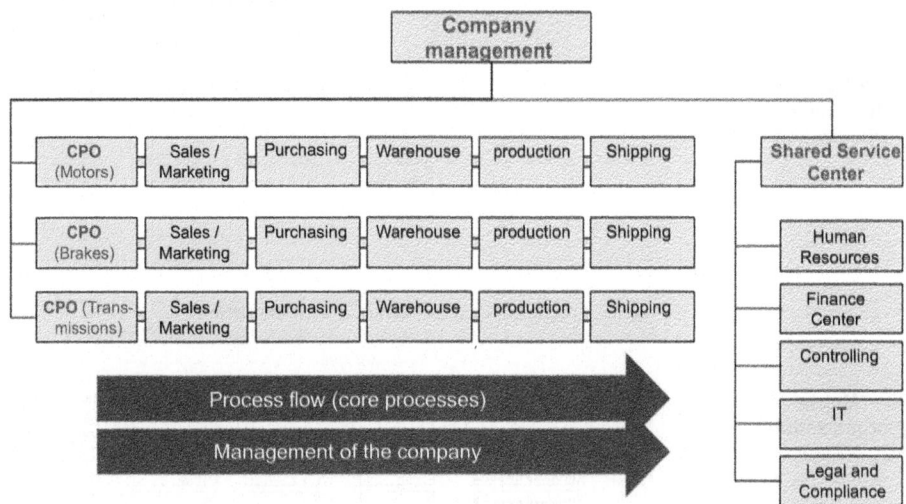

Fig. 3.4 Forms of Process Organization—Process Organization with Shared Service Centers

remains in place, meaning the organization is still fundamentally function-oriented. The effectiveness of this model is therefore not considered particularly high in terms of process management, but with appropriate leadership skills of the Chief Process Officer (head of the staff unit), it can certainly be an alternative to process organization, especially when process management is being introduced for the first time.

Practical Example: DAK

The responsibilities of the CPO at DAK (Deutsche Angestellten Krankenkasse), established as a staff unit within corporate development, include "moderation, documentation, and the derivation of concrete projects from the strategy." Implementation remains the responsibility of the IT manager, who is therefore also significantly involved in process management (Vogel 2004, p. 22). ◄

The example from Fig. 3.1 is shown in Fig. 3.5 as a process organization with a staff structure. The difference compared to a pure line organization is marginal.

The **matrix organization** is based on two structuring principles: activity/function and object/process, according to which activities are organized. Here, process managers (Process Officers) are responsible for aligning processes along the functional organization in such a way that they operate smoothly. They compete with the heads of the functional departments for resources, which is intended to lead to ongoing coordination conflicts.

The well-known example of the engine manufacturer from Fig. 3.1 is shown in Fig. 3.6, in a variant with shared service centers.

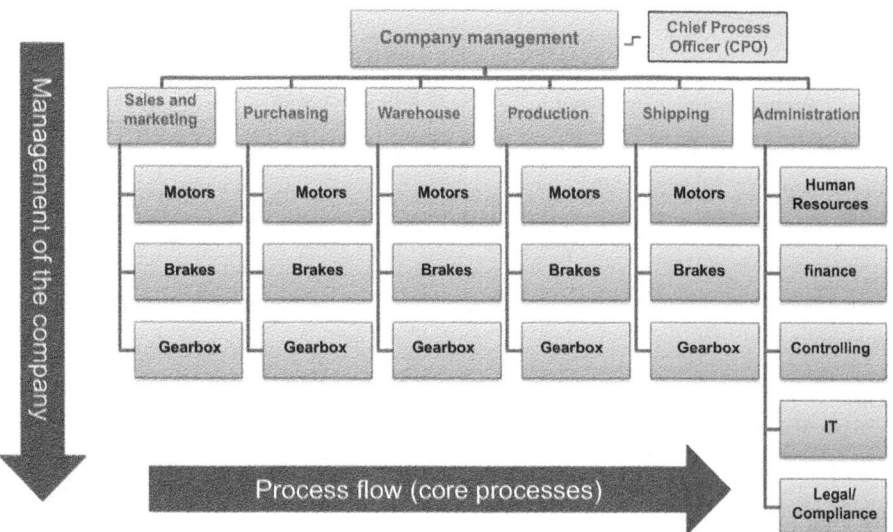

Fig. 3.5 Process organization as a staff structure

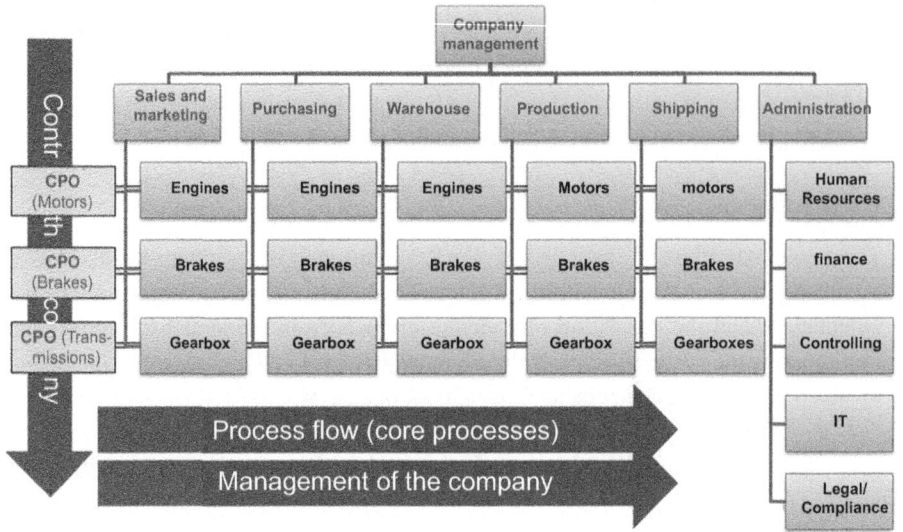

Fig. 3.6 Process organization as a matrix organization

Another example of the use of the matrix organization, using a hospital as an example, is shown in Fig. 3.7.

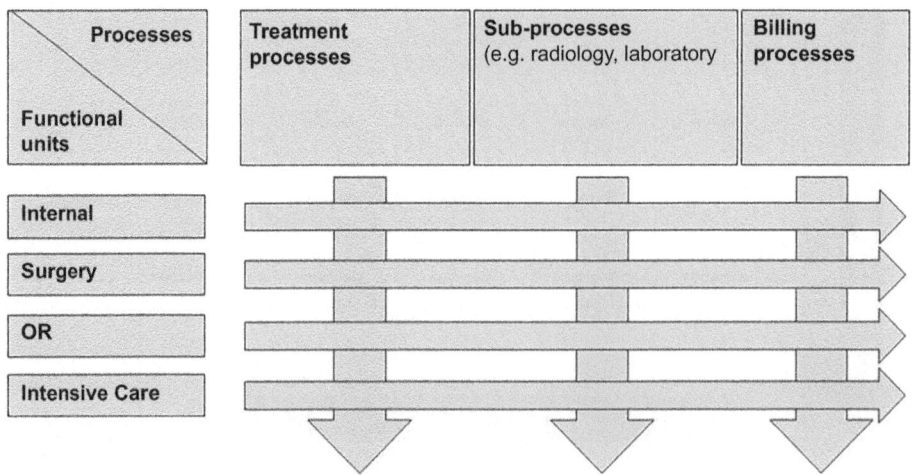

Fig. 3.7 Matrix organization in a hospital

3.1.2   Evaluation

The **pure process organization** is considered the ideal form, but is practically unattainable in real-world settings due to its high complexity. It is particularly difficult to implement in organizations with an existing functional structure. This is due to resistance and lack of understanding among employees and managers. Its characteristics are:

- Processes are customer-oriented (customer-to-customer processes),
- Processes are the primary structural element of the organizational design,
- Processes have their own organizational autonomy,
- Processes have their own resources (budget, personnel, machinery, equipment, IT systems),
- The CPO has full professional and disciplinary authority.

The impact can be summarized as follows: strong process orientation, very high process efficiency, and low resource efficiency (see Schmelzer and Sesselmann 2013).

The **staff organization**, a staff unit for process management within a functional organization, is the entry-level solution for process management. Due to the limited influence of staff units on decision-making, this variant is also referred to as the "influence process organization" according to Schmelzer and Sesselmann (2013). It is easy to implement and widely used. Its characteristics are:

- Processes are not customer-oriented (no customer-to-customer processes!),
- Functions are the primary structural element of the organizational design,
- Processes have only very limited organizational autonomy,
- Processes have only limited resources of their own (budget, personnel, machinery, equipment, IT systems),
- The Chief Process Officer (CPO) has only coordinating authority.

The impact of this variant is therefore limited: strong functional orientation, low process efficiency, and high resource efficiency. In most cases, a more pragmatic solution is chosen in practice: the **matrix organization**. Its characteristics are balanced:

- Processes are customer-oriented (customer-to-customer processes),
- Processes and functions are equally important structural elements of the organizational design,
- Processes have limited organizational autonomy,
- Processes have extensive resources of their own (budget, personnel, machinery, equipment, IT systems),
- The CPO has full professional but only limited disciplinary authority, as the latter remains with the functional management.

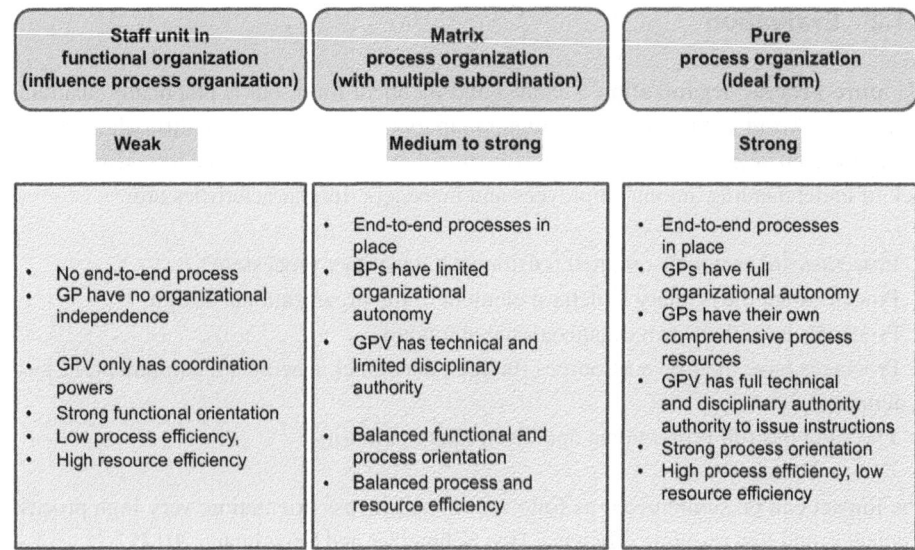

Fig. 3.8 Summary characterization of process management organizational forms according to Schmelzer and Sesselmann (2013)

The effect of the matrix organization is a balanced process and functional orientation, as well as process and resource efficiency (see Schmelzer and Sesselmann 2013).

The main arguments for and against the different organizational design options are summarized in Fig. 3.8.

3.2   Roles and Stakeholders

Process management is characterized by the interaction of a wide range of participants in different roles at various levels of an organization, such as an industrial enterprise or a university. The overview in Fig. 3.9 first assigns the key stakeholders in abstract form to the previously introduced concept of business process and workflow management. Since there are numerous German and English synonyms, both German and English terms are provided where appropriate. In the following, the terms most commonly used in practice, according to the author, will be used more frequently.

The illustration in Fig. 3.9 distinguishes between roles in day-to-day operations (run the business) and change projects (change the business) aimed at improving efficiency and quality. In addition, there are overarching roles such as the *Process Steering Board* or the *Process Auditors*.

The following section describes the roles based on Schmelzer (2005). In every organization, these roles must be specifically defined and assigned to concrete positions. Depending on the situation, this may also require the creation of new positions.

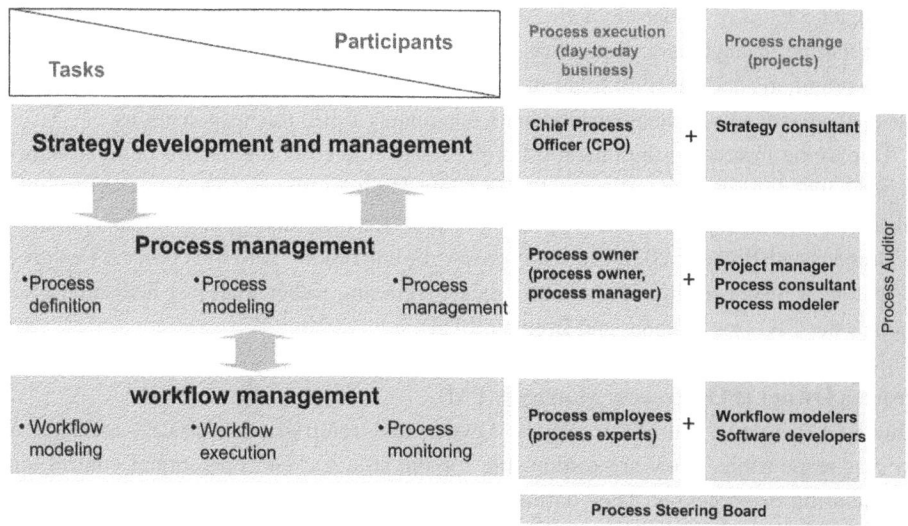

Fig. 3.9 Roles in process management

Head of Process Management or Chief Process Officer (CPO)
The person with overall responsibility for the processes within an organization is the Chief Process Officer (CPO). The CPO ensures organization-wide documentation, restructuring, and monitoring of processes, advises organizational units, and oversees the process-oriented design of the organization. The CPO is not responsible for individual processes, but rather for the effective interaction of all processes with a focus on the customer or patient. The main responsibilities include:

- Process documentation: Identification and description of relevant processes,
- Process analysis: Business-oriented simulation and analysis of weaknesses in business processes,
- Process optimization: Identification, definition, initiation, and monitoring of process improvements,
- Process monitoring: Ongoing analysis of process metrics with regard to achieving process objectives,
- Design and implementation of a process-oriented organizational structure, including the assignment of process responsibility to so-called Process Owners,
- Ensuring process-oriented IT systems through collaboration with the CIO (Chief Information Officer).

The actual appointment of the CPO role varies across industries. Not all companies have a dedicated position with the job title "CPO" within their organizational structure. The proportion of companies with a role that holds overall responsibility for all processes is just under 28% (see Gadatsch et al. 2016). As a result, the CPO role often remains with the executive management in practice. In smaller organizations, this can still be considered a pragmatic and sensible solution. In larger companies, however, this leads to a situation where executive management cannot adequately fulfill this responsibility.

Due to the increasing digitalization of processes, the CPO role is also being assumed by the Chief Information Officer (CIO) or Chief Digital Officer (CDO), as the responsibilities cannot always be clearly separated in practice (see interviews with several CIOs in Brenner and Brenner 2022). In many cases, digitalization—and thus process design— is seen as a responsibility of the entire executive team, rather than just dedicated roles such as the CIO (see Brenner and Brenner 2022).

Process Owner (PO)/Process Manager (PM)
Another key role is that of the Process Owner, also referred to as process manager or process responsible. They are responsible for the strategic and operational control and restructuring of processes. They define process objectives and ensure their achievement through goal-oriented leadership of process-supporting staff. If both roles are defined, the Process Owner is typically responsible for the strategic aspects, while the Process Manager (PM) focuses more on day-to-day operations and their management.

Process Staff/Process Expert/Process Participant
Process staff or process experts (e.g., a sales clerk, an administrative employee) support the initial implementation of business process management and its further development during major restructuring of the process organization. They are generally involved as specialists in one or more processes and, in this role, primarily perform operational tasks related to the process.

Process Consultant
The main focus of internal or, more commonly, external process consultants is the execution of conceptual and operational project work packages, such as knowledge transfer of best practices for processes, application of specialized methods and tools, and conducting workshops and training sessions.

Process/Workflow Modeler
The tasks of process or workflow modelers include IT-supported collection, modeling, and specification of processes, detailed analysis and optimization, as well as implementation in workflow management systems (WFMS).

Project Manager
Project managers are recruited from internal or external specialists or executives and are responsible for leading the business process management project, coordinating project objectives, ensuring goal achievement, managing project staff, and informing management.

Ideally, the project manager has interdisciplinary knowledge relevant to the specific industry (business administration, computer science, engineering, etc.).

Process Auditor
The process auditor is responsible for the independent review of workflows and process change projects. This role should be filled by an external or independent internal party.

Process Steering Board
The Process Steering Board is a group of senior executives from line management (functional perspective) and process management (process perspective) that addresses cross-functional issues. It is typically established in larger companies and corporate groups.

Process Controller
The role of the process controller is covered in a separate chapter (see Chap. 4). It is usually performed by the Process Owner or Process Manager. For this reason, it is not explicitly included in Fig. 3.9. The responsibilities primarily include metric-based management and control of processes at both the strategic and operational levels.

Assignment of Roles in the Life Cycle
Process management is a team effort. The roles defined above work together in various constellations. The primary assignment of roles within the process management life cycle, as previously presented in Fig. 2.4, is shown in Fig. 3.10. The strategic design of business processes is driven by the process strategy of the Chief Process Officer. Process Owners, process staff, and process modelers (possibly supported by external consultants) analyze processes, identify weaknesses, and modify the process. The subsequent technical implementation of processes is the responsibility of software developers or workflow modelers. The execution of processes is carried out by process staff. Monitoring compliance with process objectives is the responsibility of the Process Owners.

3.3   Project Organization for Process Management

3.3.1   Classical Forms of Project Organization

Indicators for necessary restructuring measures include declining profits, decreasing sales, increasing inventories of finished goods, and business management key figures (see Maurer and Versteegen 2001, p. 27). These measures are implemented in the form of projects. For the execution of projects with a focus on process management, reference is made to the collection of methods by Leyendecker and Pötters (2022). A practical example of the organization of a restructuring project is shown in Fig. 3.11.

The members of the Steering Committee are managing directors, board members, process owners, project managers, or external experts (consultants). Their tasks include

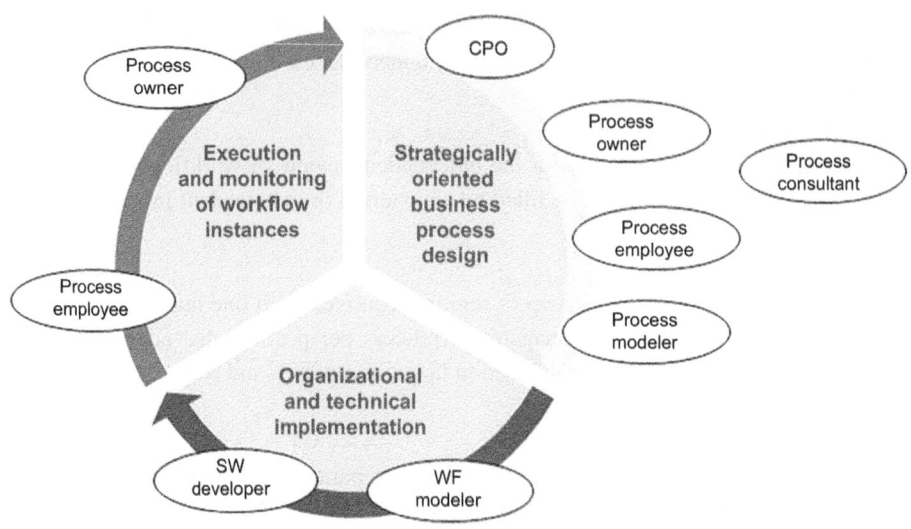

Fig. 3.10 Roles in the life cycle of process management

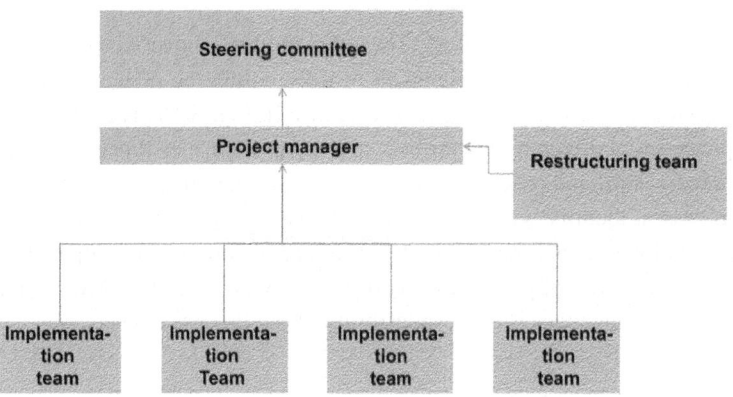

Fig. 3.11 Project organization for restructuring projects (see Schmelzer and Sesselmann 2013)

providing the necessary resources, reviewing and approving the project plan, resolving cross-project issues, and making necessary decisions. The position of Project Manager is often filled by the process owner or someone from their area of responsibility. Their tasks consist of planning, managing, and controlling the project, managing resource allocation, and reporting to the Steering Committee. Additional responsibilities include external communication and representation of the project, as well as motivating the Implementation Teams. The Restructuring Team forms the full-time core of the project. It is composed of sub-process owners, the heads of the Implementation Teams, and, if necessary, external experts (consultants). The main tasks of the team are the analysis of

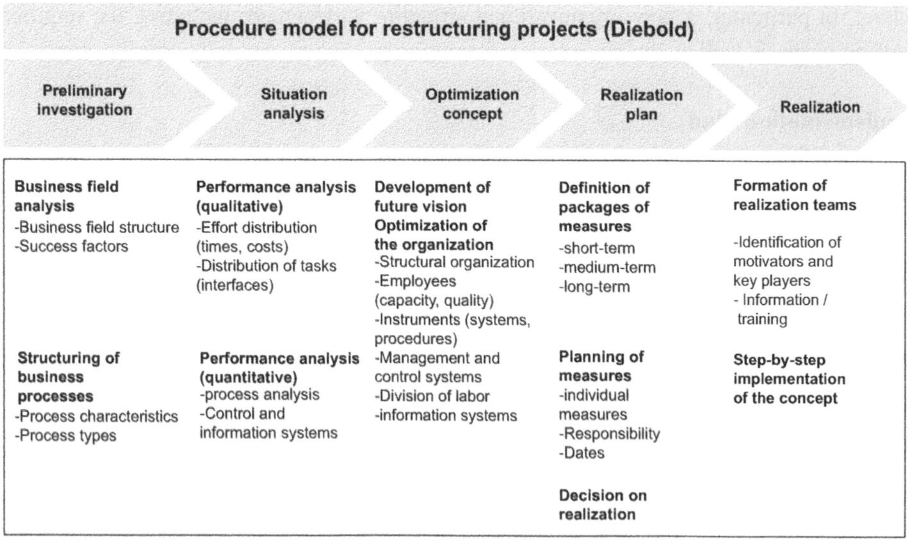

Procedure model for restructuring projects (Diebold)

Preliminary investigation	Situation analysis	Optimization concept	Realization plan	Realization
Business field analysis -Business field structure -Success factors	**Performance analysis (qualitative)** -Effort distribution (times, costs) -Distribution of tasks (interfaces)	**Development of future vision** **Optimization of the organization** -Structural organization -Employees (capacity, quality) -Instruments (systems, procedures)	**Definition of packages of measures** -short-term -medium-term -long-term	**Formation of realization teams** -Identification of motivators and key players - Information / training
Structuring of business processes -Process characteristics -Process types	**Performance analysis (quantitative)** -process analysis -Control and information systems	-Management and control systems -Division of labor -information systems	**Planning of measures** -individual measures -Responsibility -Dates	**Step-by-step implementation of the concept**
			Decision on realization	

Fig. 3.12 Process model for restructuring projects (Diebold n.d.)

the current processes and the design of the target processes. It is common to divide the overall project into subprojects to implement the overall concept in a distributed manner. The members of the necessary Implementation Teams are employees from the sub-processes as representatives of the sub-process owners, external experts (consultants), and, if required, IT experts. Their tasks include the detailed design of the target processes, the implementation of the subprojects, i.e., the introduction of the target processes (live operation), and reporting to the Restructuring Team. The project proceeds in several phases (see the proposal by the consulting firm Diebold n.d., p. 19 in Fig. 3.12).

Preliminary Study
In the first phase, a "Preliminary Study" is conducted, in which the objectives are initially developed and then jointly defined with the decision-makers.

Situation Analysis
In the second phase, "Situation Analysis," a performance analysis of the company is carried out, including the determination of times and costs. In this phase, the information systems and information flows involved are also analyzed.

Optimization Concept
The next phase, "Optimization Concept," serves to develop a vision for the future and to "optimize" or, more precisely, "improve" the organization according to meaningful criteria such as process costs, throughput times, process quality, resource utilization, and

others. In particular, a new organizational structure is designed, including the required staffing levels as well as the necessary information, management, and control systems.

Implementation Plan

In the fourth phase, "Implementation Plan," the concrete planning of individual measures with short-, medium-, and long-term timelines is carried out as a package of measures and submitted to the decision-makers for approval.

Implementation

The project concludes with the fifth phase, "Implementation," which is responsible for the concrete execution of the action plan. This phase brings about the critical changes in the company and requires the full attention of management. Key to successful implementation is identifying the key performers affected in the company, motivating them to provide support, and adequately preparing all affected employees for the changes.

3.3.2   Agile Methods of Project Organization

3.3.2.1 Software Development as the Initiator of Agile Methods

Traditional, well-known concepts of software development, such as the waterfall model (see, e.g., Pomberger and Blaschek 1993), assume that software clients know what they need at the outset and software developers know how to implement these requirements, with no major changes to the plan occurring during the project. Unfortunately, reality is often different. Frequently, software clients only discover what they need during the course of the project, and software developers devise solutions much later and with different methods and tools than originally planned. Moreover, project plans are usually only up to date for a short period; they are quickly overtaken by reality.

Agile Methods as a Solution Approach

The fundamental idea behind agile methods is: if traditional methods do not work, they should not be used. Instead, a mixed team of experienced members should be given the freedom to solve the problem. Transparency, autonomy, daily or timely team coordination, and decentralized responsibility replace detailed central planning.

Paradigm Shift

The core idea of all agile methods is a paradigm shift. The approach moves away from the concept of "complete planning of a product, process, or software" and its implementation (Plan-Built-Try) toward "experimental iteration," in which small, usable artifacts are continuously produced. In aggregate, these artifacts form the finished end product, the complete process, or the full software (multiple, iterative Plan-Built-Try cycles) (see Fig. 3.13).

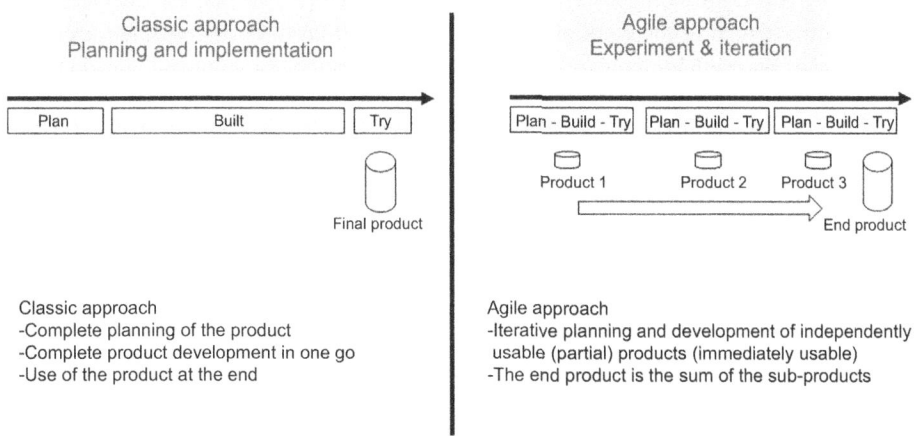

Fig. 3.13 Comparison of Traditional and Agile Methods

Agile Manifesto

In an Agile Manifesto, renowned software development experts have set down revolutionary principles that, in their view, can overcome the weaknesses of traditional process models (see Agile Manifesto n.d.). The concept proposes a fundamentally different approach to project execution.

In general discussions, "agile" is sometimes equated with "unplanned," but in reality, only the planning approach has been reversed to address the problem of time overruns (Hanschke 2016, p. 70). This has led to criticism that "adherence to deadlines and schedules" is considered a higher goal than the quality of the software produced (Mertens and Bissantz 2021, p. 4).

In traditional waterfall-oriented planning, the content is specified by the client. The project costs are then estimated based on this, which in turn determines the project timeline—a timeline that is often exceeded. In agile planning, the approach is different: the budget is specified. Given the available resources (personnel), this determines the timeline, and ultimately, the deliverable content (see Hanschke 2016). Put simply, in agile planning, the client knows what the project will cost and how long it will take. However, the deliverables are open and depend on the performance of the team.

Agile methods became particularly well known through the SCRUM methodology. SCRUM is a term from rugby, referring to the close formation of the team as they attempt to gain possession of the ball after a throw-in.

Applied to process management, this means that the entire project team must work together to achieve the goal of process restructuring. Obstacles that arise must be removed, not regarded as problems.

SCRUM defines three central roles: the Product Owner, the Team, and the Scrum Master (see Sutherland n.d.). The Product Owner is comparable to the process owner, acting as the "advocate" for the software product to be developed and is responsible for defining and prioritizing work packages. The Team is responsible for independently delivering the results of the work packages. The Scrum Master is responsible for correct application of the methodology and supports the team with methodological questions.

3.3.2.2 Agile Project Organization in Process Management

More than 25 years of experience with traditional process management methods have shown that the strong orientation toward waterfall models from software development also has a negative impact on process management. It is therefore logical to transfer the concept of agility to process management (see Bernardo Junior and Dallavalle de Padua 2023).

Traditional process management models attempt to fully document, analyze, revise, and adapt processes, and, if necessary, provide new information systems for this purpose—these, in turn, are to be fully planned, designed, developed, tested, and delivered. Since there is not enough information available at the start of projects, feedback loops and delays are inevitable in practice, and in the worst case, the conditions have changed so much by the time the "new process is delivered" that the revised process is already outdated.

Agile Process Management

According to a recent analysis of relevant scientific literature (see Bernardo Junior and Dallavalle de Padua 2023, p. 23), the core elements of agile process management are characterized by the following features:

- Use of agile methodologies,
- Ability to respond,
- Coverage of all types of processes,
- Consideration of changes in the competitive environment.

The scope of agile methods such as SCRUM is illustrated in Fig. 3.14.

The use of SCRUM within process management primarily covers the phases of process documentation, analysis, and restructuring. Fig. 3.15 presents an "agile" perspective on the classical BPM life cycle introduced in Fig. 2.4 and the associated application potentials.

The roles in the classical SCRUM concept require only minor adjustments for use in process management (see Fig. 3.16), while the SCRUM process itself can be adopted without modification. The Product Owner in standard SCRUM corresponds to the *Process Owner*. The role of the *SCRUM Master* remains unchanged. The SCRUM team (comprising business department staff, database experts, software developers, and, if necessary, consultants) is slightly adapted to form the *BPM team*, consisting of process staff, process and workflow modelers, software developers, and, if required, external process consultants.

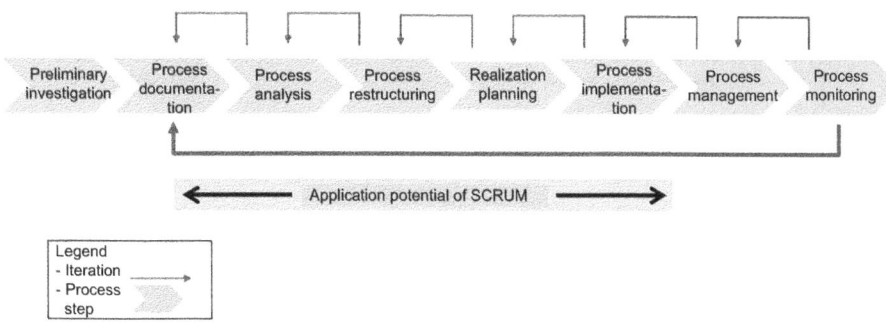

Fig. 3.14   Scope of agile methods in process management

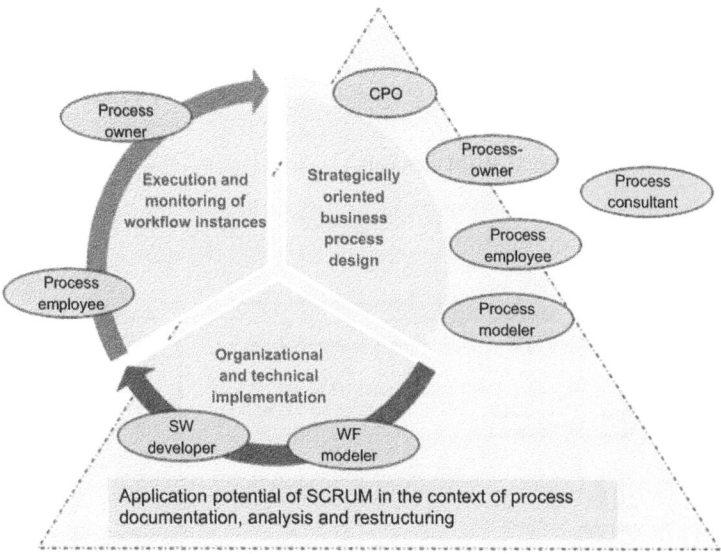

Fig. 3.15   An agile perspective on the BPM life cycle

Hybrid Model for Agile Process Management

The life cycle of agile process management is depicted in the hybrid model in Fig. 3.17. The process is methodically guided by the SCRUM Master. At the beginning of each cycle, the *Process Owner* prepares a summary of prioritized requirements as a user story and records it in the *Process Backlog*. The process requirements are documented in business language (user story), for example as flowcharts, EPC models/BPMN models, or rough process sketches, depending on the required level of detail.

Subsequently, the BPM team and the process owner discuss the next steps as part of *Sprint Planning*. The results achieved by the team are recorded in the sprint backlog. The team then works on the tasks during the *Sprint*. Each sprint is scheduled for 2–8 weeks.

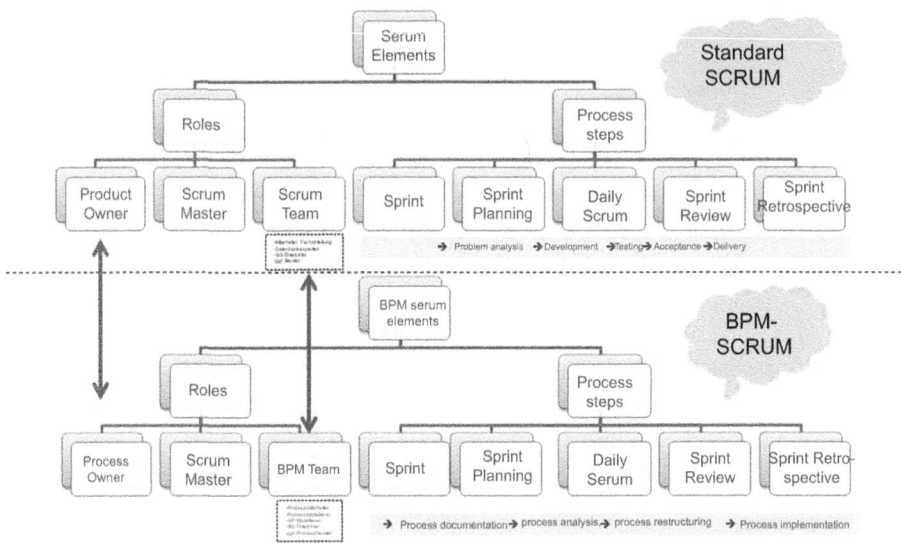

Fig. 3.16 BPM perspective on SCRUM elements

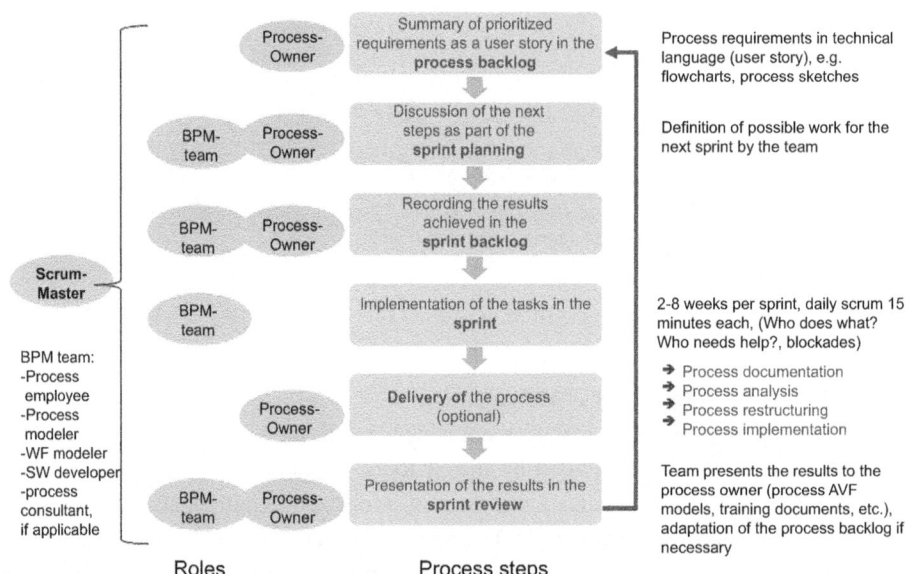

Fig. 3.17 Hybrid model of an agile process management life cycle

Table 3.1 Differences between classical and agile process management (Bernardo Junior and Dallavalle de Padua 2023, p. 24, abridged selection)

Analysis Element	Classical Process Management	Agile Process Management
Flexibility in implementing changes	Periodic review of changes	Adaptive change as needed
Reliability of results	Processes may become out-dated between "requirements analysis" and "change"	Updated processes
Work speed	Medium/long-term, in phases	Short-term, in cycles
Delivery of results	Complete, only at the end of phases/activities	Continuous, in smaller increments during development
Environmental requirements	Stable environment required	Any type of environment (stable, agile) possible
Approach to change	Provision of complete target processes	Provision of minimally viable process changes

[Table footer—please overwrite]

In a daily team meeting, the *Daily Scrum* (maximum 15 minutes), the team briefly exchanges updates. Key topics include:

- Who is responsible for what in the team?
- Who needs assistance?
- Where are there obstacles?
- What is the status of process documentation, process analysis, process restructuring, and process implementation?

After a process cycle, the process owner may decide to "deliver" a new or modified process version. In the sprint review, the results of the sprint are presented to the process owner. The team presents the detailed outcomes to the process owner (e.g., process/workflow models, training materials, etc.). If necessary, adjustments to the process backlog are made jointly.

The key differences between classical and agile process management were examined in a literature review and are presented in Table 3.1.

3.4   Review Questions and Answers

Questions
1. Describe the **key roles in process management** and distinguish them from one another.
2. Explain why an **influence-based process organization is not sufficient in the long term**, but is acceptable during the initial phase.

3. Why is the **"pure" process organization an ideal** that often fails in practice?
4. Why is the **matrix process organization a good compromise** that many companies choose for implementing process management?
5. How do **agile methods** in process management differ from **traditional approaches?**

Answers

1. The most important roles are the **Chief Process Officer (CPO), the Process Owner (PO)**, as well as **process, modeling**, and **workflow experts.** The CPO is a role with overall responsibility for process management across all departments and should be positioned as high as possible within the organization. The **role of the Process Owner** is responsible for one or more processes, also spanning departmental boundaries. The other roles mentioned perform **specialized tasks** within a process management organization. These roles are not necessarily associated with personnel or budget responsibility; this depends on the type of process organization.
2. The **influence-based process organization**, also known as a **staff organization,does not have authority to issue directives** and serves only an advisory function. In the long term, this can lead to conflicts that undermine end-to-end processes.
3. The "pure" **process organization** recognizes only processes; all **activities and resources are** subordinated to a **process.** In practice, this leads to costly redundancies that are not economically viable.
4. The **matrix process organization** features **two lines of authority:functional responsibility** by department or group, and **process responsibility across departmental boundaries.** This method, known for over 100 years, enables the balanced implementation of multiple responsibilities.
5. **Agile methods** are based on **incremental work concepts**, where flexible teams iteratively approach a solution. Changes in requirements or conditions are part of the concept and even encouraged. In **traditional approaches**, detailed planning is carried out at the beginning, which is then followed throughout the project. It is difficult or even impossible to respond to changes in conditions.

References

Manifesto, A. (Autorenteam): Manifesto for agile software development. http://agilemanifesto.org (o. J.). Accessed 11 Mar 2011

Bernardo Junior, R., Dallavalle de Padua, S.I.: Toward agile business process management: description of concepts and a proposed definition. Knowl. Process. Manag. **30**(1), 14–32 (2023). https://doi.org/10.1002/kpm.1737

Brenner, W., Brenner, B.: Digitalisierung: Welche Rolle spielen CIOs heute und in Zukunft? HMD. https://link.springer.com/content/pdf/10.1365/s40702-022-00868-7.pdf (2022). Accessed 17 Mar 2022

Diebold (Hrsg.): Geschäftsprozessoptimierung, Der neue Weg zur marktorientierten Unternehmensorganisation, Eschborn (o. J.)

Gadatsch, A., Komus, A., Mendling, J.: BPM-Compass 2016, Eine wissenschaftliche Studie der Hochschule Koblenz, Hochschule Bonn-Rhein-Sieg und der Wirtschaftsuniversität Wien in Zusammenarbeit mit der Gesellschaft für Prozessmanagement e. V., Koblenz, Bonn-Rhein-Sieg, Wien (2016). www.project-and-process.net/BPM-Compass

Hanschke, I.: Agile Planung—nur so viel planen wie nötig. In: Wirtschaftsinformatik & Management, **4,** 70–78 (2016)

Leyendecker, B., Pötters, P.: Werkzeuge für das Projekt- und Prozessmanagement. Klassische und moderne Instrumente für den Management-Alltag, Wiesbaden (2022)

Maurer, T., Versteegen, G.: Werkzeuge für Geschäftsprozessoptimierung, ein Allheilmittel? In: IT-Management, **11,** 26–34 (2001)

Mertens, P.: Ist Deutschland wirklich ein „Digitales Entwicklungsland"—Ob die Institutioneninflation hilft?, Arbeitsbericht Nr. 2/2021, Universität Erlangen-Nürnberg, Wirtschaftsinformatik I (2021)

Mertens, P., Bissantz, N.: Hänschenklein oder Mondscheinsonate: Geraten wir in eine Komplexitätskrise?, Arbeitsbericht Nr. 1/2021, Universität Erlangen-Nürnberg, Wirtschaftsinformatik I (2021)

Pomberger, G., Blaschek, G.: Grundlagen des Software Engineering, München und Wien (1993)

Schmelzer, H.J.: Wer sind die Akteure im Geschäftsprozessmanagement. ZfO, **5**(74), 273–277 (2005)

Schmelzer, H.J., Sesselmann., W.: Geschäftsprozessmanagement in der Praxis, 8. edn. München (2013)

Sutherland, J.: Scrum Handbook. http://jeffsutherland.com/scrumhandbook.pdf (o. J.). Accessed 28 July 2016

Vogel, M.: IT-Chefs müssen sich Geschäftsprozessen widmen. Comput. Ztg. **35**(22), 22 (2004)

Process Controlling

4

Process controlling supports the achievement of strategic objectives in process management

Abstract

Process management is inconceivable without process controlling. Process controlling sets objectives, regulates collaboration between project partners through process agreements, and monitors compliance with targets using key performance indicators. In the event of deviations from the objectives, IT controllers ensure that appropriate proposals for corrective actions are submitted. The section concludes with review questions and exercises.

4.1   Development of a Process Strategy

Definition

Controlling should be understood as a management concept for future-oriented corporate and profit management, but also as a strategy for securing the existence of the company and jobs (Gadatsch and Mayer 2013, p. 1). It is therefore a management task that supports corporate leadership in fulfilling its responsibilities.

Process controlling is a subtask of controlling with a particular focus on business processes. It ensures that process objectives are met and that process execution is of high quality. To this end, process controlling regularly analyzes target/actual deviations and thus supports continuous business process management (Scheer and Heß 2009, p. 149).

© The Author(s), under exclusive license to Springer Fachmedien Wiesbaden GmbH, part of Springer Nature 2026
A. Gadatsch, *Business Process Management*,
https://doi.org/10.1007/978-3-658-49339-4_4

A key prerequisite for carrying out this task is a strategic directive from corporate management. Strategic process controlling is therefore based on a process strategy. By planning, implementing, and monitoring suitable process-related measures, it supports the achievement of strategic corporate objectives, i.e., the corporate strategy.

Approach

Various strategies are systematically derived from the general corporate strategy, including the IT strategy and the process strategy, both of which are important for the organization's performance (see Fig. 4.1).

A strategy consists of several elements, such as formulating a target state (Where do we want to go?), identifying the need for action (What do we need to do? Where are the weaknesses?), outlining options for action (What alternatives do we have?), setting objectives and defining measures (What exactly should be done? By when must the measures be completed? Who is responsible for implementation?), and establishing metrics for goal monitoring as well as determining when the objectives have been achieved (When have we reached our goals?).

Strategic Process Controlling

Strategic process controlling requires a holistic management cycle that, starting from the previously defined business strategy, leads to strategic process planning, in which the key processes and their objectives are detailed and described in the form of metrics (see Fig. 4.2). During process execution, the achievement of objectives is monitored. For this purpose, process reporting is used as a data source and, within the framework of strategic process control (analysis of deviations), is employed for process management. Process

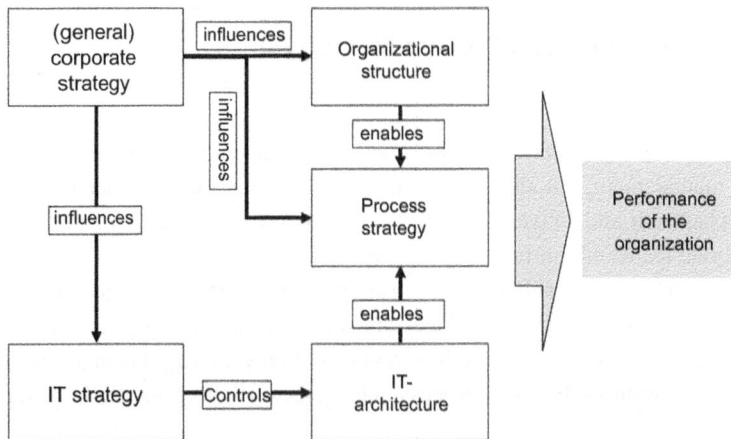

Fig. 4.1 Relationship between process strategy and organizational performance (Krcmar 2005)

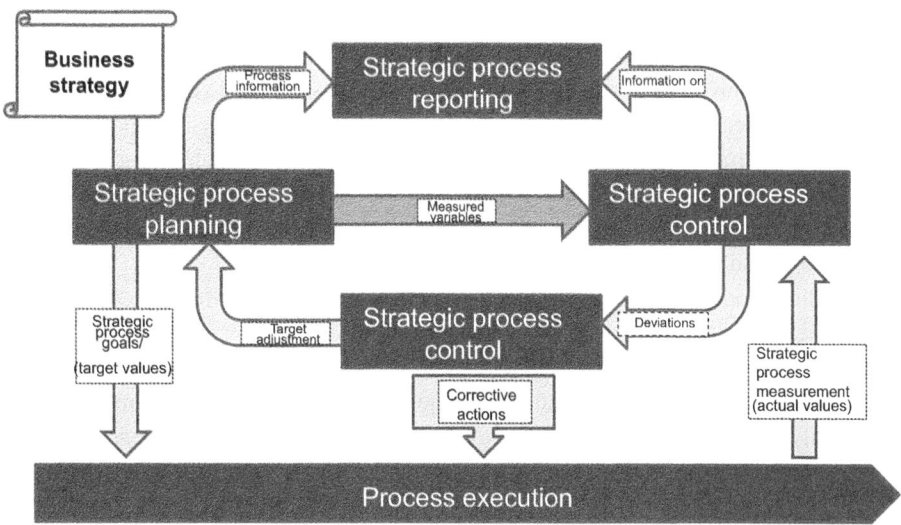

Fig. 4.2 Strategic process controlling as a management cycle according to Schmelzer and Sesselmann (2013)

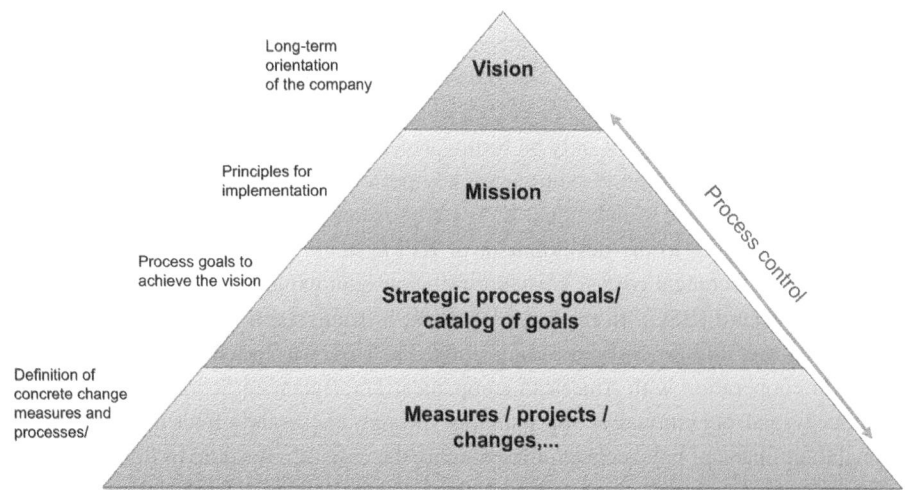

Fig. 4.3 From Mission to Action

management directly influences the executed processes through corrective actions, which in turn feed back into process control in the form of actual values.

Strategic process management requires a strategy process in a four-level hierarchy: First, top management formulates an abstract vision for the company's long-term direction (see Fig. 4.3).

Example of a Vision

For a university, the vision could be: "We will become the leading provider of industry-oriented digital university products in the region." This statement is still very general and needs further specification. This is done in the form of a mission, i.e., more concrete intentions are formulated. These could be statements such as: "Establishing digital university process management," "Analysis and digital restructuring of management, core, and selected support processes," or "Utilizing modern ICT technologies for student-centered research and teaching."

From this, process objectives are defined, which are then described by concrete processes or measures to change the situation. One process objective could be that student enrollment should be digital, barrier-free, and completed within very short, competitive turnaround times, in accordance with legal requirements. A specific measure to improve accessibility could be a project to revise the university's social media presence (website, Facebook page, etc.).

4.2   Process Scorecard

For the successful implementation of a process strategy, alignment with the corporate strategy must be ensured. The process strategy needs to be interconnected with company-related elements at multiple levels, from strategy and objectives to budgets and individual measures (see Fig. 4.4). The Balanced Scorecard was developed as an instrument for this purpose.

A process strategy must not only be formulated, but also continuously monitored with regard to its implementation. Traditionally, key performance indicators (KPIs) are used for this purpose. The use of individual KPIs has proven ineffective due to the risk of misinterpretation, leading to the development of KPI systems that initially focused mainly on financial and technical issues. This approach was later expanded by the concept of the Balanced Scorecard (BSC). In the early 1990s, R. S. Kaplan and D. P. Norton developed the BSC as a new tool for corporate controlling. The BSC was based on years of research projects in cooperation with American companies. The Balanced Scorecard links corporate strategy and operational action planning through cause-and-effect chains to create and maintain financial balance (see, for example, the case of a hospital in Fig. 4.5).

The process scorecard is a variant of the general Balanced Scorecard, which was developed as a KPI-based management and control system for general corporate controlling (see Schmelzer and Sesselmann 2013). It consists of a mutually coordinated, interdependent system of objectives, described by KPIs, target values, and measures across different perspectives (see Schmelzer and Sesselmann 2013). The perspectives, also called views, describe the areas of impact of business processes, which should support corporate objectives in a balanced manner. Examples of objectives in the "Process Finance" perspective include process value contribution, process revenue, and process costs. Objectives in the "Process Customer" perspective include customer satisfaction

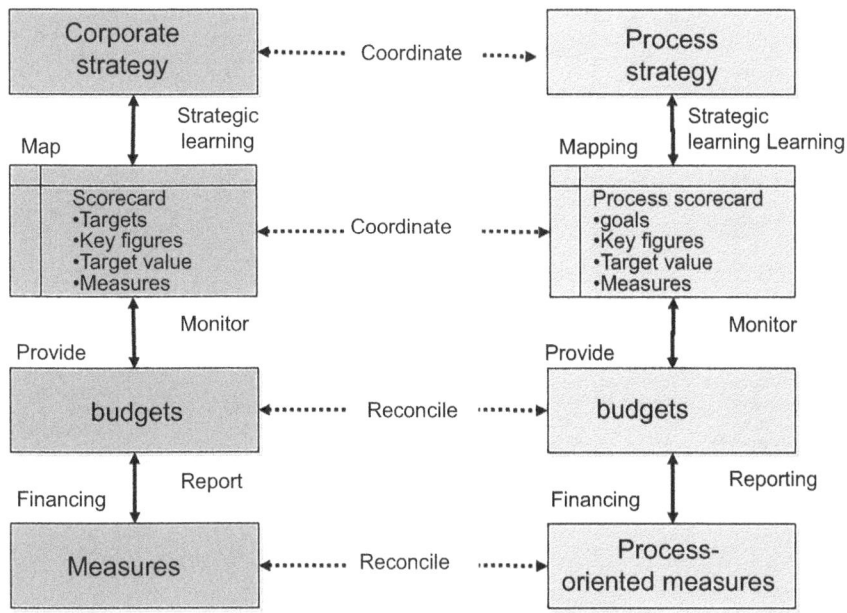

Fig. 4.4 Anchoring the process strategy within the corporate strategy

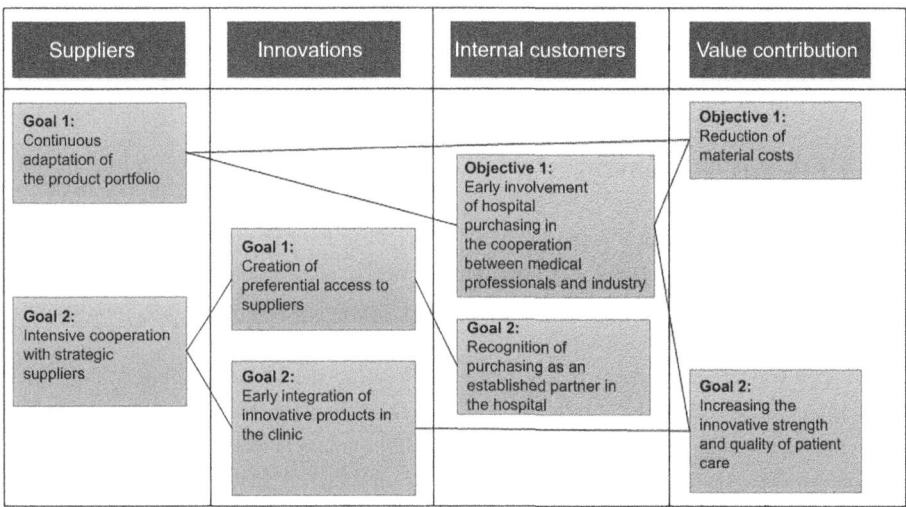

Fig. 4.5 Cause-and-effect chains in a hospital (see Stachel and Eltzholtz 2018, p. 92)

Customer							
Goal	Key figures	Target values	Measures	Target	Key figures	Target values	Measures
Achieve high customer satisfaction	Customer turnover compared to previous year	+2%	Survey customers Analyze requirements Analyze customer events Analyze and track complaints	Perfor-mance -Capability better than competition competition	Throughput runtime	< 1 day	Process analysis and benchmarking with competitors carry out
	Number of customer complaints	Share < 1%			Capacity	> 1000 processes per day	Automate processes

Resources/personnel				Finances			
Target	Key figures	Target values	Measures	Target	Key figures	Target values	Measures
Staff trained and ready to work as required	Number of training days / employee	10 days per year	Update job descriptions Compare requirements with training status Create training plan	Positive deca- sion contribution	DB% / turnover per customer	DBk > 30%	Carry out product analysis Customer ranking Revise calculation
	Adherence to agreed deadlines	Percent-age > 95%			DB % / per product	DBp > 30%	

Fig. 4.6 Process scorecard example (product sales)

and customer retention. "Process Performance" can be managed, for example, through objectives such as process times, process quality, and process reliability (see Schmelzer and Sesselmann 2013). Figure 4.6 presents a simplified process scorecard for the "Product Sales" process.

4.3   Process Agreements

Business process agreements have become established for the operational management of processes. They essentially document the internal customer-supplier relationships within process management and describe in detail the process performance, quality level, and costs, or, in the case of agreements with external partners, the price.

The term process agreement is also widely known in the IT sector under the English designation "Service Level Agreement" (SLA). The principle of establishing customer-supplier relationships based on business process agreements is illustrated in Fig. 4.7.

Each process owner coordinates with their internal "customers" and "suppliers" regarding the services to be provided (e.g., number of examinations, number of operations, number of transports) and the associated quantities. The planning of service relationships can take place annually as part of the planning process and, if necessary, be adjusted during the year. When using internal cost and performance accounting, internal transfer prices for services should be added in order to subsequently determine process costs. An example of a business process agreement from the healthcare sector is

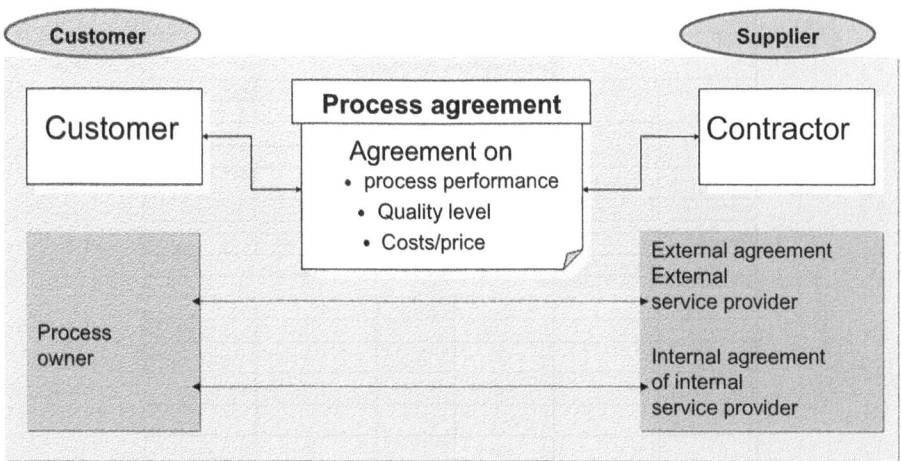

Fig. 4.7 Process agreement – schematic representation

shown in Fig. 4.8. It also demonstrates the possible level of detail in business process agreements. The business process agreement contains information about the process, the service to be provided including the required specifications, the parties involved, and contact persons. The service must be documented in such a way that all parties have a clear understanding of the content and quality level.

The use of process agreements improves clarity regarding the process inputs to be provided and the outcomes of processes. In addition, it facilitates coordination among the parties involved.

4.4   Process Metrics

Metrics (or, in English, Key Performance Indicators) are of great importance for controlling. In the control cycle of process controlling (see Fig. 4.9), they serve as the basis for managing the implementation of strategy. Without metrics, controlling is not possible.

Procedure

Starting from the corporate strategy, a process strategy is developed. To manage its implementation, metrics are defined, which are to be achieved through specific measures. The actual values from real operations are compared with the target values of the metrics, resulting in a deviation analysis. Various activities may result from this. For example, corrective action may be taken with respect to the measures (adjustment of resources, deadlines, objectives, etc.), or changes to the process strategy may be made.

Klinik-Logo

Abt.

Geschäftsprozess-Vereinbarung

Prozess:	Operative Behandlung des Zervixkarzinoms	Prozess-ID:	OBZ
		Schnittstellen-ID:	OBZ 3-4
Schnittstelle	Teilprozess: Transport	Lieferant Stationsleitung Pflege	
	Teilprozess:	Kunde Stationsleitung OP	
Version vom:	10.06.2014	Gültig ab:	20.06.2014	Versions-ID:	OBZ 3-4 20120610
Modifiziert am:	25.09.2014			Modifiziert durch:	Prozessteam

| Review von: | Qualitätszirkel | Review am: | 15.07.2014 | Genehmigt durch: | Direktor |
| Verteiler: | Prozessteam, Mitarbeiter der Teilprozesse, Intranet | | | | |

Beteiligte Personen des Prozessteams:

	Name:	Funktion:	Abteilung:	Telefon-Nr:	E-Mail:
Prozess-Owner:	Schmidt	Prozessbegleiter	Management	7234521	schmidt@klinik.net
Teilprozess-Owner, Lieferant	Müller	Stationsleitung	Onkologie-Gynäkologie	7234565	müller@klinik.net
Teilprozess-Owner, Kunde	Meier	Stationsleitung	OP-Pflege	7234567	meier@klinik.net
Weitere Permanente Mitglieder:					
1.	Schulz	Assistenzarzt	Onkologie-Gynäkologie	7234598	schulz@klinik.net
2.	Raider	Krankenpfleger	Onkologie-Gynäkologie	7234585	raider@klinik.net
Weitere fakultative Mitglieder:					
1.	Bucher	QMB	Qualitäts-sicherung	7234512	bucher@klinik.net

Leistungsumfang:

Der Leistungsumfang erstreckt sich auf die Qualität, die Zuverlässigkeit, die geforderte Menge, die Kooperation, Beratungstätigkeiten und Flexibilität des Lieferanten

Anforderungen an den Lieferanten:

Patient:
Körperpflege, Nabelreinigung, Nagelpflege/Nagellack entfernen
Enthaarung von Bauch, Intimbereich und Oberschenkeln
OP-Hemd, Einmalslip
Blasenentleerung, abführende Maßnahmen
Schmuck- und Prothesenentfernung
Patientenarmband mit Namen
...

Labor:
Blutbild: Hb/Hk, Thrombozyten, Blutgruppe, BSG
Leberstatus: SGOT, SGPT, Gamma-GT, alkalische Phosphatase, Transaminasen
Gerinnungsstatus: Quick, PTT
Elektrolytstatus: Kalium
...

Untersuchungen:
Röntgen-Thorax in zwei Ebenen
EKG
Sonographie und intravenöse Pyelographie
Zystoskopie, Rektoskopie

Anforderungen an den Kunden:
Einhaltung des Übergabezeitpunktes an definierter OP-Schleuse
Falls der Patient telefonisch abgerufen wird, ist der zeitliche Vorlauf von 45 Minuten zu berücksichtigen
Abnahme der geforderten Leistung durch examiniertes Fachpersonal

Nichterfüllung der Anforderungen:
Ausrichtung der nächsten Sitzung

Nächste Sitzung am:	25.11.2016
Münster, den 25.09.2016	
Ort, Datum	Prozess-Owner
	Teilprozess-Owner, Kunde	Teilprozess-Owner, Lieferant

Fig. 4.8 Example of a business process agreement from the healthcare sector (Kölking 2007)

Structure of Key Performance Indicators

Key performance indicators (KPIs) exist in various forms. They can be structured into absolute and ratio-based KPIs (see Fig. 4.10). Absolute KPIs refer to quantifiable facts, such as the number of employees involved in a process. Their informational value is

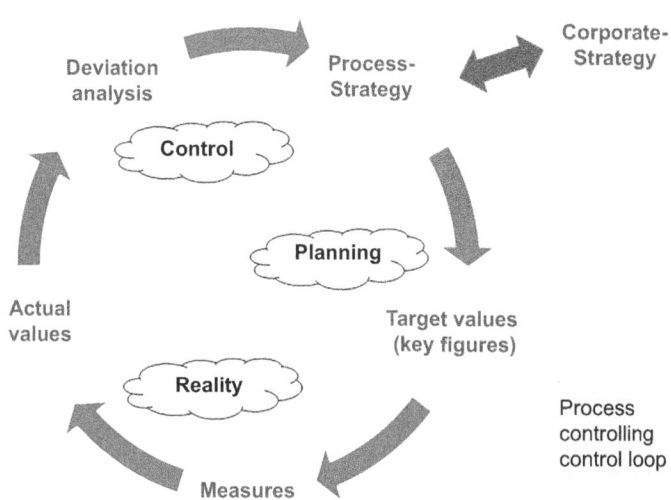

Fig. 4.9 Control cycle of process controlling

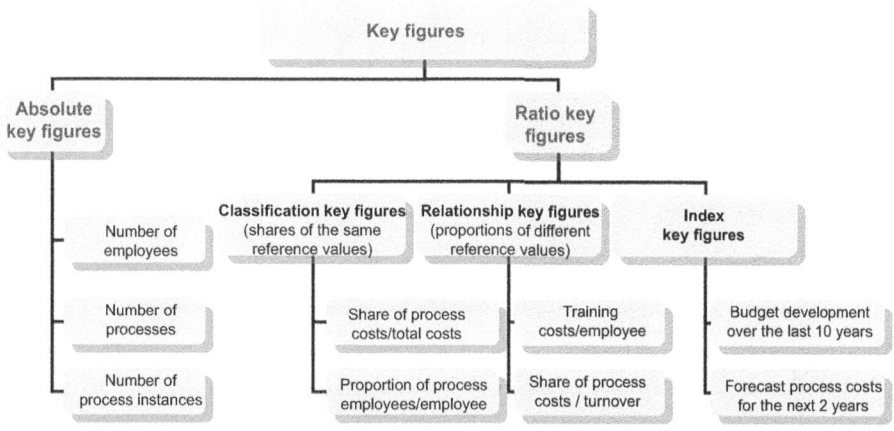

Fig. 4.10 Structure of Key Performance Indicators

limited, as they lack a basis for comparison. Ratio-based KPIs relate multiple indicators to each other and can thus describe relationships between different aspects. These, in turn, are differentiated into composition, relationship, and index KPIs. Composition KPIs represent proportions of quantities with the same dimension, for example, the share of process costs in the company's total costs. Relationship KPIs relate quantities of different dimensions, such as process costs per employee. Index KPIs are normalized developments of indicators over longer periods, for example, the trend in process costs for office supply procurement.

In process controlling practice, it is important to assess KPIs based on their quality, calculability and analyzability, cost-effectiveness, and the feasibility of organizational implementation. Potential KPI candidates should be critically evaluated. The checklist for KPIs in Fig. 4.11 (adapted from Kütz 2011) provides guidance for this purpose. The results of this assessment should be taken into account when selecting KPIs.

Documentation

KPIs must be described precisely to ensure their meaningful use within the company. Otherwise, there is a risk of misinterpretation. For example, the KPI "Order Processing Time" can be measured differently depending on the perspective of the stakeholders from various departments:

- Time span from receipt of the order to entry in the SAP system (IT perspective),
- Time span from receipt of the order to dispatch of the order confirmation to the customer (sales perspective),
- Time span from receipt of the order to dispatch of the goods to the customer (end-to-end process perspective).

The quality

- Which objective is to be achieved and managed with the KPI?
- Does the KPI measure the right effect?
- Are the key figures understandable for the recipient?
- How should the quality of the basic data be assessed, is it necessary to prepare the raw data?
- Does the KPI measure objectives relevant to the strategy?

Predictability and analyzability

- Can target and target values or expected values be defined?
- Can corresponding actual values be determined?
- Can tolerance values be defined?
- What must happen if the target values are exceeded or not met, what processes must be initiated?
- Who needs to take action and how?
- Are the key figures "benchmarkable"?
- How sensitive are the key figures to changes?
- Can the necessary basic data be determined, and if so, can this be automated?
- Can the key figures be drilled down, i.e. can changes be traced back to their origin?

Economic efficiency

- Is the cost of determining basic data for the target/actual calculation economically justified?
- Is the cost of determining the key figure offset by an appropriate benefit?
- Can pragmatic substitute values be determined?

Organization

- Can those responsible for data provision, calculation, reporting and for the content of the indicator itself be named?
- Can those responsible be appointed to take action and initiate countermeasures if target values are exceeded or not met?
- Are the key figures tamper-proof, e.g. are there control variables?
- How do the key figures react to organizational or technological changes?

Fig. 4.11 Assessment Criteria for KPIs (adapted from Kütz 2011)

It is necessary to clarify how the KPI is to be calculated and interpreted. The description should cover numerous aspects, including a meaningful technical description, the validity period of the KPI, those responsible for its content, the intended target groups for reporting, the reporters, and the data providers. Additional information includes the KPI category (e.g., finance, production, IT), the target values (e.g., 90% of orders entered on the day of receipt), possible tolerance thresholds for deviations, and associated escalation rules for outliers (e.g., notification to the process owner if target achievement is up to 90%, notification to management if below 80%).

Of particular importance is the precise specification of data collection methods to ensure consistent and uniform KPIs. Documentation of data sources should include

- the IT system providing the data,
- the measurement method (manual if necessary, automatic at regular intervals, indirect by deriving from complementary values), and
- the exact measurement points.

The following aspects should be considered when using KPIs:

- Type of presentation (text, graphics, numbers, etc.),
- Frequency of data provision (on occurrence, hourly, daily, weekly, etc.),
- levels of data aggregation (individual data, summary data per department, summary data per day/month/year), and
- type and duration of archiving (location, medium, duration).

Optionally documented information includes complaints (e.g., incorrect or contradictory values), feedback on the use of KPIs, and changes to calculation logic to enable retrospective traceability of values.

Process Metric Profile

Process metrics should be consistently documented in a standardized process metric profile and stored centrally on a permanent basis. This serves both as a general source of information and to ensure consistency and the assignment of responsibilities. The profile provides an exact definition and description of a metric for process management purposes.

The following information can be recorded in the profile:

- Objective and scope of the metric
- Responsibility and organizational aspects
- Target values and thresholds
- Documentation of data sources and information distribution (reporting), including access rights
- Notes on the use of IT tools

Process name:	Record customer order	
Process owner	Process manager Sales	
Process key figure:	Lead time	
Person responsible for the key figure:	N. N.	
Recipient of the key figure (reports):	Director Sales, Process Manager Sales, Sales Manager	
Objective of the key figure		
What should be controlled with the KPI?	Time from receipt of the order to handover to shipping for delivery	
Which target values should be achieved?	Minimum processing times depending on the type of goods (10 min. to 60 min.)	
What happens if tolerances are breached?	Information to Director Sales	
Determination of the key figure		
Calculation / Formula	Time stamp "Order entered" minus "Order received" (BPMN model events)	
Tolerance values	+/-20%	
Data sources	SAP document database, order type "O"	
Publication / Reporting		
Frequency of provision	Director Sales: monthly, by customer group	Process manager, sales manager
Level of detail / aggregation	Country, region, customer group	Customer group, customer
Information technology		
Source system(s): SAP document database (ERP)	Receiver system(s): SAP BI (Data Warehouse)	Reporting tool(s): Power BI

Fig. 4.12   Process Metric Profile – Example

Storage should take place in a central database. The profiles should be published on the intranet and made visible to process participants (CPO, process owners, process experts). An example of a process metric profile for the metric "lead time" in the process "recording customer orders" can be found in Fig. 4.12.

Significance of Individual Metrics
The significance of isolated metrics should be critically examined. For example, in a cartoon related to controlling, two managers describe a glass of water as half full or half empty. The controller's third opinion is: "For me, it's twice as big as necessary," meaning that the interpretation of metrics depends on one's perspective (Verlag für Controlling-Wissen 2006, p. 162). The commonly used metric in practice, "IT costs in relation to revenue" (see, e.g., Gadatsch et al. 2013), can serve as an example of the limited significance of individual metrics.

Example

An example of misinterpretation based on the metric "IT costs/revenue" is documented in Kütz (2003, pp. 20–21). A comparison of two companies led to the interim result that company A had a cost share of 0.8% and company B 1.2%. The resulting recommendation was that company B should adopt company A's IT systems to reduce its IT costs. Further detailed analysis revealed that company A was operating an outdated IT architecture that had not been maintained for years. The IT costs mainly consisted of maintenance for legacy systems. In contrast, company B had a modern and significantly more powerful IT architecture. The proposal to adopt company A's IT systems was therefore abandoned. ◄

Metric Systems
As described, individual metrics are only of limited significance. For this reason, metric systems have been developed to establish interdependencies between individual metrics and provide analysts with a comprehensive overview. A metric system places individual metrics in a logical context. General requirements for such metric systems are as follows:

- Objectivity and consistency, i.e., an appropriate structure of metrics supports consistent statements.
- Simplicity and clarity, i.e., a simple structure supports dissemination and use within the company.
- Information consolidation, i.e., metrics should be structured according to management levels and allow for top-down or bottom-up analyses. The individual values of subordinate metrics sum up to the aggregate value at the next level.
- Multicausal analysis, i.e., higher-level metrics should be able to be broken down into different perspectives at lower levels. The company's IT costs are explained by various cost categories and quantities at subordinate levels (projects, initiatives) (Gladen 2008, pp. 92–93).

Assignment of Metrics to Main and Subprocesses
For process controlling, it is advisable to align and define metrics based on the objectives and requirements of the process. Metrics enable the process owner to manage the process in a targeted manner. This is made possible by assigning metrics to main and subprocesses or process steps.

An assignment of metrics to sub- and main processes is illustrated in Fig. 4.13 using the example from Daxböck for the "Order-to-Cash Process" (Daxböck 2014, p. 60). The metric "On Time In Full (OTIF)" controls the process steps "availability check," "order confirmation," "create delivery," and "planning and transport," while the metric "Order-to-Cash total costs" applies to the entire process.

Example Calculation of Process Metrics
The following provides a calculation example that draws on several process metrics from Schmelzer and Sesselmann (2013). The basic data are summarized in Table 4.1, and the formulas for the metrics can be found in Fig. 4.14.

The average process time for the three orders already completed is 33 days. This is calculated from the total number of days' difference (99 days) divided by the number of completed orders (three) (see Fig. 4.15).

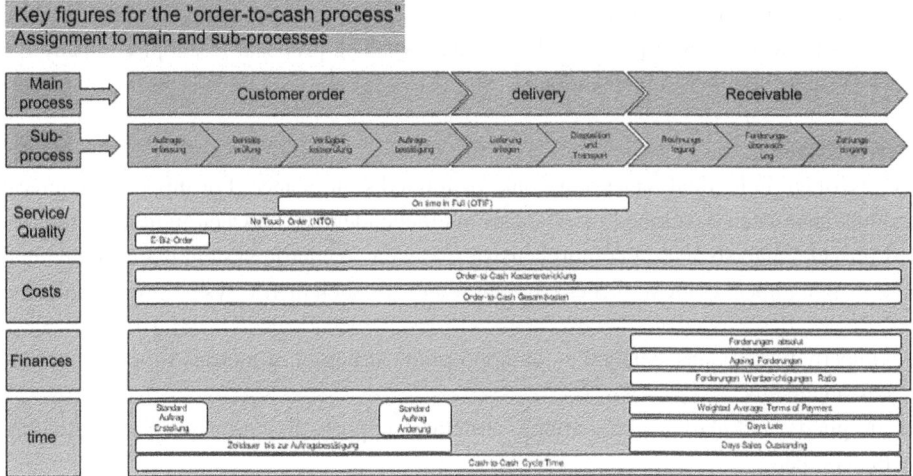

Fig. 4.13 Process metrics for an Order-to-Cash process (Daxböck 2014, p. 60, modified)

Tab. 4.1 Order data (Analysis date: 15.06.2016)

Order No.	Customer	Start Date	Planned Duration	Planned End Date	Actual End Date	Rework (Yes/No)
100	Berger	01.04.16	40	11.05.16	20.05.16	Yes
200	Müller	01.05.16	30	31.05.16	Open	No
300	Schmitz	01.02.16	10	11.02.16	11.02.16	Yes
400	Zeppelin	01.03.16	40	10.04.16	10.04.16	No
500	Meiner	01.06.16	30	01.07.16	Open	No

The average schedule adherence of the orders is 66% (2/3*100), as two orders were completed without schedule deviation. In total, three orders have been completed (see Fig. 4.16).

The average process quality of the orders is 33% (1/3*100), as one order was completed without rework and three orders were fully completed (see Fig. 4.17).

4.5 Process Cost Accounting

The business analysis of processes requires the inclusion of cost information. Process cost accounting is proposed as an instrument for this purpose (see Hirschmann and Scheer 1994, p. 189). Process cost accounting was developed in the early 1990s as a supplement to traditional cost accounting methods such as cost center, cost type, and cost unit accounting, in order to enable the evaluation of processes. Traditional cost accounting methods allocate costs from indirect business areas that cannot be directly assigned

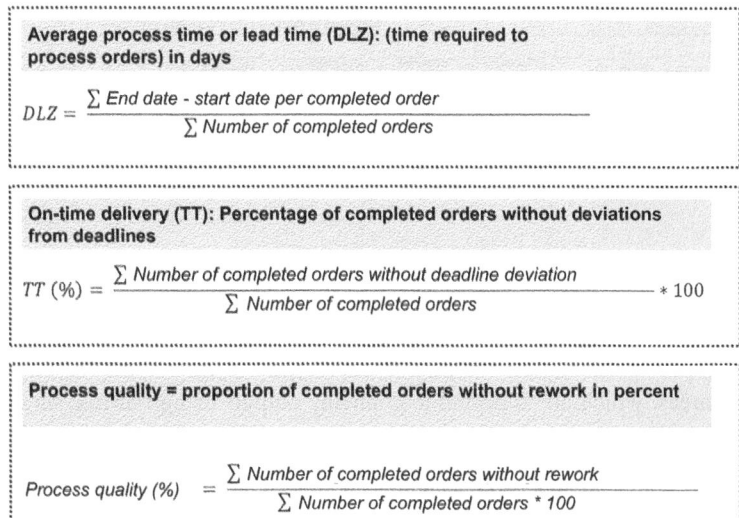

Fig. 4.14 Process metrics (formulas)

Order data					Analysis date	15.06.2020		
Order no.	Customer	Start date	Planned duration	Planned end date	Actual end date	Rework Y/N		Date deviation Y/N
100	Berger	01.04.2020	40	11.05.2020	20.05.2020	J		J
200	Miller	01.05.2020	30	31.05.2020		N		J
300	Schmitz	01.02.2020	10	11.02.2020	11.02.2020	J		N
400	Zeppelin	01.03.2020	40	10.04.2020	10.04.2020	N		N
500	Meier	01.06.2020	30	01.07.2020		N		J
5					3	3		2
(total)					(completed)	(without NA)		(without dev.)

Fig. 4.15 Determining process time (according to Schmelzer and Sesselmann 2013)

Order data					Analysis date	15.06.2020		
Order no.	Customer	Start date	Planned duration	Planned end date	Actual end date	Rework Y/N		Date deviation Y/N
100	Berger	01.04.2020	40	11.05.2020	20.05.2020	J		J
200	Miller	01.05.2020	30	31.05.2020		N		J
300	Schmitz	01.02.2020	10	11.02.2020	11.02.2020	J		N
400	Zeppelin	01.03.2020	40	10.04.2020	10.04.2020	N		N
500	Meier	01.06.2020	30	01.07.2020		N		J
5					3	3		2
(total)					(completed)	(without NA)		(without dev.)

Fig. 4.16 Determining schedule adherence (according to Schmelzer and Sesselmann 2013)

Order data						Analysis date	15.06.2020	
Order no.	Customer	Start date	Planned duration	Planned end date	Actual end date	Rework Y/N		Date deviation Y/N
100	Berger	01.04.2020	40	11.05.2020	20.05.2020	J		J
200	Miller	01.05.2020	30	31.05.2020		N		J
300	Schmitz	01.02.2020	10	11.02.2020	11.02.2020	J		N
400	Zeppelin	01.03.2020	40	10.04.2020	10.04.2020	N		N
500	Meier	01.06.2020	30	01.07.2020		N		J
5 (total)						3 (completed)	3 (without NA)	2 (without dev.)

Fig. 4.17 Determining process quality (according to Schmelzer and Sesselmann 2013)

to outputs. These include, for example, overhead costs incurred in administrative and commercial areas, which are allocated to company outputs using flat-rate surcharges. In contrast, process cost accounting seeks to identify allocation bases for the costs of indirect areas as well, enabling a more differentiated allocation of costs.

Unlike traditional cost accounting approaches, process cost accounting enables the evaluation of processes (see, for example, Hirschmann and Scheer 1994, p. 190). It provides allocation rates for valuing the outputs generated by processes. Process models are well suited as a basis for process cost calculation (see Berkau and Flotow 1995, p. 203). Process cost accounting derives allocation rates based on process models, which contain time and quantity information for process evaluation. This relationship between business process and workflow management and process cost accounting is illustrated in Fig. 4.18 by the integration of process cost accounting into the business process and workflow life cycle.

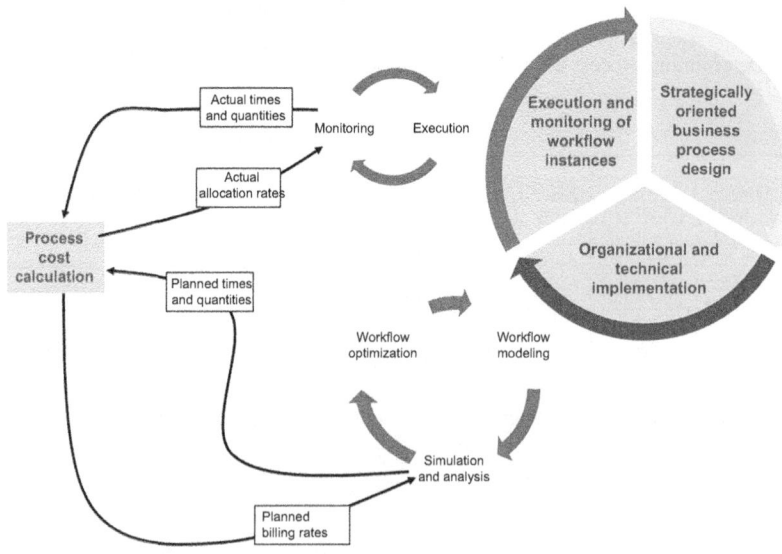

Fig. 4.18 Process cost accounting

Calculation of Process Costs

Process costs are determined according to the principle of allocation rate calculation. For this purpose, the process cost rates from process cost accounting are multiplied by the quantity of usage. The process cost rates can be broken down into cost-type-specific components, such as personnel costs, energy costs, depreciation, interest, and costs for the use of information technology. Determining the quantity of resources used by the process requires suitable reference quantities for each process step.

Examples from the procurement area include "number of reminders" or "number of processed orders" (see, for example, Scheer 1998, p. 67). The cumulative process costs of the workflow steps yield the process costs at the workflow level, which can then be aggregated to the business process level.

For process modeling, the above considerations lead to the requirement that the modeling concept must be able to assign process cost rates to process steps at the desired level of detail, i.e., the data model must be extended with attributes for modeling process cost rates.

4.6   Review Questions and Answers

Questions

1. What requirements must **"good" process metrics** fulfill?
2. Explain the concept of the **"Process Scorecard"** and its possible applications in process controlling.
3. Name some metrics for assessing the **quality and efficiency of processes.**

Answers

1. **Good process metrics** must be able to support **process control**. They must measure a relevant aspect (e.g., processing time) that enables goal-oriented management of the process.
2. The **Process Scorecard** is a **multidimensional metric system** (e.g., finance, performance) that serves process analysis and process control in a balanced manner.
3. **Metrics** for assessing the quality and efficiency of processes include, for example: **"rework rate," "on-time delivery," "throughput time,"** and **"productivity."**

References

Berkau, C., Flotow, P.: Kosten- und mengenorientiertes Management von Prozessen. Manage. Comput. **3**(3), 197–206 (1995)

Daxböck, C.: Supply chain controlling: kennzahlenbasierte mehrdimensionale steuerung des order-to-cash-prozesses. Controller. Mag. **2**, 58–61 (2014)

Gadatsch, A., Kütz, M., Juszczak, J.: Ergebnisse der 4. Umfrage zum Stand des IT-Controlling im deutschsprachigen Raum. In: Schriftenreihe des Fachbereiches Wirtschaft Sankt Augustin, Hochschule Bonn-Rhein-Sieg, Bd. 33, Sankt Augustin (2013)

Gadatsch, A., Mayer, E.: Masterkurs IT-Controlling, Wiesbaden, 5. edn (2013)

Gladen, W.: Performance measurement, controlling mit Kennzahlen, 4. edn Wiesbaden (2008)

Hirschmann, P., Scheer, A.-W.: Entscheidungsorientiertes Management von Geschäftsprozesse. Manage. Comput. **2**(3), 189–196 (1994)

Kölking, H.: DRG und Strukturwandel in der Gesundheitswirtschaft, 1. edn Stuttgart (2007)

Krcmar, H.: Informationsmanagement, 4. edn Berlin (2005)

Kütz, M. (Hrsg.): Kennzahlen in der IT, Heidelberg (2003)

Kütz, Martin: Kennzahlen in der IT, Heidelberg, 4. edn (2011)

Scheer, A.-W.: ARIS – Modellierungsmethoden, Metamodelle, Anwendungen, 3. edn Berlin (1998)

Scheer, A.-W., Heß, H.: Business process/performance management im rahmen eines ganzheitlichen controlling-ansatzes. In: Controlling Zeitschrift für erfolgsorientierte Unternehmenssteuerung, **21**(3), 145–151 (2009)

Schmelzer, H.J., Sesselmann., W.: Geschäftsprozessmanagement in der Praxis, 8. edn München (2013)

Stachel, K., Eltzholtz, L. (Hrsg.): Strategisches Einkaufsmanagement Krankenhaus, Berlin (2018)

Verlag für Controlling-Wissen (eds.): Controllers Pocket Guide 2007/2008, Offenburg (2006)

Modeling and Analysis of Processes

5

Models simplify daily work through abstraction

Abstract

Models serve to simplify real-world phenomena. They abstract from unnecessary details and provide stakeholders in process management with a tool for documenting, analyzing, and improving processes. This article introduces fundamental questions regarding the modeling and analysis of processes and subsequently discusses modeling methods commonly used in practice: process map, process profile, tabular notation, swimlane diagrams, extended event-driven process chain (eEPC), and Business Process Model and Notation. Finally, aspects of proper modeling are addressed and the presented methods are compared. Review questions and exercises ensure learning success.

5.1 Fundamental Questions of Modeling

5.1.1 Overview of Selected Modeling Concepts

Models simplify our view of complex reality. As an example, consider planning a train journey in an unfamiliar city, which typically requires some form of assistance. As a traveler, one could, for instance, ask passersby for directions or consult a timetable.

A timetable is a simplified model of reality that focuses on enabling interested users to navigate the transportation system. Figure 5.1 shows an excerpt from the timetable of the Cologne public transport system, which can be used to plan and undertake a train

© The Author(s), under exclusive license to Springer Fachmedien Wiesbaden GmbH, part of Springer Nature 2026
A. Gadatsch, *Business Process Management*,
https://doi.org/10.1007/978-3-658-49339-4_5

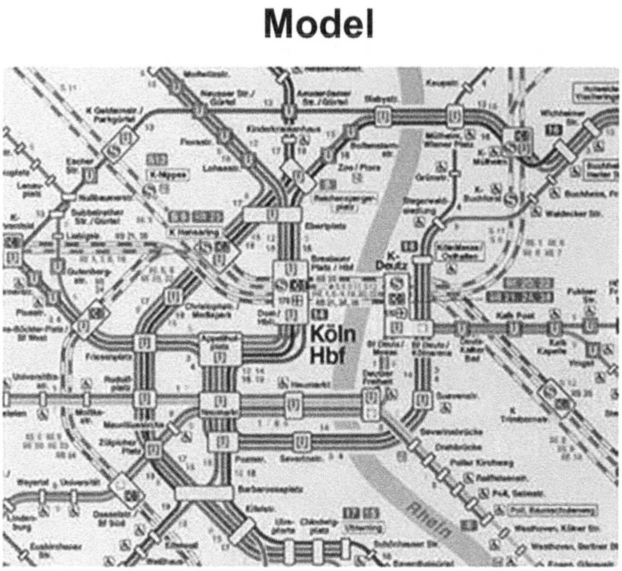

Model

Fig. 5.1 Model of a train journey (Image source: Kölner Verkehrsbetriebe (ed.), City of Cologne)

journey within the city. This "model" facilitates navigation by concentrating on the essential aspects. In this context, these would be, for example, the following two questions:

- How do I get from "A" to "B"?
- Which train do I need to take?

The symbols used in the "timetable" model are standardized, allowing users of various age groups to work with it without requiring extensive prior knowledge.

As previously discussed, business processes are often highly complex and involve a division of labor. Over the past decades, various methods have been developed to systematically represent processes in order to reduce this complexity.

In the context of business reengineering and business process optimization, both the current and target business processes are analyzed, designed, and documented. For this purpose, business process models are created to formally describe the business processes. Workflow models are derived from business process models through refinement. They serve to provide a detailed specification of business processes with the aim of execution by a workflow management system (WFMS).

Formal Methods

Formal methods can be used for process modeling. These are divided into script-based methods (scripting languages) and graphical methods (diagram languages).

Scripting languages allow process models to be described using a formal notation similar to programming languages. This enables a very high level of precision in model specification. However, process scripts are not very intuitive, and their interpretation requires detailed methodological knowledge, which makes practical application more difficult.

Compared to scripting languages, diagram languages are much more intuitive and can be differentiated into data flow, control flow, and object-oriented approaches (see Fig. 5.2). In practice, they have become more widely adopted than scripting languages, especially in contexts where models are created in collaboration with business users (e.g., employees from sales, accounting, or manufacturing).

Data-Oriented Methods

Data flow-oriented methods do not describe the process itself, but rather the flow of data—that is, the movement of data in the interplay of individual activities. The process is only indirectly derived from these representations, and the sequence of process steps is difficult to discern from the diagrams. As a result, the significance of data flow-oriented methods has declined considerably in recent years. Nevertheless, it remains necessary to

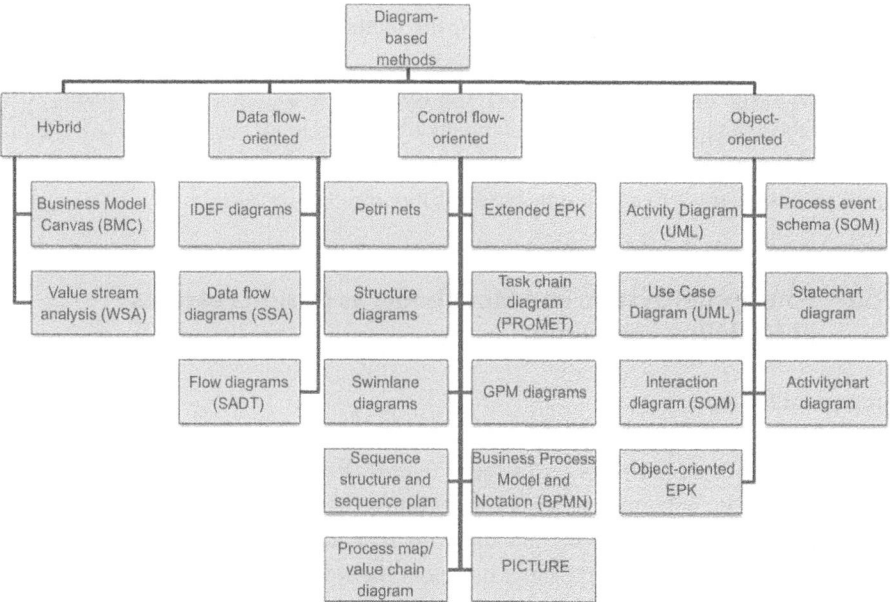

Fig. 5.2 Overview of selected modeling methods

adequately consider data aspects in process models. However, data flow-oriented methods are not very expressive with regard to process management aspects, since the process itself is not the focus of the modeling effort (Meyer, Smirnov, and Weske 2011, p. 5).

Control Flow-Oriented Methods
Control flow-oriented methods focus on the sequence of activities, i.e., process modeling. In practice, process maps, swimlane diagrams, value chain diagrams (WKD), the extended event-driven process chain (eEPC), and the Business Process Modeling and Notation method (BPMN) have become established.

Object-Oriented Methods
The idea of integrating functions and data into so-called objects originates from software development. This has led to the development of object-oriented modeling methods. In practice, the Unified Modeling Language (UML), particularly the Activity Diagram, has become widely adopted.

Hybrid Methods
Hybrid methods include value stream mapping (WSA) and the Business Model Canvas (BMC). Value stream mapping is primarily used in manufacturing and production to analyze processes. Its goal is to identify waste resulting from unnecessary overproduction, transportation, waiting times, excess inventory, errors, and the resulting rework (see Wagner and Lindner 2022, p. 4 ff.). It is particularly suitable for analyzing mass production processes, as it was developed for this purpose (see Wagner and Lindner 2022, p. 135). Due to this narrow application focus, the method will not be discussed further in this book.

The relatively new Business Model Canvas (see Osterwalder and Pigneur 2010) describes the key characteristics of a company's business model at a level above the process layer. It is therefore an excellent starting point for process management, as a company's processes are derived from its business model.

5.1.2   Conceptual System and Metamodel as Design Features of Modeling Languages

Conceptual System
The purpose of a conceptual system is to delineate and categorize modeling-relevant phenomena and to assign them terms (see Gehring 1998). Examples include the naming of information, activities, process relationships, or assignment relationships. These are reflected in the notation of the modeling method and thus in its expressive capabilities. Business process models typically represent the following aspects (see Kurbel et al. 1997):

- **Process steps** represent the activities required to deliver process outputs. Synonymous terms for an individual process step include operation, task, function, and work step.
- **Objects** are processed within process steps and exchanged between them. Examples include orders, complaints, or quotations. Objects are represented by information carriers in various forms, such as email, fax, voucher, document, etc. The transfer of objects is referred to as object flow. Equivalent terms include information flow, data flow, and document flow.
- **Dependencies** between process steps, which may be temporal, logical, or technological in nature, define the process logic of a business process. Analogous terms include control flow and steering flow.
- **Actors** perform activities within process steps. Actors can be, for example, users, machines, or programs. Alternative terms include department, organizational unit, role, etc.

Metamodel

Models are used to analyze and design real-world systems. They map an original or object system to a model system. Since a model should reflect the structure and behavior of an object system as faithfully as possible, special requirements must be met in the mapping process. The ability to formally describe model systems makes it possible to introduce the higher-level modeling layer of meta-modeling (see Gehring 1998) (see Fig. 5.3). A metamodel represents an entire class of model systems; each class element is an instance of the metamodel. In addition, notation rules for creating the model system are specified. This allows the model system to be checked for completeness and consistency with respect to the object system.

5.1.3 Process Modeling in Practice

Many companies use complex, historically evolved software systems that are undocumented or insufficiently documented. Cumbersome workflows and inefficient organiza-

Fig. 5.3 Meta-modeling (see Gehring 1998)

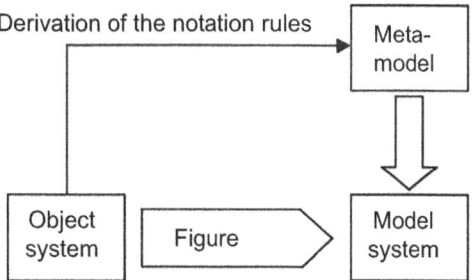

tions force them to reorganize their business processes and to redevelop or replace their software. The introduction of standard software to reduce costs can only lead to rationalization success if it is accompanied by an analysis and redesign of workflows. For this reason, especially larger organizations consider developing an enterprise process model.

Companies
- Capturing and documenting business processes
- Weakness analysis of the overall organization
- Requirements definition for new information systems
- Selection and implementation of standard software
- Development of an enterprise process model

Customers of standard software vendors require information about the functional scope of products when making purchasing decisions. Process models can be considered an additional component of the software product and offer added value to customers during deployment analysis. These analyses can be simplified by the data and process descriptions. Even later, during operation, the models can serve as a reference resource.

Standard Software Vendors
- Data and process models as product documentation
- Support for deployment analysis at the customer site
- Basis for individual enhancements (modifications)
- Basis for comparison in the software selection process
- Training aid and reference for users

For consultants, the primary focus is on supporting clients in reorganizing their workflows and structures. Another key area is providing implementation support during the introduction of standard software or workflow management systems. There is often also a need to compensate for a lack of expertise on the client side.

Consulting Firms
- Implementation of IT systems for clients
- Conducting weakness analyses
- Supporting consulting in organizational projects
- Conducting business reengineering projects

5.1.4   Case Study: "General Practitioner's Office"

The following case study on taking over a general practitioner's office serves as the basis for comprehensive modeling examples. All information is designed to be realistic, but does not refer to any specific real-world case.

Basic Data

A physician is planning to take over a general medical practice from a predecessor who has retired. He is considering which economic fundamentals he must take into account in order to achieve a sustainable and adequate income (business model), as well as how the day-to-day operations in the practice should be organized (business processes). To this end, he intends to use modern business process management methods. The practice will treat patients with statutory and private insurance, as well as international patients. In addition to the usual on-site services, innovative online services will also be offered, such as appointment scheduling, downloads, prescription orders, and even an "online consultation."

Initial Analysis

An initial analysis by the physician resulted in a structured process list and preliminary details for the two processes "Schedule Appointment" and "Change Dressing." Additional processes still need to be identified.

- Management processes (for practice management)
  - Planning practice operations,
  - Managing staff deployment,
  - Managing finances
- Core processes (for patient-facing service delivery)
- Service delivery
  - Providing treatments: appointment scheduling, examination, treatment, documentation
  - Conducting preventive check-ups: appointment scheduling, data collection, check-up, documentation
  - Administering vaccinations: online appointment scheduling, patient information, vaccination, issuing vaccination certificate
- Support processes (for general support)
  - Procuring materials and services,
  - Analyzing laboratory samples,
  - Providing IT support,
  - Cleaning and maintaining the practice,
  - Posting receipts, calculating and paying salaries,
  - Writing medical reports.

Detailed Process: "Schedule Appointment"

The "Schedule Appointment" process takes place either on-site at the practice or by phone. It serves to prepare for examinations and treatments in the practice. The process can be described as follows.

Process objective: Appointment is scheduled with the patient.

Process steps (responsible persons in parentheses)

- Greeting (reception assistant or by phone),
- Clarifying the request (assistant),
- Checking resources/available appointments (assistant),
- Scheduling the appointment (assistant with patient)
- Saying goodbye to the patient (assistant)

Result: Appointment is scheduled, or the process is discontinued.
   Participants (roles): Patient, assistant.

Detailed Process: "Change Dressing"
The "Treatment" process occurs in various forms, such as scheduled treatment, emergency treatment, or routine procedures like "changing a dressing in the doctor's office." The process can be described as follows.
   Process objective: New dressing is applied correctly and protects the patient's wound.
   Process steps (responsible persons in parentheses)

- Recording patient data (reception), waiting (patient),
- Inquiring about symptoms, removing dressing, examining and disinfecting wound, applying new dressing, checking pressure/fit (assistant),
- If complications arise, consult physician if necessary (assistant), perform examination and treatment (physician)
- Documenting the procedure (assistant)

Result: Wound is treated, dressing is applied and checked.
   Participants (roles): Patient, reception, physician, assistant.

5.2   Business Model Canvas (BMC)

5.2.1   Notation

The Business Model Canvas is a method for the simple graphical modeling, structuring, and optimization of business models. It was developed as recently as 2010 by Alexander Osterwalder as part of his dissertation (see Osterwalder and Pigneur 2010).
   Its range of applications has expanded significantly. The BMC was originally developed as a strategic tool to support the founding of startups, but is now used by small and medium-sized enterprises as well as large corporations across all industries. For startups, it is used to move from a business idea to a business model, as well as for further development and realignment of the company. For established companies, it supports

the analysis of the current state, identification of optimization potential, and adaptation to changing customer needs or market requirements (see Lukas 2018). In the meantime, additional areas of application have been developed for the Business Model Canvas, such as data science (see Neifer et al. 2020).

5.2.2 Modeling Example

The Business Model Canvas provides a clear description of nine aspects of value creation: business partners, business activities, resources, value propositions, customer relationships, distribution channels, customer segments, as well as cost structure and revenue streams (see Maisch and Valdés 2022). Figure 5.4 presents a small example that describes the business model of a medical practice based on the case study in Sect. 5.1.4.

5.2.3 Evaluation

The method helps to identify relationships within the business model and to highlight strengths and weaknesses. However, it is easy to remain at a very abstract level and neglect the derivation and implementation of concrete measures (see Lukas 2018).

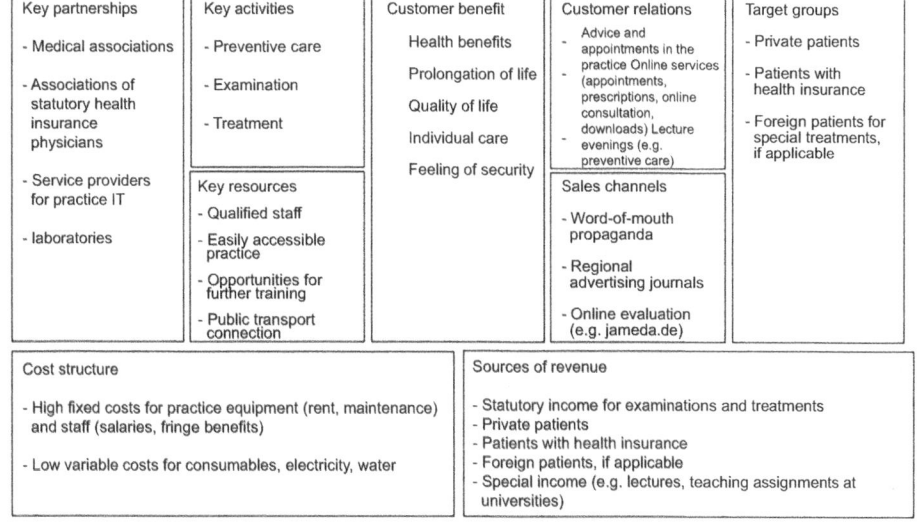

Fig. 5.4 Business Model Canvas modeling example for a general practitioner's office

5.3   Process Map

5.3.1   Notation

Business processes are often differentiated based on their proximity to a company's core business (see e.g. Seidlmeier 2002, pp. 2 f.). Process maps have become established as a clear way to present the essential processes, highlighting the defining business processes of a company. The purpose is to provide a high-level overview of important workflows (processes) within an organization. Target audiences can be internal (management, employees) or external (suppliers, applicants). The processes depicted are usually divided into management, core, and support processes.

Management Processes
Management processes are responsible for the integrative coordination of business processes (e.g., strategy development, corporate planning, operational management). They provide the organizational framework for value-creating and supporting processes.

Core Business Processes
Core business processes are those with a high value creation share. They are typically critical to competition and constitute the value creation process, starting from customer demand through procurement, storage, production, assembly, and delivery.

Support Processes
Support processes are business processes with little or no value creation. They are generally not critical to competition. Examples include financial accounting, cost accounting, reporting, human resources, cafeteria, vehicle fleet, information processing, and legal services.

5.3.2   Modeling Examples

Figure 5.5 shows an example of a possible notation for a process map. It was briefly mentioned in Sect. 1.4.4. The management processes are depicted at the top of the map, with the support processes at the bottom. The central element of a process map is the core processes of an organization, which are shown in the middle section with their main process steps.

Figure 5.6 shows an example of a process map based on the case study from Sect. 5.1.4. It presents three core processes (conducting treatments, performing preventive examinations, and administering vaccinations). In this example, the customer is represented by the patient. In addition, typical management and support processes are shown.

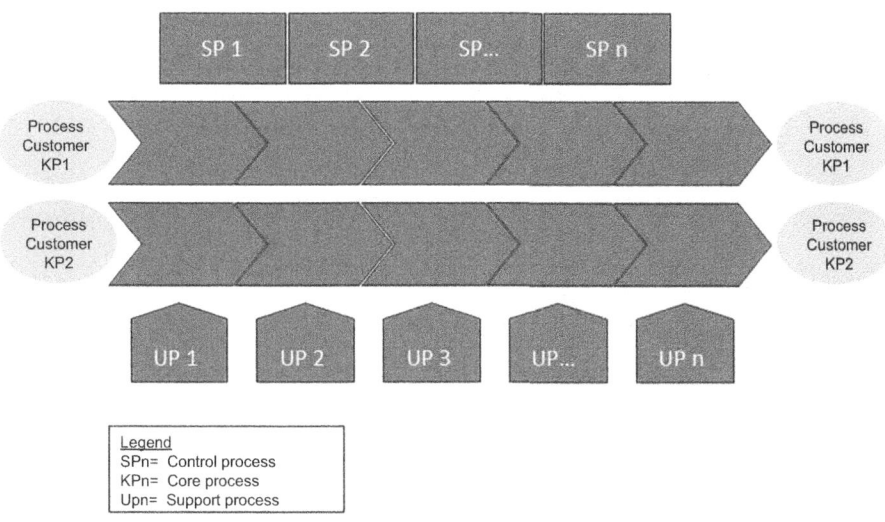

Fig. 5.5 Process map—notation

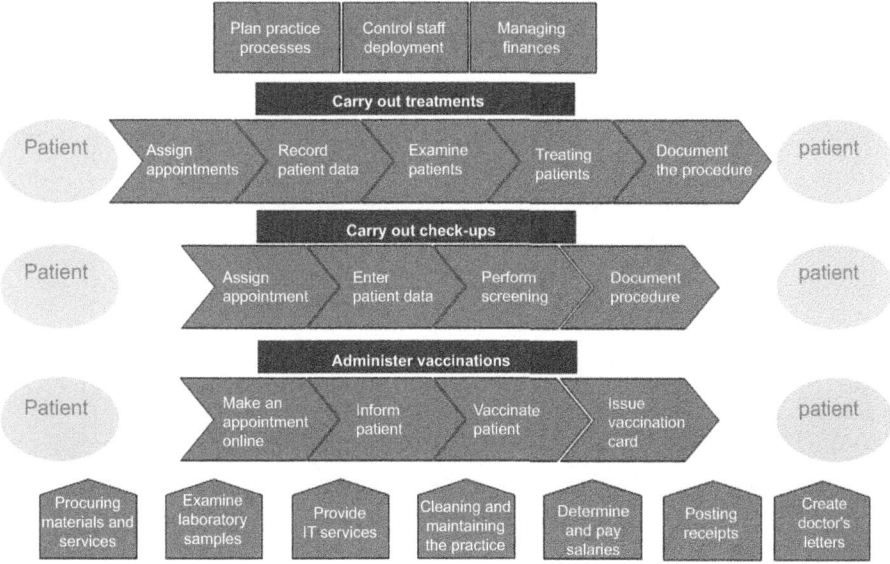

Fig. 5.6 Process map—example of a general practitioner's office

Figure 5.7 shows an example of a process map for an automotive business, which was also introduced in Sect. 1.4.4. The company has two main processes: the sale of new or used vehicles, and the service process (repairs, maintenance, vehicle inspection, etc.).

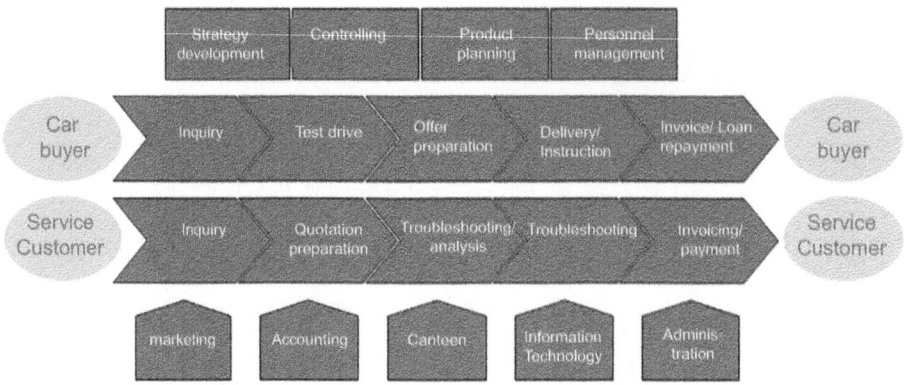

Fig. 5.7 Process map—example: automotive business

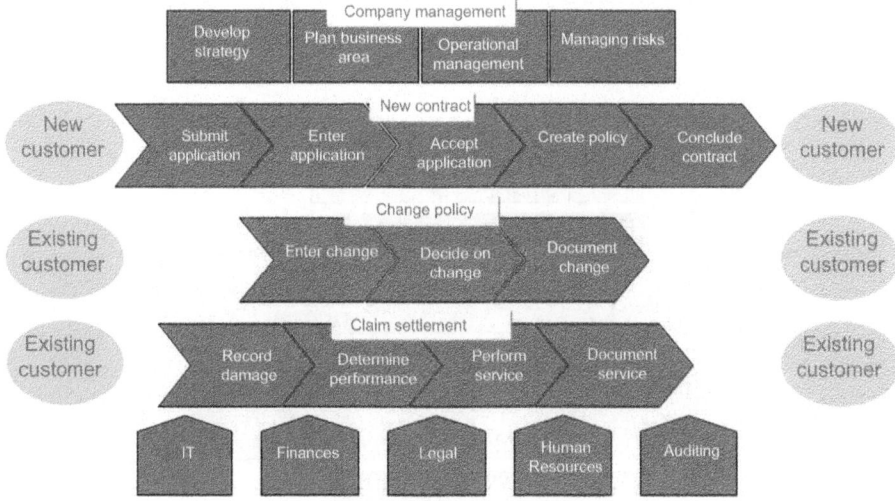

Fig. 5.8 Process map—example: insurance company

Another example is shown in Fig. 5.8. The three core processes—"New contract," "Contract modification," and "Claims settlement"—describe the typical workflows of an insurance company.

Since there is no standardized method for describing process maps, many variants have emerged in business practice. The previous examples are often adapted in practice using custom symbols or visualization techniques.

The modeling example for a general practitioner's office (see Fig. 5.6) was created for illustration purposes using the modeling tool "Bic Design," which is, for example, used in courses at Bonn-Rhein-Sieg University of Applied Sciences (see Fig. 5.9). Each of the tools available on the market (see also Sect. 6.1.2) defines its own graphical standards.

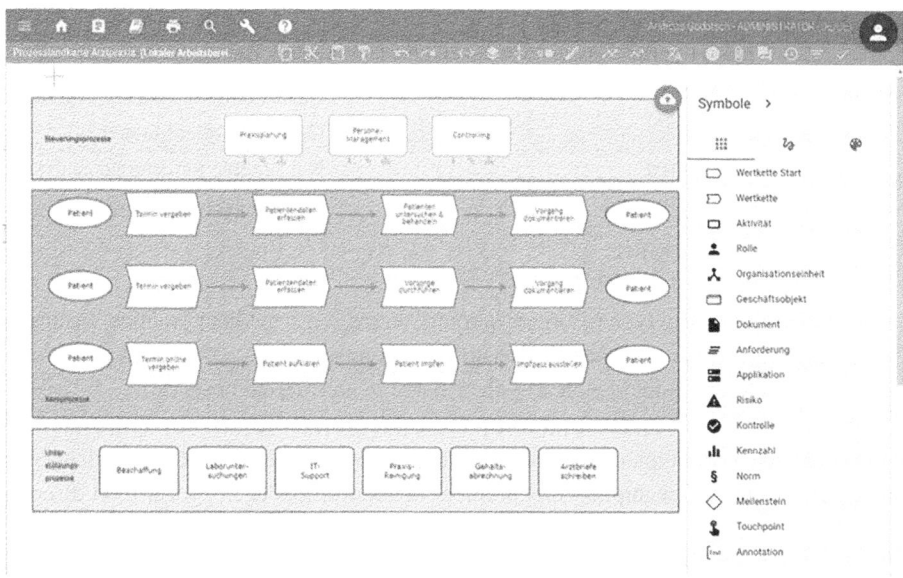

Fig. 5.9 Process map for a general practitioner's office—modeled with Bic Design

In practice, it is often difficult to decide whether a process should be included in the process map. Wagner and Lindner (2022) refer to this as "process suitability." The following guiding questions can serve as orientation. If most of them can be answered with "yes," the process should be included in the process map (see Wagner and Lindner 2022, p. 145):

- Are different units, departments, or areas affected by the process (high division of labor)?
- Are there interfaces to other processes?
- Are there interfaces to the customer or customer processes?
- Can a process owner be designated?
- Is the process frequently executed?
- Does the process tie up many resources that are also relevant for other processes?

5.3.3   Evaluation

The following characteristics define a "good" process map:

- **Clarity:** The representation should ideally fit on a single page. The model excerpt should clearly describe the subject matter, while details and process variants should be avoided.

Tab. 5.1 Evaluation of the Process Map

Advantages	Disadvantages
Easy to use	Usable only for process overviews
Clear and concise	Cannot represent branches
Little or no training required	Not suitable for detailed analysis
No tools required	Limited expressiveness

[Table footer—please overwrite]

- **Recognizability:** The type of organization depicted (e.g., medical practice, insurance company, university) or a specific division of a company (e.g., a branch of an automobile manufacturer) should be clearly identifiable to an external observer.
- **Conciseness:** Use of meaningful labels for process steps. Generic descriptions without reference to the type of organization should be avoided (Not: "Procurement-Storage-Sales," but, for example, "Procurement of food products ..." for a food discount retailer).
- **Core processes:** Organizations are primarily distinguished by their core processes. Therefore, these should be highlighted in the process map with more detail and the central process steps.
- **Symbols:** Use of simple symbols, differentiated by process types (with legend).

Conclusion A "good" process map is characterized by the fact that a reader immediately gains an overview of the key processes and thus the core business of the organization.

The process map is a widely used tool for providing a clear overview of overall relationships. It enables a company and its key processes (management processes, core processes, support processes) to be presented in an illustrative manner.

The method can also be applied to specific areas, such as sales, IT, or a corporate unit. However, it is not suitable for detailed representations of processes or subprocesses.

The effort required to create and especially to use the process map passively is minimal, as only a few symbols are used. In addition, this method is not standardized, which allows for the development and use of custom symbols. On the other hand, the lack of standardization limits comparison with reference models or representations from other organizations. The arguments are summarized in Table 5.1.

5.4   Process Profile

5.4.1   Notation

As a supplement to the process map, process profiles describe the overall process and each process step with additional textual information and, if applicable, further content such as statistical indicators or an explanatory video. A standardized notation or scope of description has not yet been developed. Important and commonly used contents of process profiles in practice include:

- Process name,
- Process description,
- Process owners and other contacts,
- Triggers and outcomes of the process,
- Additional explanations that go beyond the formal process models, and
- Key figures, such as number of transactions per time unit, number of employees, or process controlling metrics.

5.4.2 Modeling Examples

A good example of a process profile is documented on the website of Freie Universität Berlin. The university uses process profiles for internal purposes and has made them publicly available alongside a process map published on the internet. Figure 5.10 shows an excerpt from the interactive process profile "Establishing New Degree Programs."

5.4.3 Evaluation

The process profile complements the process map by providing detailed descriptions of processes. Since not all aspects of a process can be captured in a graphic, the process profile offers a simple and generally understandable way to document details and special issues of a process. The content can be tailored to the needs of the organization. Ideally, a process profile is created for every process and subprocess and made available to employees and, if necessary, external stakeholders (e.g., "Quotation Processing Process for Customers"). The contents are not standardized, so custom variants can be created without difficulty. In practice, the intranet has proven to be an effective publication medium.

5.5 Tabular Process Modeling

5.5.1 Notation

Graphical modeling methods require the use of specialized software tools for long-term application. The use of conventional graphics programs leads, in the long run, to significant effort for creation and modification.

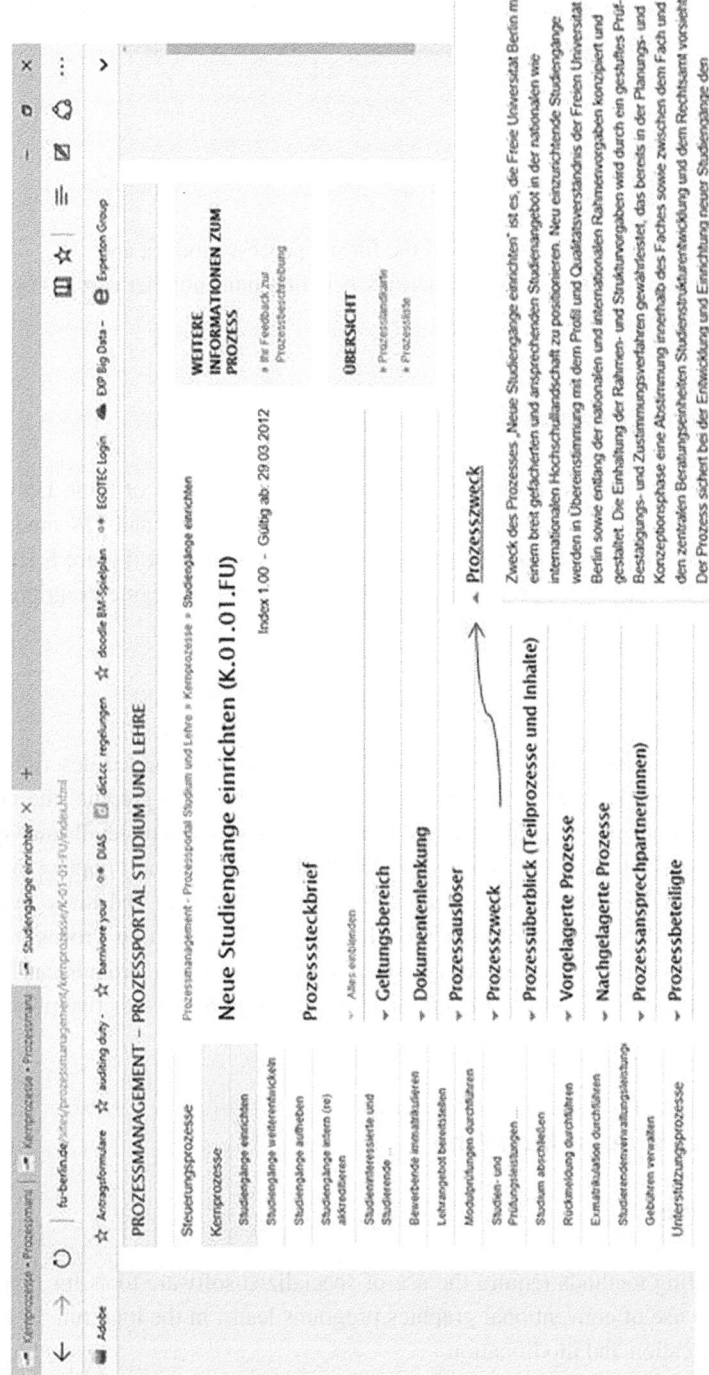

Fig. 5.10 Process profile Freie Universität Berlin (2015)

Process name		Process date		Creator	
Trigger			Process results		
Roles		Role Description			
Process owner					
Participants					
To be informed					
Process step	Responsible	Input	Output	IT deployment	Measured variable
Comments					

Fig. 5.11 Tabular process documentation form

For the "quick" documentation of processes, simple "process documentation forms" in tabular format are also used in practice. Even though the formal requirements for such concepts are not very high, their practical value is considerable. The ease of understanding and straightforward presentation of the content are aspects that are highly beneficial for initial documentation or for providing a clear overview of the essential process elements.

A simple form for collecting process information is provided in Fig. 5.11. The notation of tabular models is not standardized and is kept relatively simple. The header section of the form provides a general description of the process with several attributes such as "Process Name," "Date," and "Author." The "Results" attribute is particularly important, as it describes the fundamental output of the process. The section below describes the process steps sequentially, where for each process step at least a designation, a responsible person, the required input (information, resources), the output (information, results), and the software used should be recorded. It may also be useful to define a metric for process controlling (see Chap. 4) in order to monitor the success of process execution.

5.5.2   Modeling Examples

Figure 5.12 presents an example of a process that has been "modeled" in tabular form. The example concerns "Appointment Scheduling in a Medical Practice." The table

Process name: Appointment allocation	Date: 06.03.2013		Creator: A. Gadatsch	
Trigger: Patient calls or enters practice		Results: agreed appointment		
Roles		Role Description		
Process owner		Med. FA		
Participants		Patient		
To inform		Laboratory, if applicable		
Process step	**Responsible**	**Input**	**Output**	**IT use**	**Measurand**
Greeting	Med. FA	-	-	-	-
Clarify the patient's concerns	Med. FA	Appointment request Insurance card		Medical practice information system	Number of patients
Clarify resources / free appointments	Med. FA	Appointment overview staff deployment plan	Appointment	Medical practice information system	
Make an appointment	Med. FA	-	-	-	-
Farewell	Med. FA	-	-	-	-
Comments: Comparable process for appointment changes. Not every patient may receive an appointment if the request is unsuitable or there is a lack of capacity.					

Fig. 5.12 Tabular process documentation: "Schedule appointment"

depicts a process that takes place at the reception area of the practice and involves, in addition to the medical assistant, the patient as another process participant. The metric defined for process controlling is the "number of patients." The overall output of the process can be modeled as an "Agreed Appointment" with the patient.

The first row serves to identify the process (process name, date, and author). This is followed by a brief description of the process triggers (e.g., "Patient enters the practice") and the outcomes ("Patient is discharged"). In addition to the process owner, other participants and parties to be informed are listed. Each process step is then documented row by row. This includes specifying the responsible party, the input (What information is used? e.g., health insurance card, medical reports), the output (What information is produced? e.g., prescription, referral), and the use of IT (e.g., medical practice information system).

The tabular process representation can be converted "at the push of a button" into graphical notations using many modeling tools, which will be discussed in Sect. 5.7 and following. Figure 5.13 shows a screenshot of the ARIS Toolset by Software AG, which displays the "Schedule appointment" process both as a table and in the EPK modeling language (see Sect. 5.7).

The process "Change dressing" from the case study is shown in Figure 5.14.

The arguments are summarized in Table 5.2.

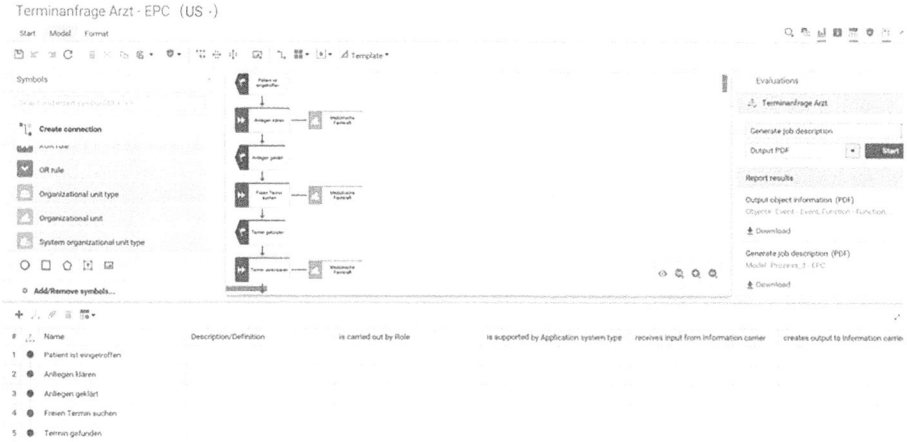

Fig. 5.13 Tabular process documentation: "Schedule appointment" alternatively represented as an EPK model

Process name: "Change dressing"		Date: 13.12.20xx			Creator: A. Gadatsch	
Trigger: Patient comes to practice			Results: Wound treated, dressing correctly applied			
Roles		**Role Description**				
Process owner		Doctor				
Participants		Patient, assistant, doctor				
To be informed		Health insurance company				
Process step	**Responsible**	**Input**	**Output**	**IT use**		**Measured variable**
Patient data record	Reception / Patient	Insurance card		Medical practice information system		Number of patients
Wait	Patient					
Examine wound	Assistant					
Examine and treat complications if necessary	Doctor					
Apply dressing, check pressure, firmness check	Assistant					
Process Document	Assistant			Medical practice information system		Number of procedures
Remarks:						

Fig. 5.14 Tabular process documentation: Change dressing

5.5.3   Evaluation

Tabular process modeling is suitable for the rapid documentation of as-is processes of simple and medium complexity. It can also be used for target process modeling. As soon as processes become more complex, especially when branches in the workflow need to be modeled, this method becomes less appropriate.

Tab. 5.2 Evaluation of Tabular Modeling

Advantages	Disadvantages
Easy to use	Only suitable for simple processes
Clear and well-structured	Branches are difficult to represent
Little or no training required	Unsuitable for comprehensive process analysis
No tools required	Only suitable for business-level modeling

[Table footer—please overwrite]

Some tool vendors use tabular process documentation to generate "raw process models" (e.g., BPMN models, see Sect. 5.8, eEPK models, see Sect. 5.6.3). This approach has the advantage that, during the as-is process documentation with the business department staff, a simple method can be used initially. Later, the work can continue with a more refined notation.

5.6   Swimlane Diagram

5.6.1   Notation

Swimlane diagrams were developed in the early 1990s by H. F. Binner to represent sequences of activities in a simple manner (see Binner 2000). The design is inspired by the view of a swimming pool from above. The pool represents the overall context, such as the company under consideration or a larger section, for example, a department of the company. The swimlanes (lanes) in this analogy stand for the areas of responsibility of actors (e.g., a department), between which the assigned responsibility for a process segment shifts back and forth until the entire process is completed.

The representation bears some resemblance to the activity diagrams of the UML notation known from computer science or to the task chain diagrams according to Österle (see Österle 1995). The notation has been further developed several times and can be adapted in different ways depending on its intended use (see, for example, Sharp and McDermott 2002, pp. 144 f. and 158 f.). Organizational units are depicted as "swimlanes" (lanes), activities (process steps) as rectangles, and decisions as diamonds. This provides a good overview of high-level processes with frequent departmental transitions (see the example in Fig. 5.15).

To reduce complexity, often only the "happy path" is modeled, that is, the standard process flow without exceptions, which occurs under normal circumstances (Fischermanns 2013).

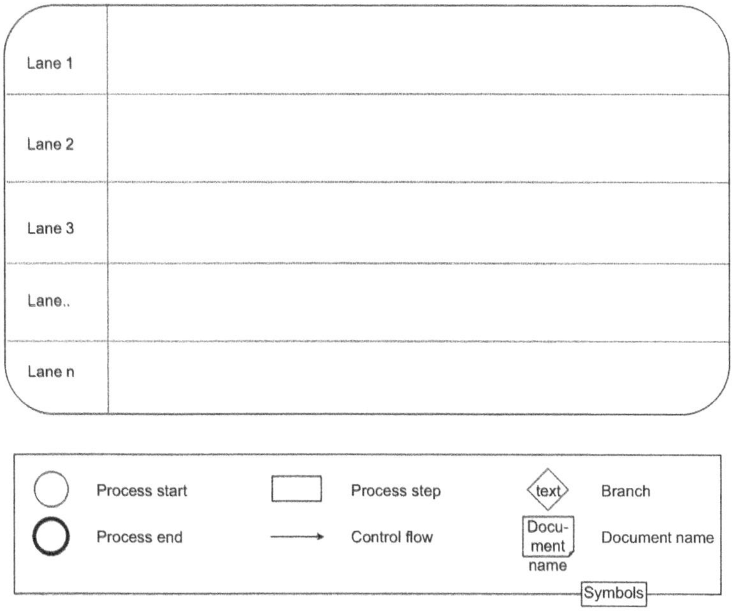

Fig. 5.15 Swimlane notation

5.6.2 Modeling Examples

The process "Scheduling an Appointment" was created using the freely available modeling tool "draw.io" (www.draw.io or diagrams.net) and is shown in Fig. 5.16. Since only two people are involved, two lanes are required for this relatively simple process.

The process "Changing a Dressing" is significantly more complex. It requires 4 lanes (reception, waiting area, assistant, physician) and involves a branching (complications yes/no?). It is shown in Fig. 5.17.

Another example of a swimlane diagram can be seen in Fig. 5.18. It shows the simplified process of treatment in a hospital. The lanes represent departments such as administration, ward, radiology, operating room, and billing. In the diagram, the process begins at the top left with the recording of patient data. The patient is then examined, and depending on the result, X-rays are taken and subsequently evaluated. This is followed by surgery and, finally, post-operative care and discharge of the patient. Subsequent activities include billing and monitoring of incoming payments.

5.6.3 Evaluation

The swimlane method provides a clear overview of processes and very effectively visualizes departmental transitions. This makes processes with frequent handovers between

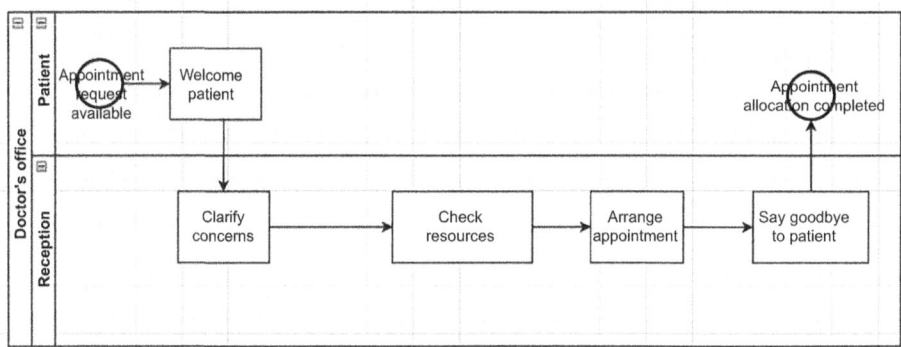

Fig. 5.16 Swimlane "Scheduling an Appointment"—modeled with draw.io

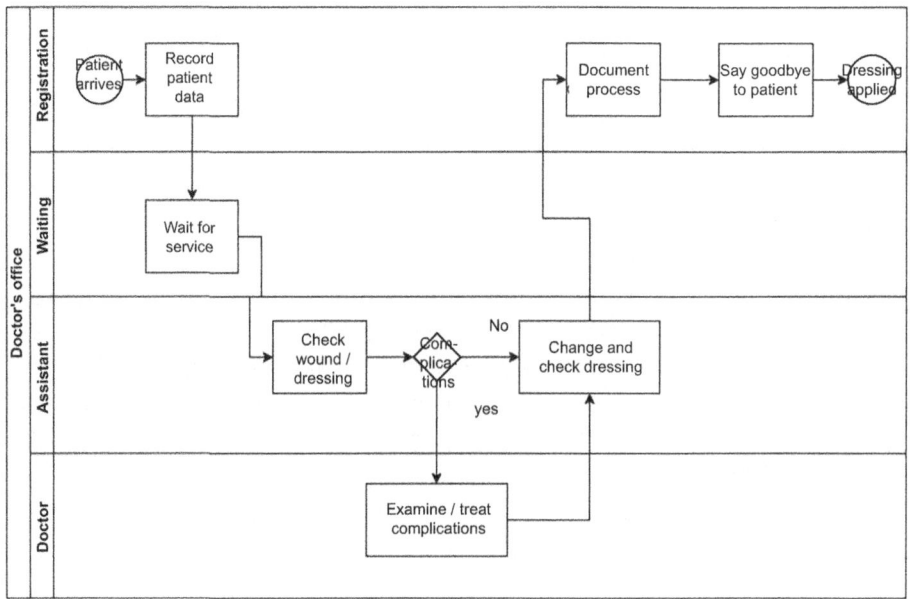

Fig. 5.17 Swimlane "Changing a Dressing"—modeled with draw.io

employees quickly apparent, which can serve as an indicator for potential optimization. It does not require any tools and can be easily used in workshops on a whiteboard or flipchart.

A disadvantage is the limited level of detail and the low information content of the representations. The focus of the visualization is on the concise depiction of control flow in the context of the involved organizational units, i.e., the sequence of individual

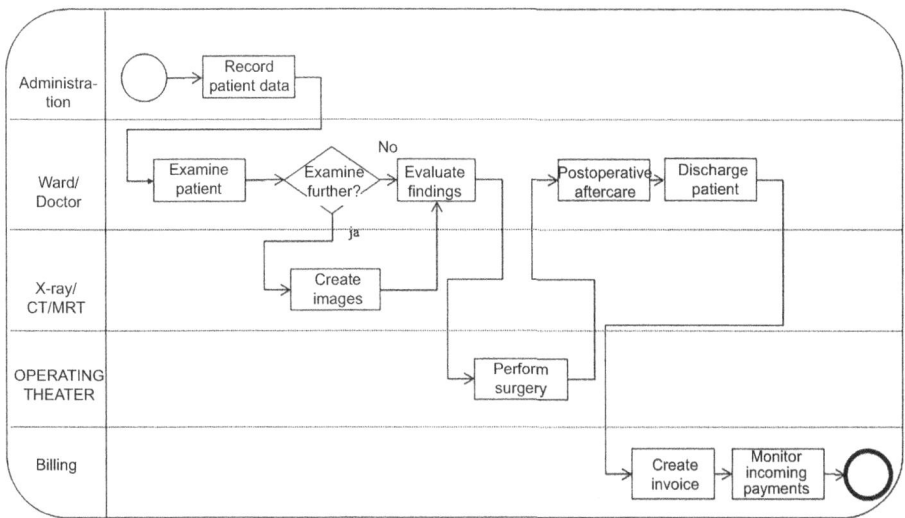

Fig. 5.18 Swimlane model: Hospital treatment

activities and their organizational assignment. The notation uses very few, non-standard-ized elements and is very easy to learn. This makes the method suitable for ad hoc use, for example on a flipchart in meetings. However, more extensive processes with many branches cannot be represented well. Additional symbols must at least be explained in a legend, but often lead to less clear representations due to limited space. The arguments are summarized in Table 5.3.

Tab. 5.3 Evaluation of Swimlane Modeling

Advantages	Disadvantages
Easy to use	Only suitable for simple and less complex processes
Clear, especially for departmental transitions	Less suitable for comprehensive process analysis, as models become confusing
Minimal training required	Notation is not standardized, i.e., symbols differ depending on the tool
Simple branches can be represented	Only suitable for business-oriented modeling
Well suited for informing new employees or external parties	
Tools are not strictly necessary, but useful for widespread adoption	

[Table footer—please overwrite]

5.7   Event-Driven Process Chain (EPC)

5.7.1   Overview

Until the early 1990s, so-called data flow diagrams were used to illustrate which data "flowed" between the organizational units of a company. They were used as tools in software development. The reason for this data-oriented approach at the time was the limited memory available. Programs supporting business processes were designed to make optimal use of the available memory. Process models for describing workflows were not yet common. Against this background, the Event-Driven Process Chain (EPC) method was developed (Hoffmann et al. 1992, p. 3) to place the process at the center of modeling and thus the design of information systems.

The Event-Driven Process Chain (EPC) is a central component of the ARIS (Architecture of Integrated Information Systems) framework for the development and description of information systems, developed by A.-W. Scheer at Saarland University (see Scheer 1998), as well as the modeling concepts anchored in the architecture, which were developed in 1991 by Keller, Nüttgens, and Scheer (see Keller et al. 1992).

▶   The original article cited above (Keller et al. 1992) is still available online on the
     institute's website and is highly recommended to interested readers. The most
     recently checked link is: https://www.uni-saarland.de/fileadmin/user_upload/
     Fachrichtungen/fr13_BWL/professuren/PDF/heft89.pdf

The EPC modeling approach quickly established itself in practice as a leading semi-formal method for modeling business processes. One reason was that SAP AG, Walldorf, used EPCs to document its successful ERP system "R/3" (Scheer 1998, p. 125). Due to the success of SAP software, this also led to the rapid spread of the EPC method (Rump 1999, p. 61). An early description of the method can be found in Keller and Teufel (1997).

The notation of the EPC method has been modified many times and published in various versions. There is no single standardized version, as is the case with BPMN 2.0 (see Sect. 5.8) (see Jannaber et al. 2016 and Riehle et al. 2016). The author therefore largely follows the original version by Keller, Nüttgens, and Scheer (see Keller et al. 1992) as well as the variants commonly used in business practice, which have been established by various modeling tools.

Classification within the ARIS Architecture by A.-W. Scheer
The ARIS architecture developed by August-Wilhelm Scheer (University of Saarbrücken) distinguishes between the data, control, function, organization, and service views for the holistic specification of information systems. In addition, the project phases of business concept, IT concept, and implementation are differentiated (see Fig.

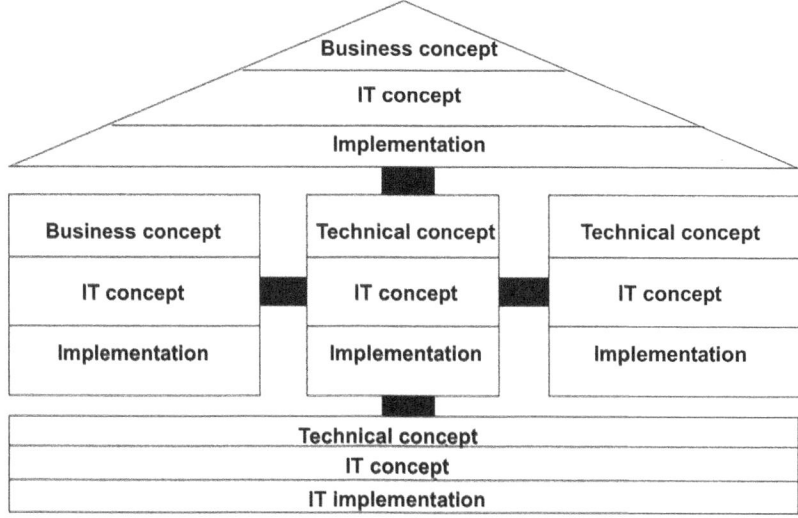

ARIS architecture ("ARIS house") according to A.-W. Scheer

Fig. 5.19 ARIS House (Scheer 1998)

5.19). ARIS is a general framework for business process modeling. It provides modeling and implementation methods specific to each layer and view (Scheer 1998, p. 1).

Modeling Phases

ARIS is designed as a method-neutral procedural model. It supports the process from the initial problem statement to a functioning program and distinguishes three consecutive modeling phases: business concept, IT concept, and implementation. The starting point of modeling is a business problem that is not formally described, which is gradually refined up to implementation. In addition to modeling methods, numerous software tools (e.g., the products "ARIS Business Architect" and "ARIS Express" from Software AG, Darmstadt) are available to support practical implementation. Due to its generic structure, ARIS can be adapted to current developments and is still considered a leading and established framework in business informatics (see Fig. 5.20).

The **business concept** serves to formally represent the business problem so that it can be translated into information technology solutions. The business concept is of a long-term nature, as it forms the substantive basis of the business application concept.

The **information technology concept** (IT concept, formerly referred to as data processing concept or DP concept) adapts the business concept to the requirements for technical implementation in a general form that is independent of the actual implementation. The business concept and the IT concept are only loosely coupled.

The **implementation** is the realization of the IT concept in concrete software and hardware components. It describes the computer-supported realization of the business

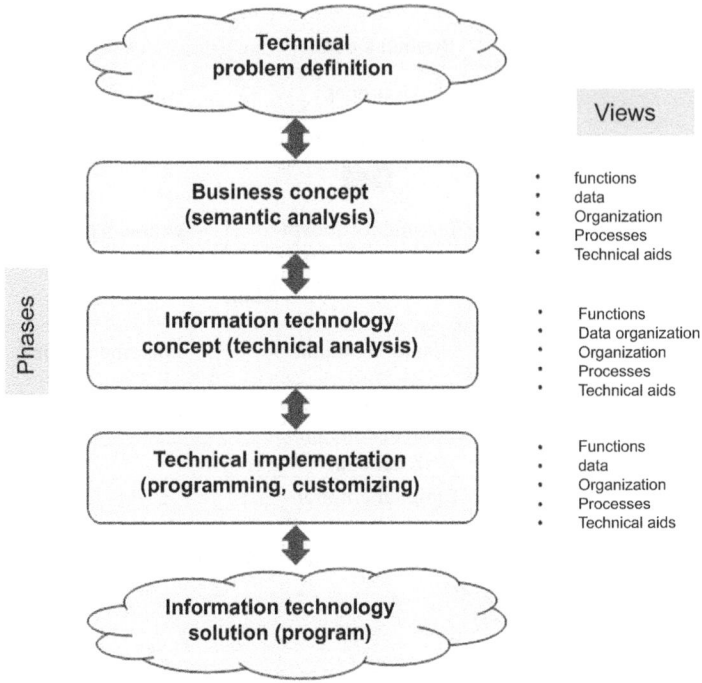

Fig. 5.20   ARIS—From Problem to Program (Scheer 1998)

concept. The ARIS concept is suitable both for custom software development and for the implementation process of standard software (see also, for example, Kirchmer 1996, pp. 66 f.).

Modeling Views

ARIS distinguishes four secondary views: the organizational view, the data view, the function view, and the product view. The integrating central view is the control view.

The **organizational view** describes the organizational structure of a company. Organizational charts are used for this purpose, which depict the hierarchical relationships.

The **data view** shows the information objects relevant for modeling and their relationships to each other. Extended entity-relationship diagrams are used for this purpose.

The **function view** comprises business activities in a structured form. Function trees are used here, which represent the relevant business functions and their relationships at different levels of aggregation.

The **product view** describes a company's products, i.e., the tangible and intangible outputs including cash flows (Scheer 1998, pp. 93 f.). The description is provided using a product model.

The **control view** represents a company's business processes. It integrates the partial views of the ARIS concept and uses, for example, the extended event-driven process chain (eEPC) to describe business processes.

ARIS as a Method for Software Development

Fig. 5.21 shows the classification of tasks that arise in custom software development or the implementation of standard software within the ARIS concept, as well as the main groups of people involved (employees from the business department, IT department staff specializing in organization or software development). All ARIS phases must therefore be completed and are affected in different ways.

In **custom software development**, the business requirements are first gathered and implemented in the form of a business concept. This is followed by the technical design of the planned information system and its implementation, testing, and acceptance.

In the **implementation of standard software**, once the decision for standard software has been made, all activities focus on the business concept level, since the software is already available. The "make or buy" decision process largely precedes the ARIS concept. Except for additional programs for business extensions and interface programs to "external systems," the development work of the software vendor can be adopted. Based on reference models that document the scope of the standard software, a business target model is created. Of particular importance here are the target process models in the form of EPC models, which will be discussed in detail later. During the IT design and implementation phases, customizing activities take place, i.e., the business model is anchored in the standard software system in the form of parameters. In addition, supplementary programs (so-called add-ons) must be designed and programmed.

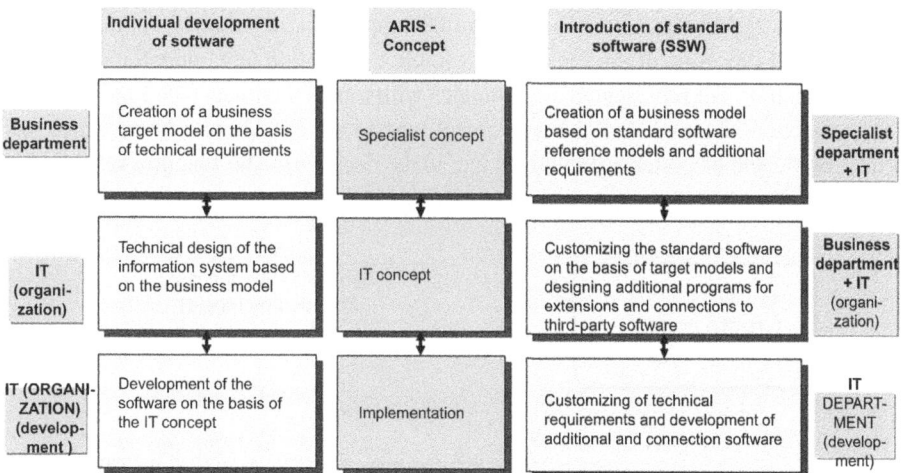

Fig. 5.21 ARIS as a Method for Software Implementation

5.7.2   Basic Notation (EPC)

5.7.2.1 Events and Functions

The basic notation of the EPC method describes the flow of a business process using only a few fundamental symbols. The starting point of every process is an event. It addresses the question of what triggers the process. This could be, for example, the receipt of an order by fax. In some cases, multiple events may be required. For instance, the payout of a life insurance policy will only occur if several preconditions are met simultaneously. After the triggering event, a function to be performed is executed.

The four basic elements of the EPC are:

- **Function,** which changes the state of objects,
- **Event,** which triggers changes in the state of objects,
- **Edge,** which links functions and events, and
- **Connector,** which combines functions and events into a process.

Function

Functions describe transformation processes of information objects to achieve business objectives. They can be described at different levels. A process or process chain is therefore a comprehensive sequence (e.g., spare parts sales). A function is a complex activity that can be further subdivided and that directly forms part of a process (e.g., order processing). The activity described by the function symbol is performed by actors (people or software).

A subfunction is an activity that can be broken down into further subfunctions or elementary functions and is part of a higher-level function (e.g., order verification). Elementary functions are activities that cannot or should not be further subdivided.

A criterion for the maximum meaningful decomposition of processes is the sensible, self-contained execution of the function at a single workstation (e.g., material availability check). Functions are represented as rectangles with rounded corners (see Fig. 5.22).

The function is a so-called "active" object type in the EPC, representing a task performed by people or systems. Functions can make decisions. The function refers to one

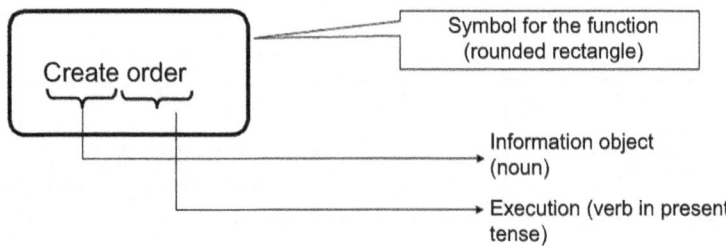

Fig. 5.22 EPC Notation "Function"

or more information objects and an activity that changes the information. For this reason, the EPC designation consists of an information object (noun) and a description of the activity (verb).

Examples of functions include "Create order," "Check order," "Evaluate employee," "Prepare calculation," "Post invoice."

Event

Events are passive object types, i.e., they represent only states and cannot make decisions. They trigger functions and are, in turn, the results of functions that have already been executed. Events can occur both within ("Applicant was rejected") and outside the company ("Application has been submitted"). Processing an object changes its state. For example, a customer order is supplemented with relevant classification features such as customer number, material numbers, etc. Events describe a state that has occurred, i.e., they describe the object that has undergone a change of state (see Hoffmann et al. 1992, p. 5). Events are represented as hexagons (see Fig. 5.23). The designation of an event consists of an information object (noun) from the underlying data model and a verb in the perfect tense, i.e., a state that has occurred. Examples of events include "Credit limit has been exceeded," "Order has been received," "Offer has been created."

5.7.2.2 Basic Modeling Rules

An EPC begins and ends with an event, with a process-triggering event described as the start event and a process-concluding event as the end event. Subsequent processes can be triggered by end events of a preceding process, i.e., an end event can also serve as a triggering start event in another process.

A simple example of an EPC is shown in Fig. 5.24. The left column shows the sequence of events and functions (each with placeholder names), while the right column presents the process of handling applications in a highly simplified form.

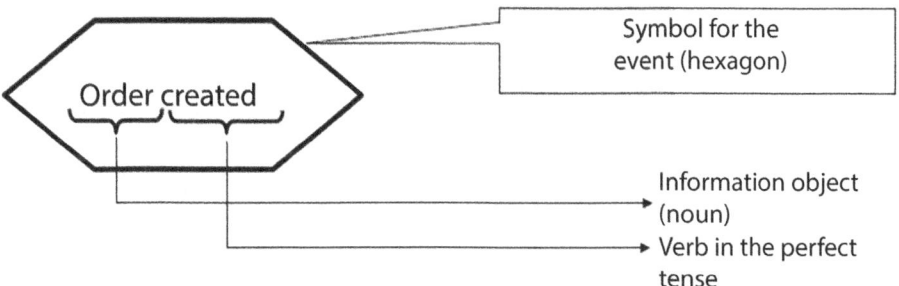

Fig. 5.23 EPC Notation "Event"

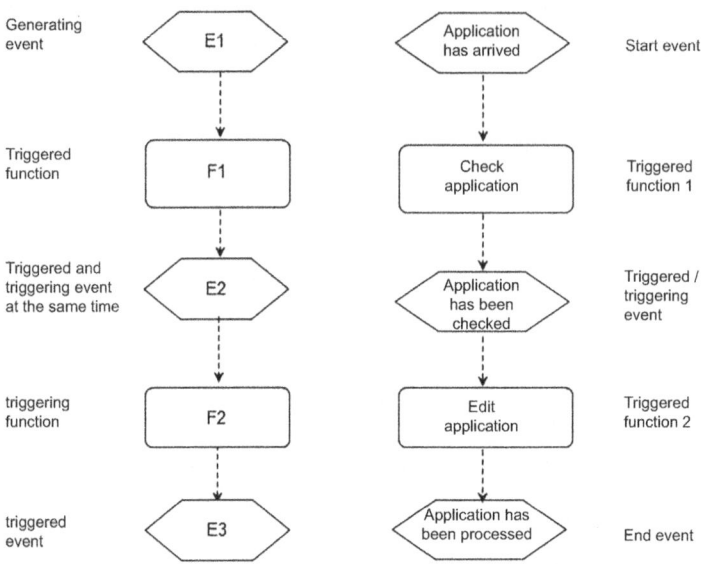

Fig. 5.24 EPC Notation "Simple Example"

5.7.2.3 Connectors

After presenting the basic structure of the EPC, the question arises as to how it can be further refined. In practice, functions can be triggered by more than one event and can also trigger multiple events. For example, the event "Customer is creditworthy" depends on several preconditions that must be checked by multiple functions. To represent such constructs using the Event-driven Process Chain, three logical connectors are used: conjunction ("and" connection), disjunction ("exclusive or" connection), and adjunction ("inclusive or" connection) (see Fig. 5.25).

Figure 5.26 shows a schematic representation of an EPC with the "XOR connector." The left column displays the formal syntax of a so-called XOR split (branching of the process flow with XOR) followed by an XOR join (merging of the process flow with XOR). The right column presents a business example. The actual process can either follow the left path from E1 to E2 via E3 and then to E6, or the right path from E1 to E4 to E5 and finally to E6. In the example of applicant evaluation on the right, the situation is illustrated more clearly: the applicant either receives a rejection or is offered a contract. Both possibilities are mutually exclusive.

Important It is not strictly necessary for the process to be closed again with an XOR join. The EPC shown could also end with two events (E3 and E5, i.e., "Candidate is rejected" and "Contract is offered"). However, if a join is used, it is important to use the same operator. For example, if an AND operation were used instead of the XOR join

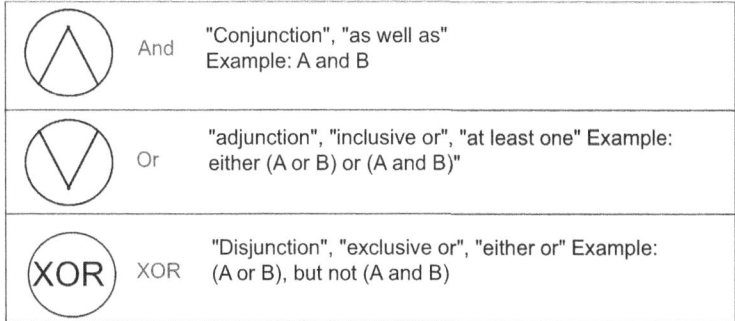

Fig. 5.25 EPK notation "Connectors"

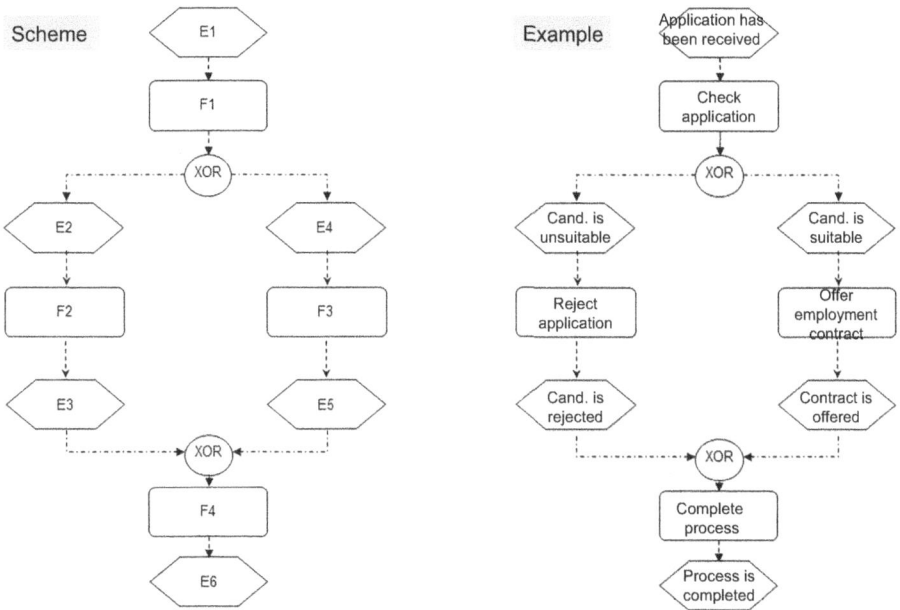

Fig. 5.26 EPK notation "Example of using the XOR connector"

before function "F4," the process would wait indefinitely, since both events cannot occur simultaneously.

Figure 5.27 shows a schematic representation of an EPC with the "AND connector." The left column again shows the modeling schema with the basic notation using the AND connector. The right column presents a relevant business example. In this case, after function F1 is executed, the process splits into two branches and is merged again before function F4. The business example on the right illustrates the application area. After the

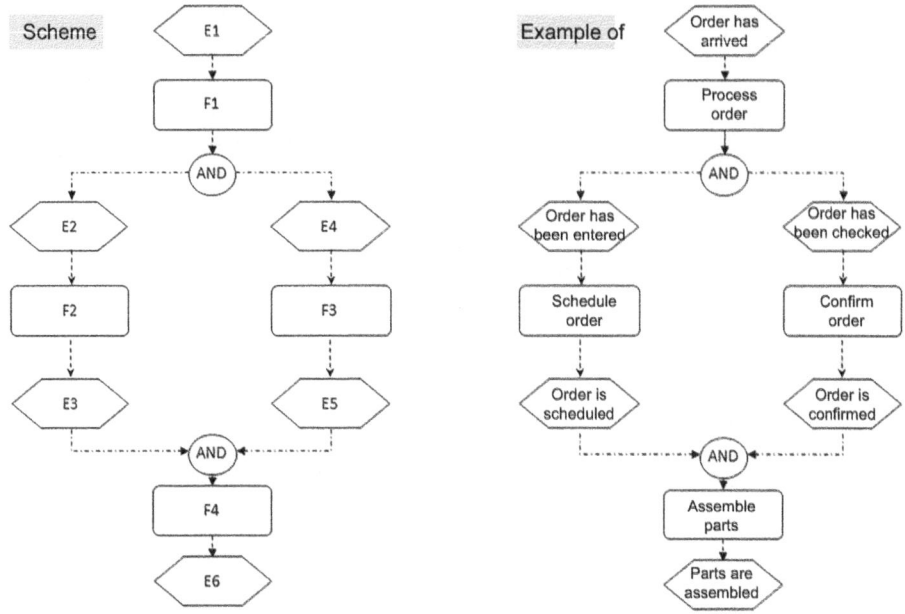

Fig. 5.27 EPK notation "Example of using the AND connector"

order has been processed, two events are established: the order has been checked and the order data has been recorded. This allows two functions to be performed in parallel, namely "Schedule order" and "Confirm order." Once both functions are completed (the AND connector waits for both), the function "Assemble parts" can begin. Once this is done, the event "Parts are assembled" occurs. This could trigger further process steps, but these have been omitted here for the sake of simplicity.

Important Here, too, it is important that the process is closed with the same connector. If, for example, an XOR connector were placed before function F4 (or "Assemble parts"), then F4 or "Assemble parts" would be triggered as soon as either event E3 or E5 (i.e., "Order scheduled" or "Order confirmed") occurs. In this application example, this could result in an order being confirmed that has not yet been scheduled.

Figure 5.28 shows a formal (left column) and illustrative (right column) representation of an EPC with the "OR connector." The possible process flows from a formal perspective (left column) are as follows:

1. Variant: (left path) E1-F1-E2-F2-E3-F4-E6
2. Variant: (left path) E2-F1-E4-F3-E5-F4-E6
3. Variant: (both paths): E1-F1-E2/E4-F2/F3-E3/E5-F4-E6

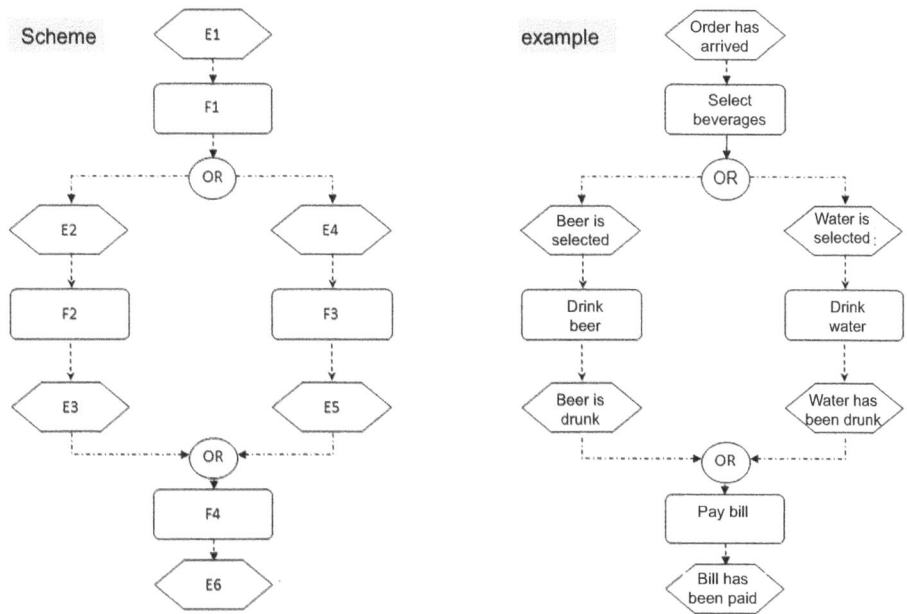

Fig. 5.28 EPK notation "Example of using the OR connector"

Looking at the right column, the use of the OR connector becomes more tangible. After the guest has selected their drinks, they either drink only beer (left path), only water (right path), or both beer and water (both paths). After the guest has finished their drink or drinks, the bill can be paid.

Important Here, too, it is important to close the split path with the same connector; otherwise, error situations may occur.

A more complex modeling example can be found in Fig. 5.29. It depicts the following scenario using the EPK notation introduced so far:

- After a customer has returned the vehicle, its condition is checked. If at least one defect is found, a defect list is created first.
- If the vehicle is damaged, it is repaired.
- If the tank is not completely filled, the vehicle is refueled.
- If the vehicle is not completely clean, it is cleaned.
- If the tire pressure is incorrect, air is either added or released.
- Afterwards, the vehicle is parked in the parking lot. It can now be rented out again.

5.7.2.4 Special Modeling Aspects
Although the basic symbols of the EPK introduced so far are quite simple, their application leads to some special cases. The standard rule of EPK modeling is: events alternate

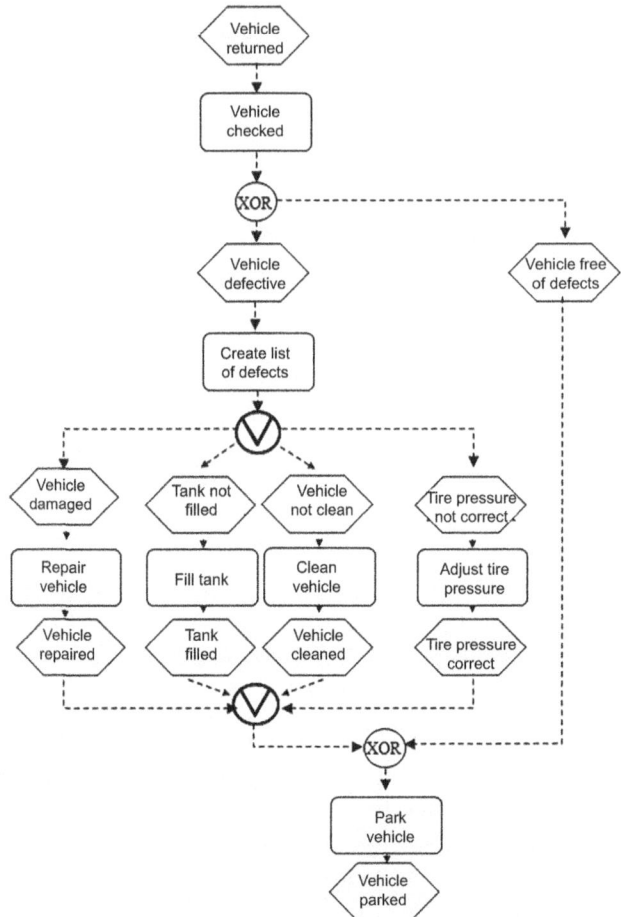

Fig. 5.29 EPK modeling example "Defect Handling"

with functions; functions must not follow functions. However, there are exceptions to this rule.

Optional Events

To further specify processes, nested connectors or optional events are also possible. Fig. 5.30 shows that events can also follow events (right column) if this provides greater clarity or is appropriate for organizational reasons.

This can be most easily explained using the business scenario shown in the lower part of the figure: As soon as the work permit and the certificate are available and the work experience is sufficient, an employment contract can be offered to the applicant (left column). To further specify the decision, the event "Person is suitable" can also be recorded (right column) to capture this situation precisely. Both models are equivalent, but differ

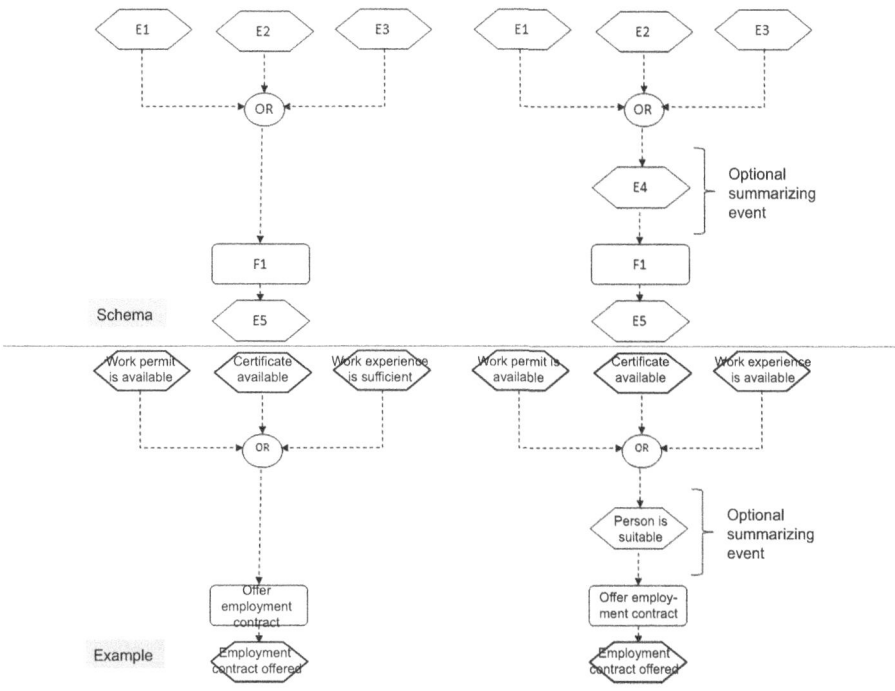

Fig. 5.30 EPK—Optional Events (Schema and Example)

in the level of detail. The upper part of the figure shows the model schematically, without reference to specific scenarios.

Nested Connectors

Not only can events follow events when necessary, but connectors can also be used in sequence. In Fig. 5.31, the upper left part of the figure shows an event E3 leading into the AND connector. The upper right part shows an alternative representation of the scenario that omits E3. In this case, the XOR connector is followed by the AND connector before F1. The lower part of the figure provides a more illustrative representation of the formal model. If "Paid in advance" or a "Guarantee is available," the customer is considered creditworthy ("Creditworthiness available") and the goods can be delivered. This event can also be omitted, as shown on the right side. It serves only to clarify the scenario.

5.7.2.5 Types of Linkages in EPC

Using the connectors introduced above, two types of linkages between functions and events can be distinguished. In **event linkage**, two or more events are linked to a function via a connector. Depending on whether the events are triggering or generated, a further distinction can be made between the linkage of triggering or generated events (see

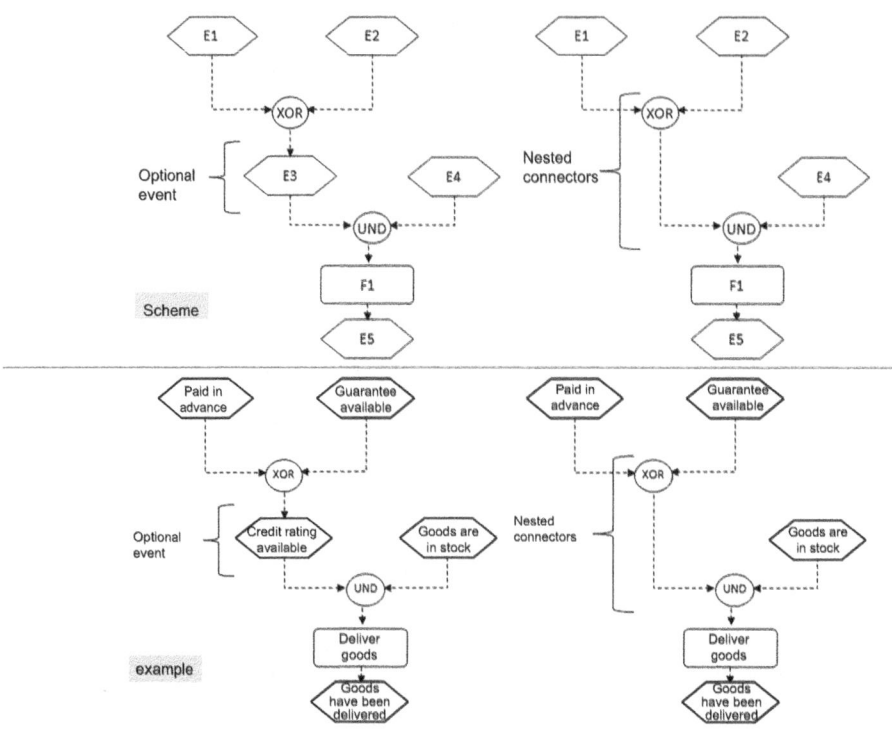

Fig. 5.31 EPK—Nested Connectors (Schema and Example)

also Hoffmann et al. 1992, p. 12). In **function linkage**, two or more functions are linked to an event via a connector. Depending on whether the functions are triggering or generated, an analogous distinction can be made, as with event linkage, between the linkage of functions with a triggering or generated event.

All combinations are possible except for the following special cases: Function linkage with a triggering event is only possible via an "AND" connector, since events, as passive model elements, cannot make decisions. The "OR" and "XOR" connectors are not permitted in this case. The possible case groups are shown in Fig. 5.32 (see also Hoffmann et al. 1992, p. 12).

Event Linkage: Linking Triggering Events to a Function First, case group 1, "Linking triggering events to a function," is presented. The common feature of this case group is that a function is initiated by one or more events as a prerequisite.

- The function in case 1a is triggered when all events have occurred. Example: If the applicant meets conditions A, B, and C, they are invited to an interview.
- The function in case 1b is triggered when at least one event has occurred. Example: If one or more of the conditions A, B, or C apply to the applicant, they are rejected.

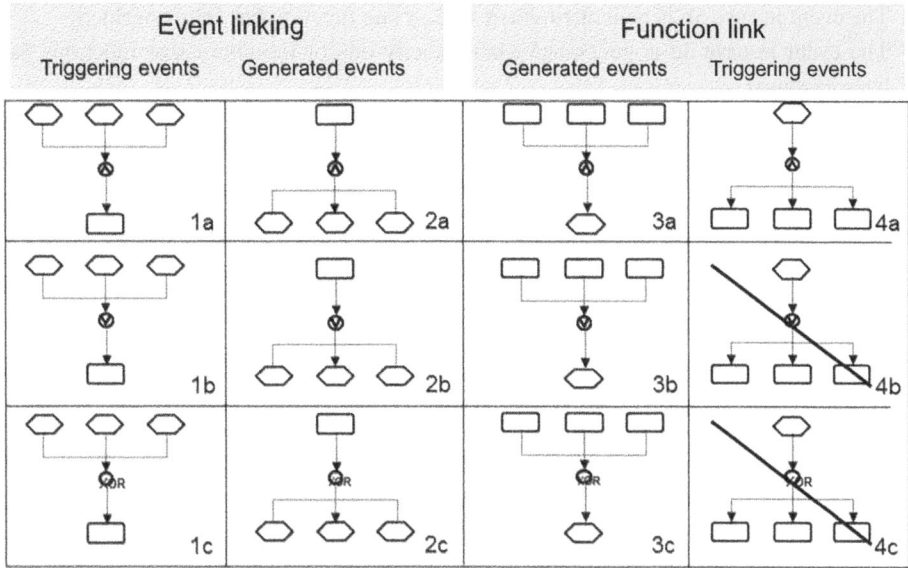

Fig. 5.32 Types of EPC linkages (see, e.g., Hoffmann et al. 1992, p. 12)

- The function in case 1c is triggered when exactly one of the alternative possible events has occurred. Example: If one of the conditions A, B, or C applies to the applicant, they are rejected.

Event Linkage: Linking Generated Events to a Function Case group 2, "Linking generated events to a function," explains the generation of one or more events after a function has been executed.

- After execution of the function in case 2a, all events are generated. Example: Once the order has been created, the master data is up to date, the order is checked, etc.
- After execution of the function in case 2b, at least one event is generated. If the order has been created, at least one of the events A, B, or C is generated.
- After execution of the function in case 2c, exactly one of the alternative events occurs.

Function Linkage: Linking Multiple Generating Functions to an Event Function linkage connects functions with generated or triggering events.

Case group 3, "Linking multiple generating functions to an event," describes the generation of an event after one or more functions have been executed as a prerequisite.

- The event in case 3a is generated when all functions have been executed. Example: The order is "released" if the order data has been entered and the credit limit has been checked.

- The event in case 3b is generated when at least one function has been executed.
- The event in case 3c is generated when exactly one of the alternative functions has been executed.

Function Linkage: Linking Functions to a Triggering Event Case group 4, "Linking functions to a triggering event," describes the generation of one or more functions by a triggering event.

Since events are passive model components and therefore cannot make decisions about the selection of relevant functions, only the conjunction "AND" ("AND" linkage) is permitted. When the event occurs, all functions are triggered.

Case 4b is not permitted, since the event, as a passive object type, cannot decide which functions to select. For the same reason, case 4c is also not allowed.

5.7.2.6 Modeling Rules of the Elementary EPC Notation

Modeling work is usually carried out collaboratively. Before a modeling project, modeling rules are typically agreed upon in practice to ensure consistent quality and comparability of the models. The following modeling rules are common for EPCs (see Seidlmeier 2002, p. 78):

- Every EPC begins and ends with one or more events.
- Events and functions always alternate in the process flow. Connectors (see below) describe branches.
- Only one control flow edge enters and leaves a function.
- No object stands alone in the model without an edge.
- An edge connects exactly two different objects.
- As a rule, an OR or XOR connector must not directly follow an event (exceptions: loop constructs, aggregation of events into higher-level events).
- Paths branched by connectors must be merged again using connectors of the same type.
- If several paths are merged with a connector, the connector may have only one outgoing edge.
- Direct connections between connectors are permitted.

5.7.2.7 Exercises on Basic Notation

The symbols for "function," "event," and the connectors "AND," "OR," and "XOR" proposed by Keller et al. (1992) are sometimes represented in color and with different graphics in software tools (e.g., ARIS Express by Software AG). Figure 5.33 provides an example of the use of the XOR connector.

Exercise for Fig. 5.33
Which of the following statements apply to the EPK model in Fig. 5.33?

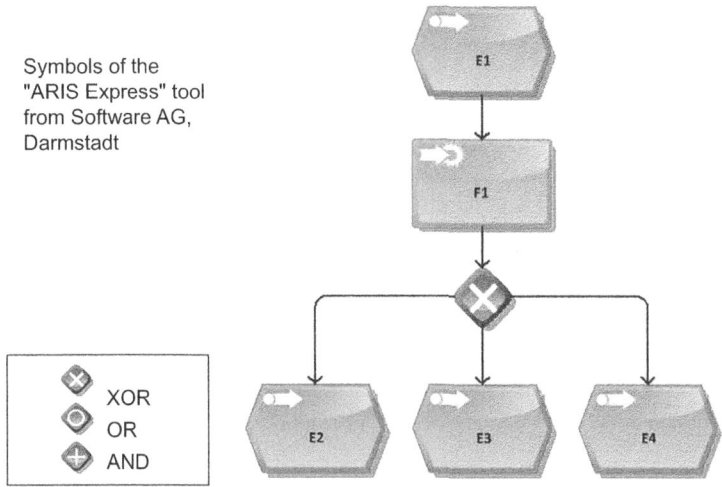

Symbols of the
"ARIS Express" tool
from Software AG,
Darmstadt

XOR
OR
AND

Fig. 5.33 EPK Example 1 with ARIS Express (Software AG, Darmstadt)

a. E2 can only occur after F1 has been completed.
b. Exactly one of the events E1, E2, or E3 always follows F1.
c. The events E1, E2, and E3 all follow F1.

Solution to the statements in Fig. 5.33:

a. E2 can only occur after F1 has been completed: Correct.
b. Exactly one of the events E1, E2, or E3 always follows F1: Correct.
c. The events E1, E2, and E3 all follow F1: Incorrect, only one of the three events is possible.

Exercise for Fig. 5.34
Another EPK model is shown in Fig. 5.34.
    Which of the following statements are correct?

a. F1 is executed when E1 or E2 occurs.
b. If E1, E2, and E3 occur simultaneously, F1 is executed.
c. If F1 has been executed, it can be concluded with certainty that E2 has occurred.

Solution to the statements in Fig. 5.34

a. F1 is executed when E1 or E2 occurs: Incorrect, E3 must also occur due to the "AND" connector.
b. If E1, E2, and E3 occur simultaneously, F1 is executed: Correct.

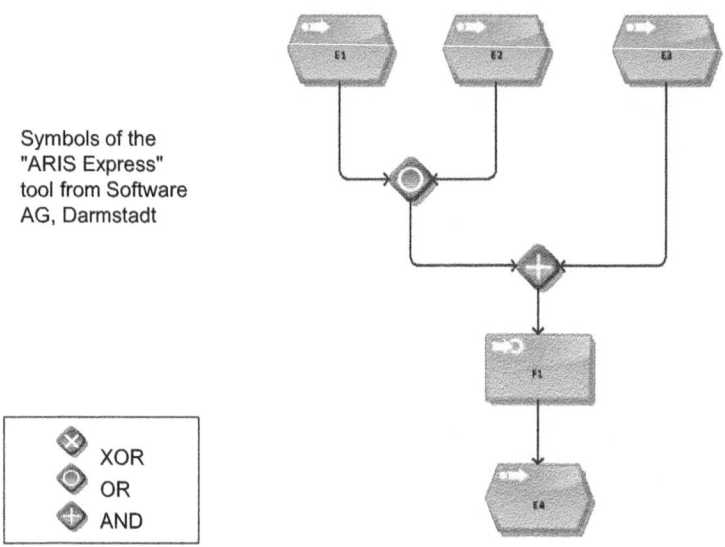

Symbols of the
"ARIS Express"
tool from Software
AG, Darmstadt

Fig. 5.34 Modeling Example 2 with ARIS Express (Software AG, Darmstadt)

c. If F1 has been executed, it can be concluded with certainty that E2 has occurred: Incorrect, the combination of E1 and E3 is also possible.

Exercise for Fig. 5.35
Another EPK model is shown in Fig. 5.35.
    Which of the following statements are correct?

a. Function F1 is executed when events E1, E2, and E3 are activated simultaneously.
b. If function F2 has been executed, then events E4, E5, and E7 have previously occurred.

Solution to the statements in Fig. 5.35

a. Function F1 is executed when events E1, E2, and E3 are activated simultaneously: Correct, but other combinations (e.g., only E1 or E1 with E3) are also possible.
b. If function F2 has been executed, then events E4, E5, and E7 have previously occurred: Correct, but E6 has also occurred (due to the AND connector).

5.7.3 Extended Event-Driven Process Chain (eEPC)

5.7.3.1 Need for Extensions
The notation of the EPC introduced so far is not sufficient to create meaningful models for practical application. At best, the method is capable of providing models with enough

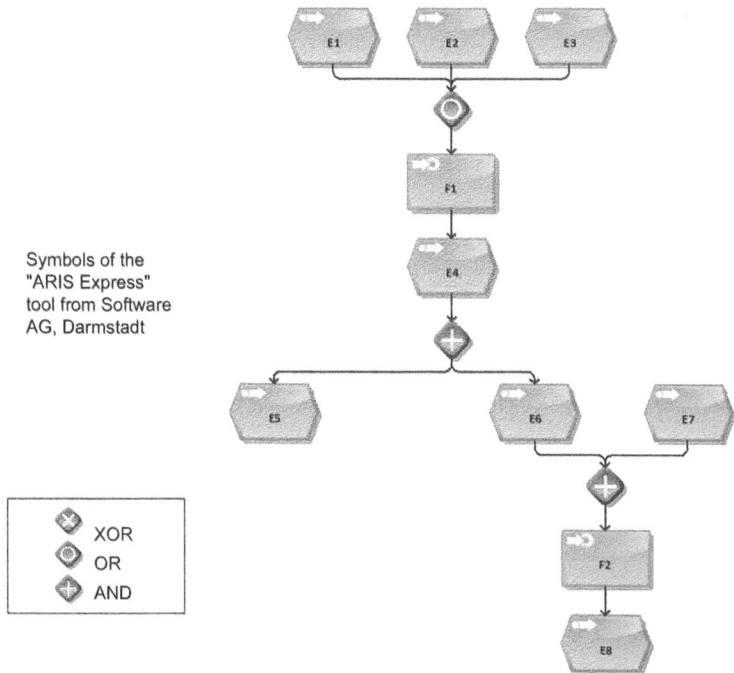

Symbols of the
"ARIS Express"
tool from Software
AG, Darmstadt

XOR
OR
AND

Fig. 5.35 Modeling Example 3 with ARIS Express (Software AG, Darmstadt)

detail for representing process logic. However, practical use requires a greater level of detail, especially when introducing or revising information systems.

The EPC method has therefore been extended by several elements, the most important of which are the "Organizational Unit," the "Information Object," the "Application System," and the "Data Flow."

The **organizational unit** is used to describe the people, roles, positions, departments, or even external partners involved in a process, such as customers in the sales process or applicants in recruitment.

The **information object** represents the information (input and output) processed by the process, which is described in more detail in the data view (ERM model).

The **application system** is used to represent the IT support for business processes.

The **data flow** links functions and information objects and indicates whether a function uses, modifies, or generates data.

Conceptual System

The complete conceptual system and the original notation derived from it according to Keller et al. (1992) is referred to as the "extended Event-driven Process Chain" (abbreviated as "eEPC") (see Fig. 5.36).

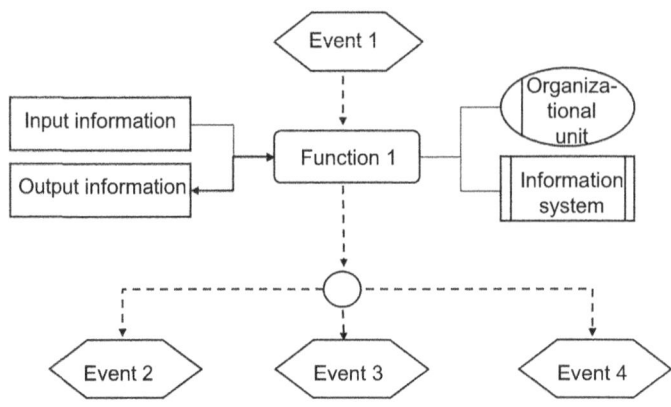

◯   = Logic operator
⊚   = either -or ("one of both")
⟨∧⟩ = and ("both")
⟨∨⟩ = and / or ("at least one of both")

Fig. 5.36   Modeling elements of the eEPC according to Keller et al. (1992)

The semantics of the symbols of the extended Event-driven Process Chain are explained in Fig. 5.37.

Verbal and Symbolic Modeling
The relationship between the verbal process description and the symbols of the eEPC is shown in Fig. 5.38. The bold terms in the textual process descriptions are assigned to the eEPC symbols.

5.7.3.2 eEPC Notation
The complete notation of the eEPC is summarized in Fig. 5.39 (see also Keller and Teufel 1997, pp. 166 ff.). The symbols can be divided into several categories: event nodes (representing events), activity nodes (representing activities), condition nodes (representing conditions that determine the further course of the workflow), organization nodes (representing the organizational units involved), control flow edges (representing the sequence of activities), data flow edges (representing input and output relationships between information objects and functions), and assignment relationship edges (assigning organizational units involved in a function).

An example of the process "Car Rental Contract Conclusion", which is outlined in text form below, can be found in Fig. 5.40:

- Upon the customer's arrival at the car rental center, the customer advisor enters the driver's license data and additional information (insurance coverage) into the ERP

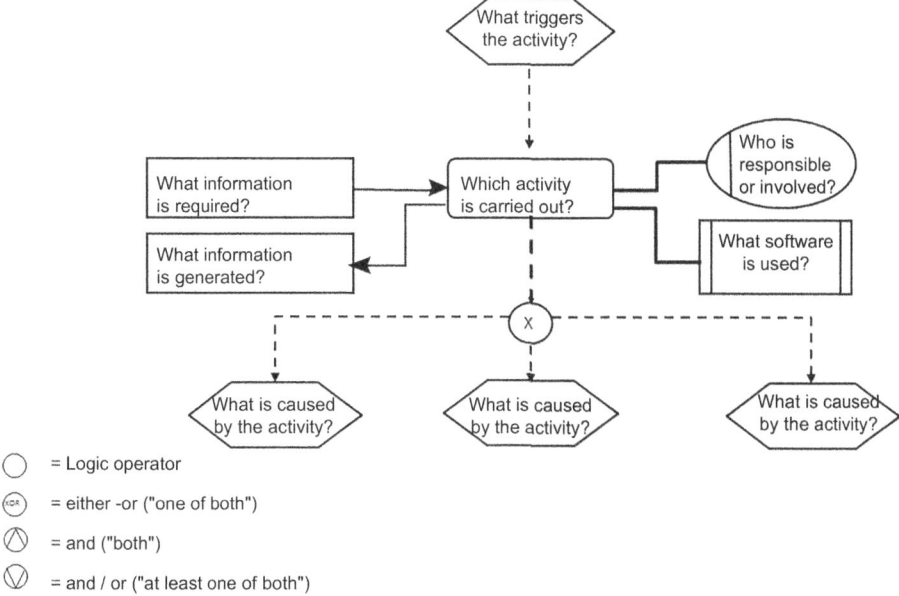

Fig. 5.37 Semantics of the eEPC

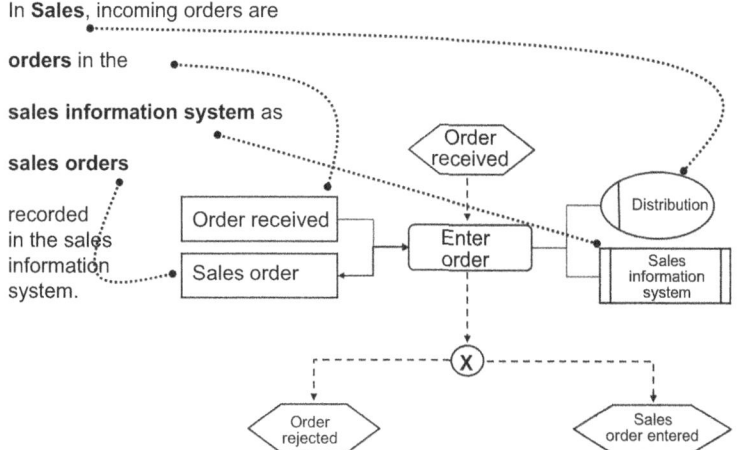

Fig. 5.38 Process description and assignment of modeling elements to the eEPC

Symbol	Designation	Meaning of	Edge/node type
⬡	Event	Description of a state that has occurred, on which the further course of the process depends	Event node
▭	Function	Description of the transformation from an input state to an output state.	Activity node
⊗	"exclusive or"	Logical link operators describe the logical linking of events and functions	Condition nodes
⊽	"or"		
⃤	"and"		
⬭	Organizational unit	Description of the organizational structure of a company	Organizational node
▭	Information object	Representation of objects in the real world	Activity node
▯▯	Application system	Application systems for process support (e.g. SAP ERP)	Activity node
‑ ‑ ‑ ▸	Control flow	Temporal-logical connection of events and functions	Control flow edge
⟶	Data flow	Description of whether a function reads, writes or changes data.	Data flow edge
──	Assignment	Assignment of resources/organizational units	Assignment reference edge

Fig. 5.39   Notation elements of the eEPC

system. If necessary, additional drivers are recorded, who must also possess a valid driver's license. The driver's license data of the additional drivers are also entered.

- The customer can choose comprehensive, partial, or no insurance coverage. If applicable, the insurance coverage and the desired deductible are recorded by the customer advisor.
- The customer hands over their credit card to the customer advisor. The credit card is checked using the credit card billing system. The card data are transferred to the customer data in the ERP system. The rental contract is then printed out and handed over to the customer.

5.7.4   Modeling Examples

The following presents two modeling examples using the modeling tool "ARIS Express" by Software AG (Darmstadt). The slightly modified symbols can be seen in Fig. 5.41.

Figure 5.42 shows the following business process, "Creation of Offers," modeled using the "eEPC method."

- After receiving the customer inquiry, the sales assistant checks, using the "SAP ERP" system, whether the customer is already known. For this, the customer and inquiry data are used.
- For new customers, a customer master record is created using "SAP ERP."
- Subsequently, the account manager creates an offer using "SAP CRM," making use of the inquiry and product data.

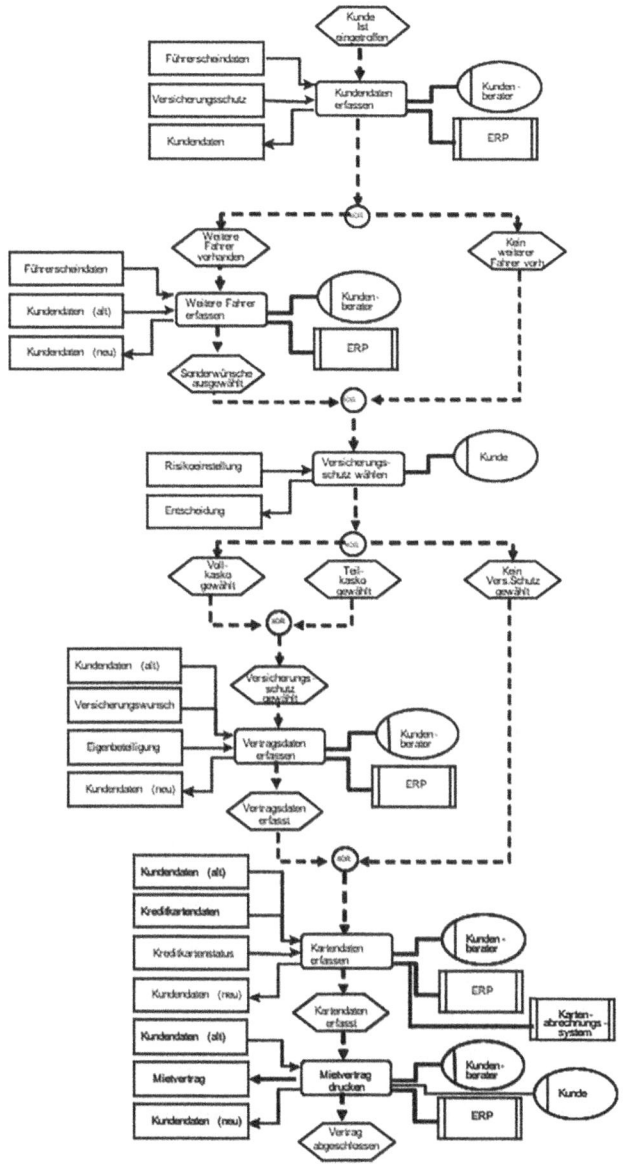

Fig. 5.40   eEPC example model "Contract Conclusion"

From the well-known case study on the takeover of a general practice, the process "Changing a Dressing" was selected and modeled as an eEPC model using the Bic Design tool. The tool uses its own symbols, mostly rectangular in shape. On the right of the illustration, the entire model is shown, and at the top left, a slightly more legible section of the model is displayed (see Fig. 5.43).

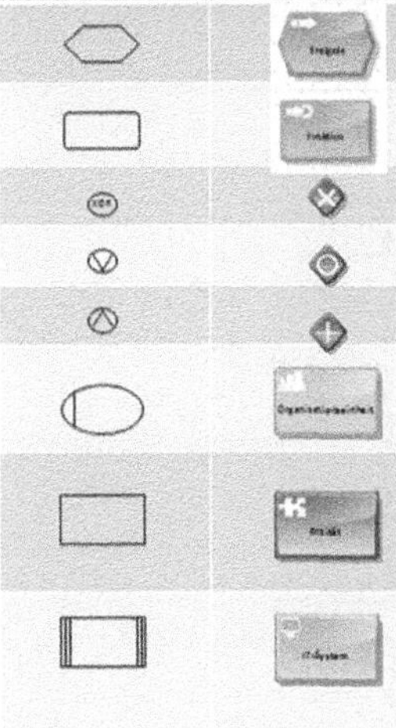

Standard Symbol	ARIS Express symbol	Name	Example
⬡		Event	Customer has rental request
▭		Function	Conclude rental agreement
◉	◆	"exclusive or"	
⊘	◎	"or"	
⊘	⬖	"and"	
⬭		Organizational unit	Train acceptance
▭		Information object (entity)	Rental contract
▯		Application system (IT system)	MS Word, SAP ERP

Fig. 5.41 Notation elements of the eEPC in the "ARIS Express" tool

5.7.4.1 Evaluation of the eEPC

The eEPC has established itself as a traditional method in German-speaking countries. It is especially prevalent where large and complex information systems are developed and maintained. It is embedded in the classic ARIS architecture and is used by many companies. Due to its limited number of symbols, it can be learned relatively quickly, which is why it is taught at many universities and vocational schools as part of business informatics education. The focus is on representing process logic, taking into account participants (organizational units), data, and information systems. Since the many model elements require a lot of "space" for the models, the use of tools is necessary to manage the models and, if necessary, display details using a "zoom function" or similar features.

The arguments are summarized in Table 5.4.

5.8   Business Process and Model Notation (BPMN)

5.8.1   Overview

Business Process Model and Notation (BPMN) is a relatively recent method, standardized worldwide by the standards organization "ISO" (www.iso.org), for representing and executing processes. The current version, BPMN 2.0, is the result of an extended development process. Key milestones in this evolution are shown in Table 5.5. Major innovations in version 2.0 included a significant expansion of the language scope and the

Fig. 5.42 eEPC example:
Offer processing (with ARIS
Express)

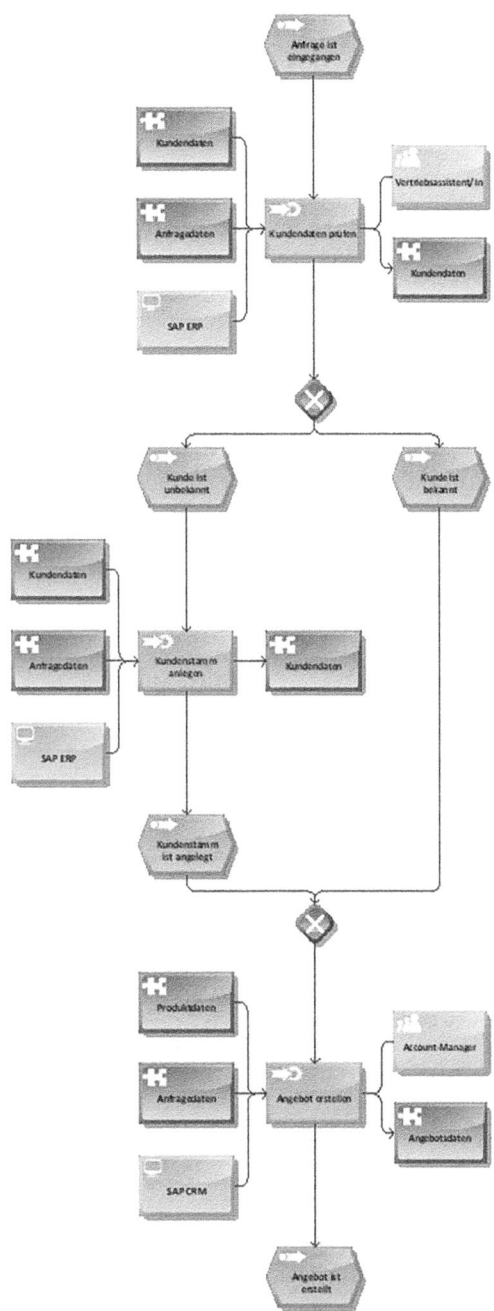

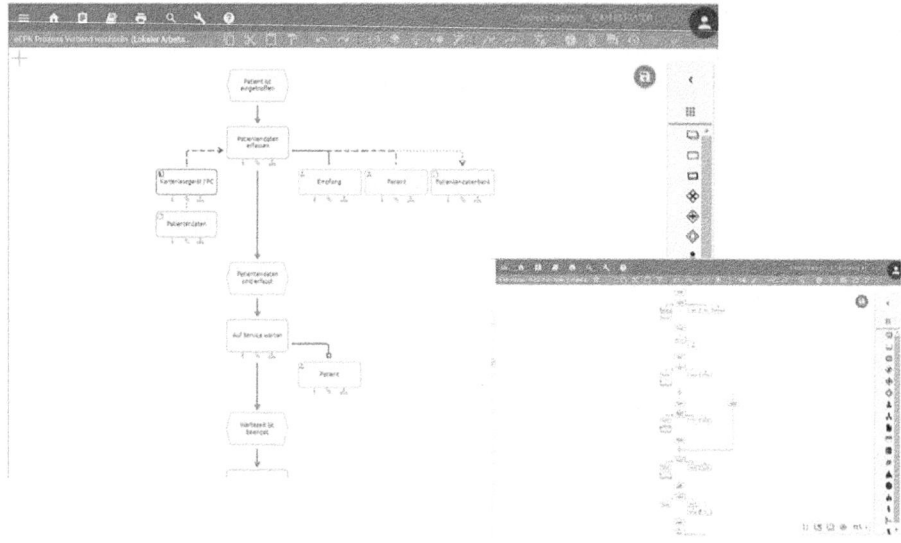

Fig. 5.43 eEPC model "Changing a Dressing"—modeled with Bic Design

Tab. 5.4 Evaluation of EPK/eEPC Modeling

Advantages	Disadvantages
High level of recognition in German-speaking countries	Training required, as notation and rules are not self-explanatory for beginners
Longstanding use in IT environments, especially with SAP software	Modeling tools are required for professional use
Compared to other professional methods such as BPMN, relatively few symbols	Complex processes require a lot of space
Tools are not strictly necessary, but are useful for widespread application	Notation is not standardized, i.e., symbols differ depending on the tool
	Only suitable for business-oriented modeling

[Table footer—please overwrite]

Tab. 5.5 Milestones in the development of BPMN 2.0

2002	Development of the method by IBM employee Stephen A. White
2005	Further development taken over by the Object Management Group (www.omg.org)
2009	Release of version 1.2
2010	Release of version 2.0

BPMN 2.0

introduction of executable elements (Spath et al. 2010, p. 16). The latest version can be accessed on the OMG website (www.omg.org).

Since the release of version 2.0, the adoption of BPMN has increased significantly. In the analysis by Minonne et al. (2011), BPMN already led in 2011 with 49%, two percentage points ahead of the previously dominant modeling method eEPK. In a survey conducted by the universities of Bonn-Rhein-Sieg and Koblenz among IT management executives and professionals, "BPMN" ranked fifth among current topics in IT management (see Komus et al. 2016). In Switzerland, BPMN has long been considered the standard method for companies and public authorities (see eCH 2016). BPMN provides a very comprehensive notation that can represent both business and technical aspects, distinguishing it from other methods.

5.8.2   Basic Notation

The basic symbols of BPMN are based on conventional swimlane diagrams (see Sect. 5.6). The core elements of the BPMN notation are shown in Fig. 3.16 (see White 2010). The symbols are easy to understand, even for inexperienced users: rectangles represent activities, circles denote different types of events (e.g., start or end), diamonds familiar from flowcharts specify possible decisions in the process, and edges indicate control and message flows. Thus, BPMN draws on many previously developed modeling languages.

Unlike other modeling languages, BPMN distinguishes between control flow (the sequence of activities) and message flow (communication between objects). This distinction between message and control flow makes it possible to represent interconnected processes and, in addition, to model interactions that cross organizational boundaries.

In addition, there are special symbols for gateways (decisions), events, textual annotations, and other detailed information (see Fig. 5.44).

A simple modeling example using the basic BPMN notation is shown in Fig. 5.45.

5.8.3   Activities

BPMN defines the basic form of an activity as well as numerous specializations (e.g., transaction, manual activity, call activity). Due to the large number of symbols and the complexity of the notation, software tools are generally required for working with BPMN.

However, the range of specializations supported by the tools and their graphical representation do not always fully comply with the original specifications of the OMG reference (OMG 2011, pp. 151 ff.). The examples in this book were created using the "ARIS Business Architect" tool, version 9.7 by Software AG (Darmstadt). They can also be created with the free "ARIS Express" tool from the same vendor.

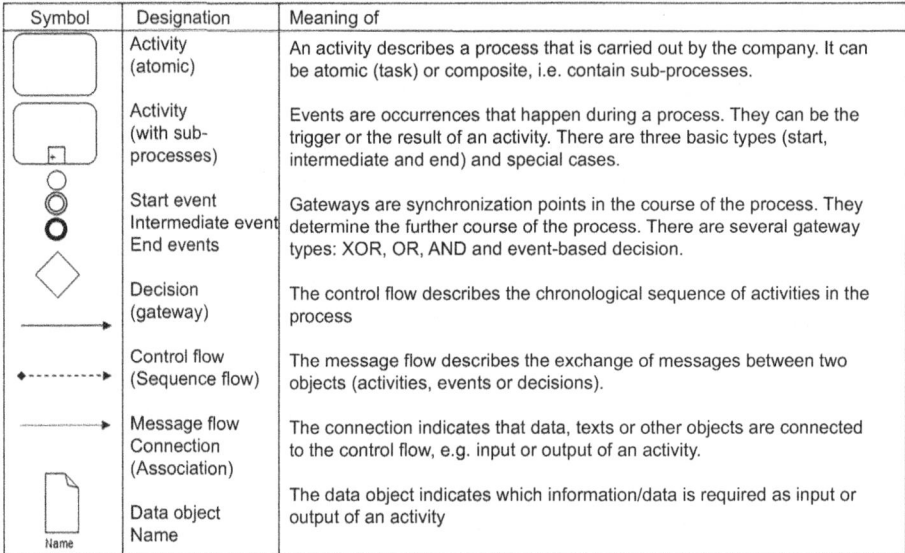

Symbol	Designation	Meaning of
	Activity (atomic)	An activity describes a process that is carried out by the company. It can be atomic (task) or composite, i.e. contain sub-processes.
	Activity (with sub-processes)	Events are occurrences that happen during a process. They can be the trigger or the result of an activity. There are three basic types (start, intermediate and end) and special cases.
	Start event Intermediate event End events	Gateways are synchronization points in the course of the process. They determine the further course of the process. There are several gateway types: XOR, OR, AND and event-based decision.
	Decision (gateway)	The control flow describes the chronological sequence of activities in the process
	Control flow (Sequence flow)	The message flow describes the exchange of messages between two objects (activities, events or decisions).
	Message flow Connection (Association)	The connection indicates that data, texts or other objects are connected to the control flow, e.g. input or output of an activity.
Name	Data object Name	The data object indicates which information/data is required as input or output of an activity

Fig. 5.44 Basic notation elements of BPMN (see White 2010)

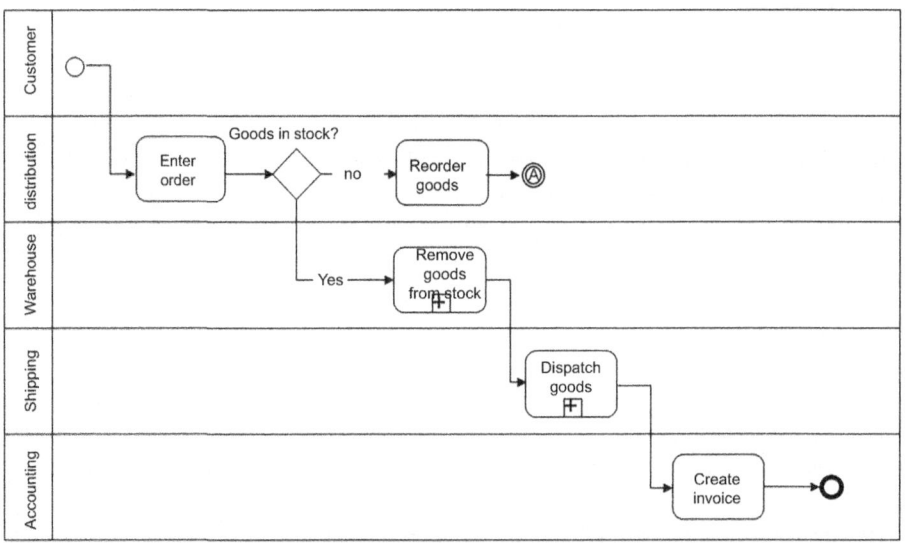

Fig. 5.45 Simple notation example with BPMN (see White 2010)

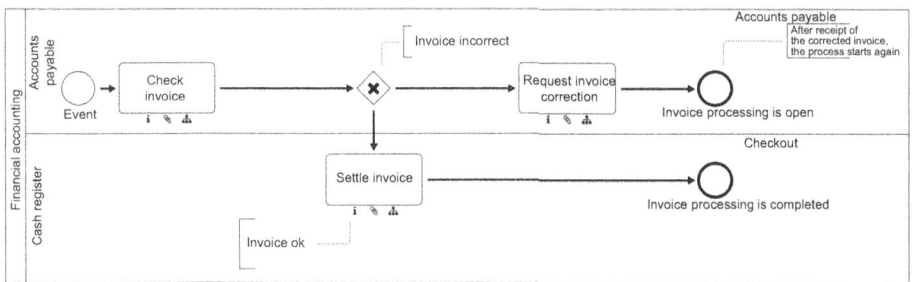

Fig. 5.46 BPMN—Example of activities (adapted from Seidlmeier 2015, modeled with the BIC Design tool)

Figure 5.46 presents an example taken from Seidlmeier (2015, p. 170). It contains three manual activities ("Check invoice," "Request invoice correction," and "Pay invoice").

The control flow, i.e., the sequence of activities in the process, is represented by arrows and can optionally be explained by annotations (e.g., "Invoice ok"). Compared to other modeling methods, BPMN offers the possibility to mark the "default flow," which is the path that is usually taken. Not all tools support this functionality. Figure 5.47 shows a process from the finance domain that makes use of this feature. The model was created with ARIS.

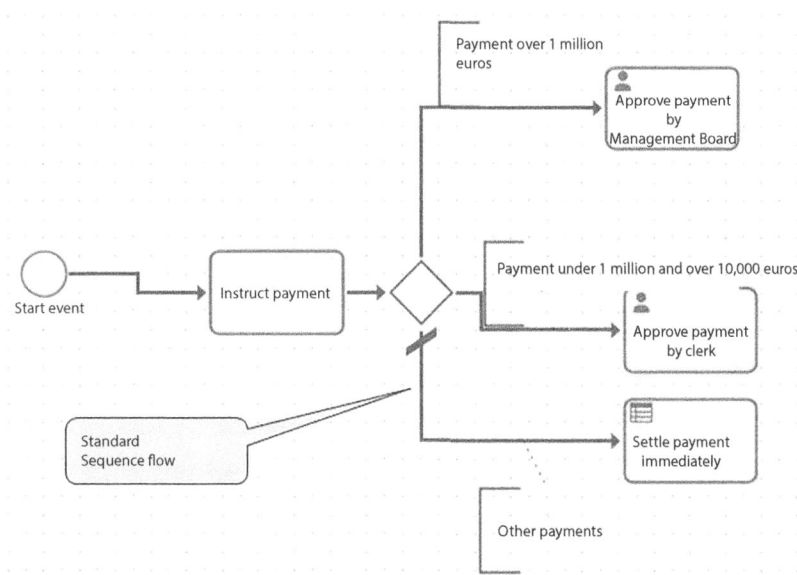

Fig. 5.47 BPMN—Example of default sequence flow

After the activity "Issue payment instruction," the activity "Settle payment immediately" is performed by default for payments up to €10,000. This control flow path is
marked as the "default sequence flow." The other two paths concern larger payments, for
which separate paths are provided.

5.8.4 Pools and Lanes

Since BPMN is based on the swimlane methodology, pools and lanes play a particularly
important role (see the schematic illustration in Fig. 5.48). A pool represents an independent process. A lane describes details of a process within a pool, differentiated by
organizational units, roles, or IT systems (see OMG 2011 pp. 109 ff.).

Fig. 5.49 shows a process structured by organizational units, taken from Allweyer
(2015, p. 22). According to the author's experience, structuring by organizational units is

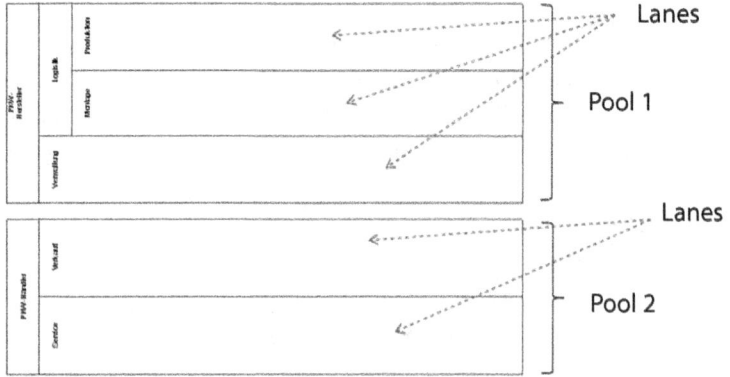

Fig. 5.48 BPMN—Pools and lanes

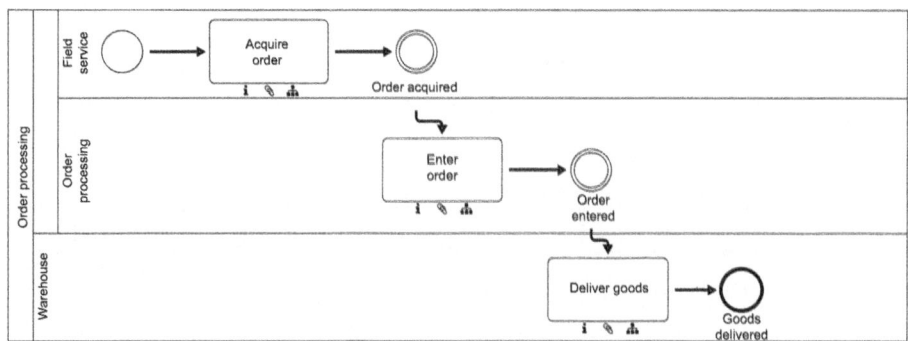

Fig. 5.49 BPMN—Pool with lanes by organizational units (adapted from Allweyer 2015, p. 22)

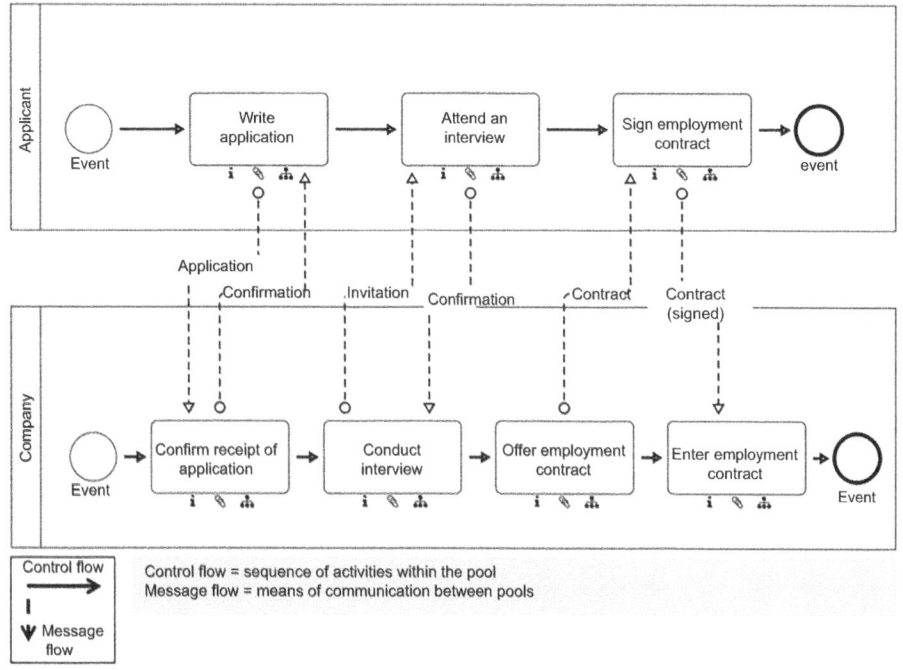

Fig. 5.50 BPMN—Message flow between pools (simplified illustration based on Allweyer 2015, p. 51)

the most commonly used method in practice. However, it is also possible to use pools for information systems.

Messages can be exchanged between pools (independent processes), which can influence each other's processes. As illustrated by the application process in Fig. 5.50, the processes running in the "Applicant" pool and the "Company" pool mutually affect each other. Each represents the perspective of a process participant on the same workflow.

5.8.5   Gateways

Gateways are used to represent possible branches (SPLIT) or merges (JOIN) of paths in processes (cf. OMG 2011, pp. 287 ff.). They map various alternatives that can arise in the course of a process. From the eEPK method (see Sect. 5.7.2), the AND, XOR, and OR connectors are known, and these are also used in the BPMN notation. The BPMN method also includes further variants, some of which are introduced here.

Exclusive Gateway ("XOR" Gateway)
The "Exclusive Gateway" corresponds to the XOR connector in the eEPK method. The XOR gateway can be described as an "either-or" selection. One path is chosen from several alternatives (select 1 out of n) for the subsequent process flow (SPLIT), or one path is selected from several incoming paths (JOIN) (cf. Fig. 5.51). In the example shown, either a flight or a train journey can be booked by the travel agency.

Parallel Gateway ("AND" Gateway)
The parallel gateway (cf. Fig. 5.52) corresponds to the AND connector (select n out of n) in the eEPK method. The process continues along all paths (SPLIT), or waits for all incoming path events before proceeding (JOIN).

Inclusive Gateway ("OR" Gateway)
With the inclusive gateway (cf. Fig. 5.53), one or more paths are selected. It corresponds to the "OR" connector in the EPK method (select x out of n, x = 1, ...n). In the process

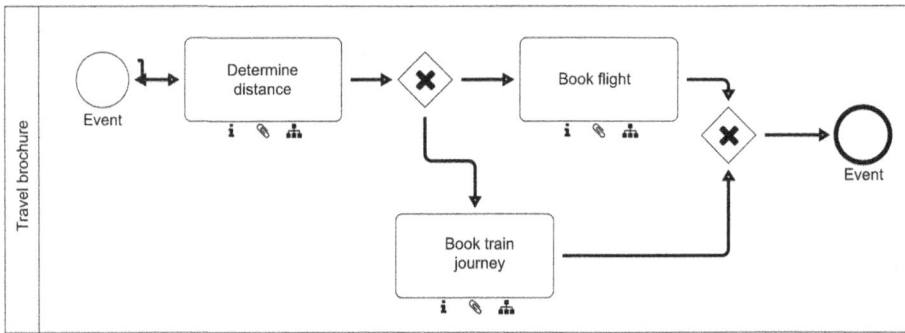

Fig. 5.51 BPMN—Exclusive Gateway (XOR Gateway, adapted from Allweyer, T.: BPMN 2.0, 3rd ed., Norderstedt 2015, p. 24)

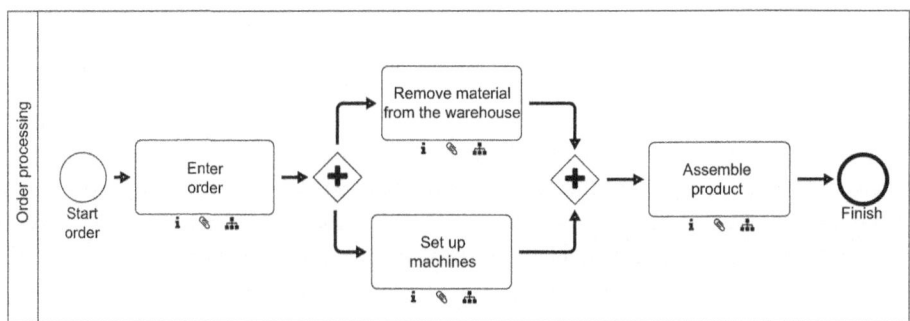

Fig. 5.52 BPMN—Parallel Gateway (AND Gateway)

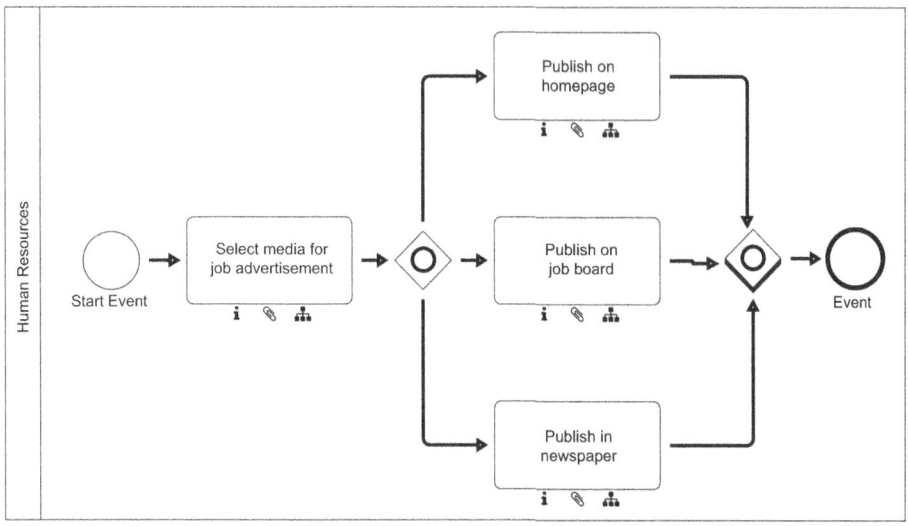

Fig. 5.53 BPMN—Inclusive Gateway (OR Gateway, adapted from Allweyer, T.: BPMN 2.0, 3rd ed., Norderstedt 2015, p. 32)

shown, after the step "media for job advertisement," several media can be selected, e.g., only the "homepage," "newspaper and homepage," or any other combination.

Complex Gateway

The complex gateway applies arbitrary (complex) rules. It is used when the classic gateways ("XOR," "AND," "OR") cannot represent a situation at all or only in a very convoluted way. In practice, the complex gateway is rarely used, as its technical implementation is difficult to realize. However, it can be used for conceptual modeling. In the process step "select applicant" in Fig. 5.54, a rule is applied that is not further specified in the model, where the contents of the applicant's references play a role.

5.8.6   Data

BPMN is a modeling language for processes, meaning the focus of modeling is on control flow (the sequence of steps) and message flow between different process steps. In principle, data modeling can be omitted if all data required within the pool is available.

An example is a pool whose process is fully supported by a BPM system (e.g., SAP ERP). If data is passed between process steps (tasks), for instance because different information systems are used, data objects must be modeled. Example: An invoice is created in the sales system and sent to the customer. The invoice data is then electronically transferred to an accounting system and recorded there as an accounts receivable invoice. BPMN provides various symbols for data modeling (see OMG 2011, pp. 203 ff.).

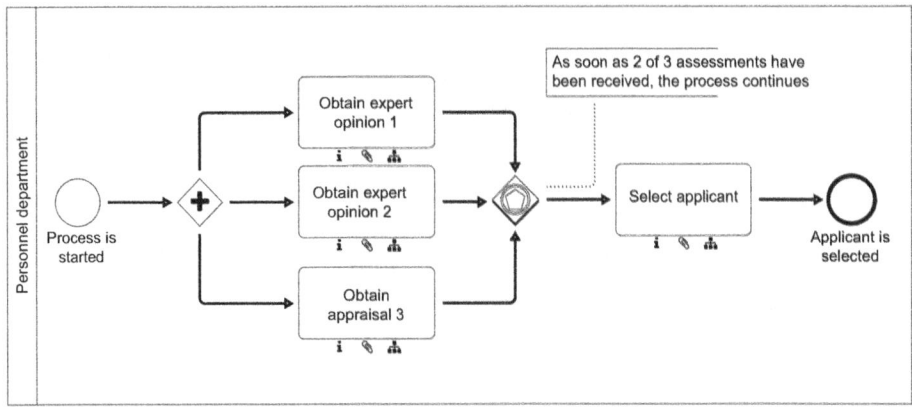

Fig. 5.54   Complex Gateway (adapted from Allweyer, T.: BPMN 2.0, 3rd ed., Norderstedt 2015, p. 37

- **Data stores** are used persistently by multiple process steps,
- **Data objects** are created or processed by process steps.

In Fig. 5.55, data objects are shown as input or output of process steps. The "application" is the input for the step "review application," while the "notification" is the output of "issue notification."

Fig. 5.56 shows data stores that have been modeled as data objects to allow access by multiple steps. The article data is read by the process step (task) "create offer." The process step "record order" writes to the data store "order data," which is then read by the process step "ship goods."

5.8.7   Events

Start, Intermediate, and End Events
BPMN defines numerous types of events. The OMG distinguishes between start, intermediate, and end events, each of which can occur in various forms (see OMG 2011, pp.

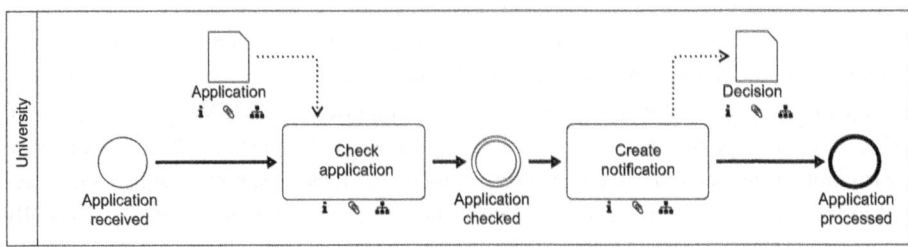

Fig. 5.55   BPMN—Data objects as input or output of process steps

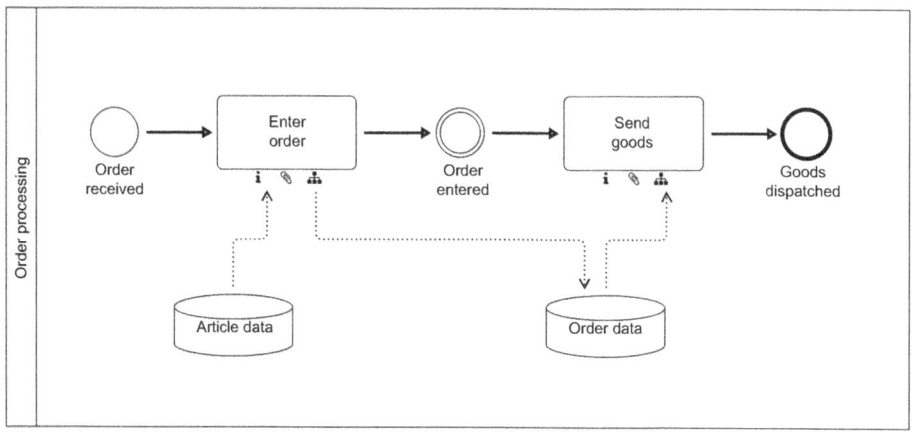

Fig. 5.56 BPMN—Data stores for multiple steps

287 ff. and Fig. 5.57). Events can be used in an undefined state (standard) or defined for specific situations.

Start and end events must be modeled, while intermediate events are optional. They are necessary if a response is required either within or outside the process. Otherwise, they simply indicate a state within the process.

Special Events

The standard symbols for start, intermediate, and end events can be replaced by special symbols that describe the situation more precisely. The use of special events as start, intermediate, and end events is illustrated in Fig. 5.58 using the example process "baking a cake in the oven." The "conditional event" is triggered when the oven temperature reaches a certain degree. Only then can the process continue. The "signal event" at the end of the process indicates that the cake is finished and can be consumed.

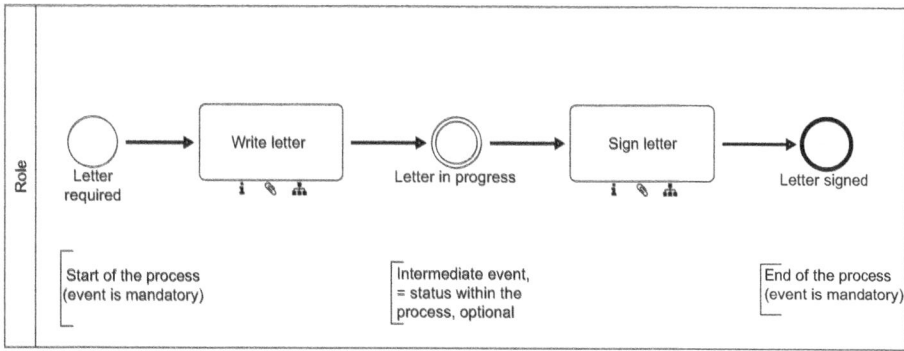

Fig. 5.57 BPMN—Standard events

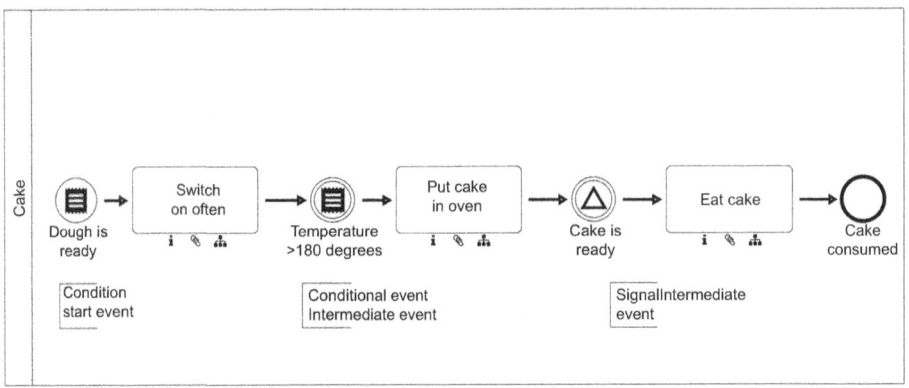

Fig. 5.58 BPMN—Special events

Modeling Messages
In BPMN, messages are also considered events. Messages connect process steps that
are interdependent. Fig. 5.59 illustrates the use of message flows using the example process "Cancellation of Process Parts" (adapted from Allweyer 2015, p. 37). Material has
already been dispatched for an order; however, subsequent steps (e.g., picking goods,
shipping goods) have not yet begun. Due to a transposed digit, the wrong order was processed. The process must be canceled.

Modeling Error Situations
Another use case for special events is error situations. The example in Fig. 5.60
describes an excerpt from production planning: The customer specified in the order does
not exist. The process cannot proceed and must therefore be terminated.

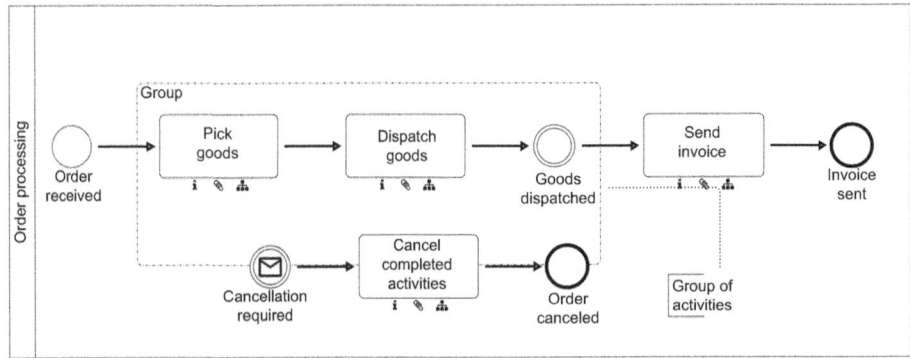

Fig. 5.59 BPMN—Use of messages to represent dependencies (cf. Allweyer 2015, p. 37)

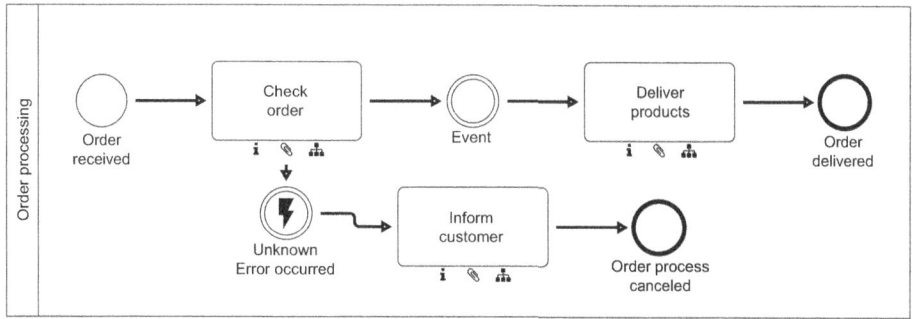

Fig. 5.60   BPMN—Error events (GI 2010)

Multiple Events
Modeling multiple events can be quite complex in other modeling languages (e.g., eEPC with the "OR" connector). In the present example of an application process in Fig. 5.61, one of the events must occur for the application to be reviewed:

- Application by letter,
- Application by email, or
- Application by phone.

Termination of Processes
The termination (completion) of concurrent processes can be described in great detail using BPMN. This is particularly relevant when events occur over time that require already running parallel processes to be aborted. In the example in Fig. 5.62, the process ends as soon as it is technically unfeasible or not economically viable. Ongoing process parts are terminated. For example, within three days, the technical manager might determine that the customer request is not feasible, in which case the ongoing commercial review would not be continued.

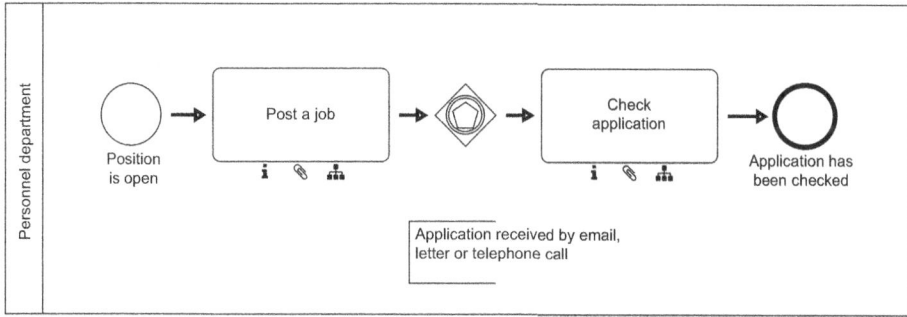

Fig. 5.61   BPMN—Multiple events

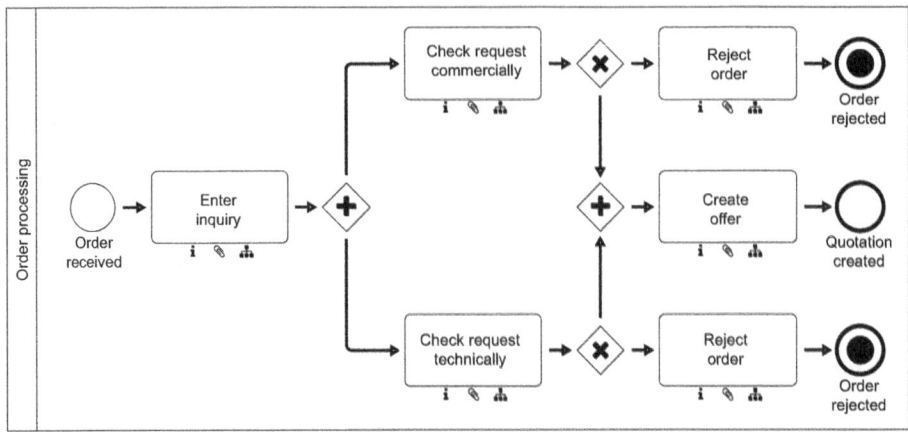

Fig. 5.62 BPMN—Termination of processes

5.8.8   Modeling Examples

The previously introduced process "Scheduling an Appointment" from the general practitioner case study is depicted as a BPMN model in Fig. 5.63 using the BIC Process Design tool. In addition to start, intermediate, and end events, activities as well as information objects (insurance card, appointment slip) and information systems (practice management information system) have been modeled.

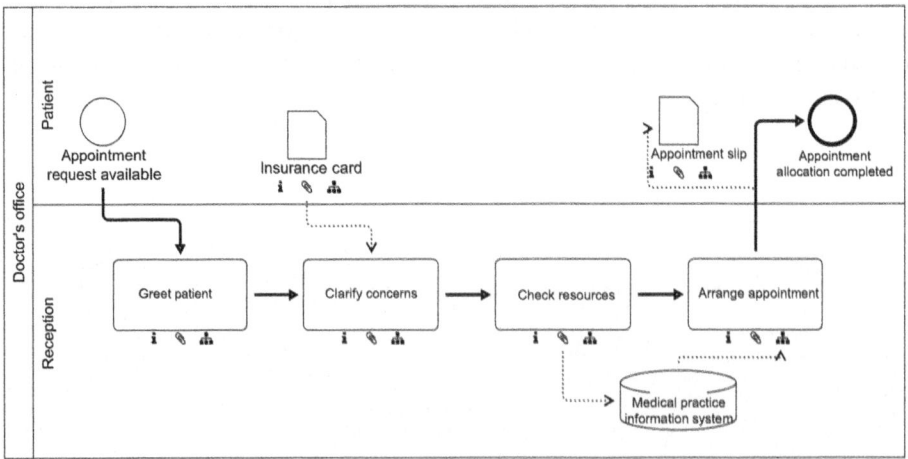

Fig. 5.63 BPMN model of the "Scheduling an Appointment" process—modeled with BIC Process Design

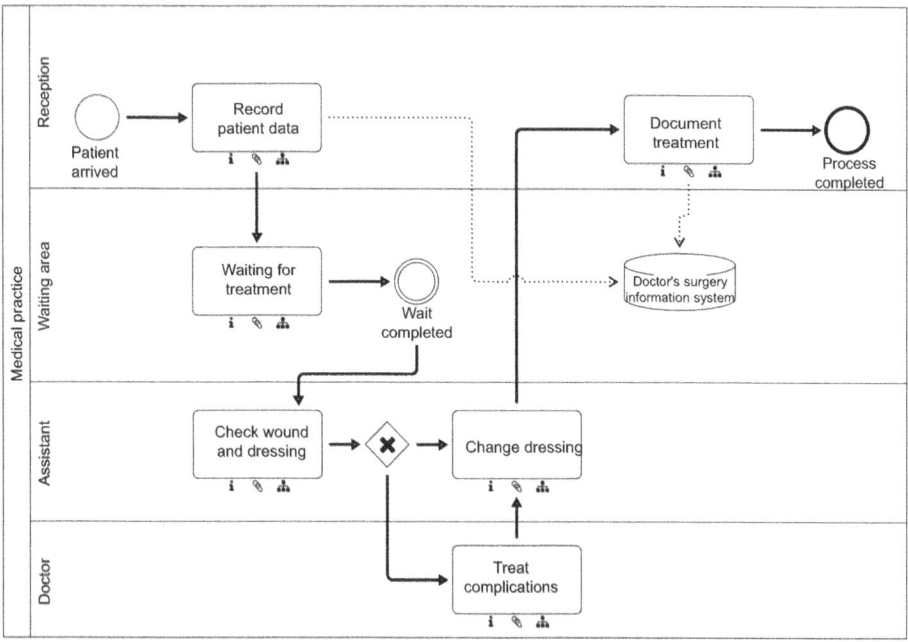

Fig. 5.64 BPMN model of the "Changing a Dressing" process—modeled with Bic Design

The somewhat more complex process "Changing a Dressing" in Fig. 5.64, also modeled with Bic Process Design, contains numerous details that can be represented with BPMN, including information systems, branching, and multiple lanes.

5.8.9   Guidelines for Creating "Good" BPMN Models

Creating "Good" BPMN Models
In practice, it is often very difficult to decide how detailed a BPMN model should be, which symbols are appropriate, and which details are important or can be omitted. In a business context, it is advisable to create a modeling guideline for the employees involved. This should provide comprehensive information about the objective, methodology, examples, and practical tips, and ideally be made available online (e.g., on the intranet). It should also explain when to use which of the more than 100 symbols. A distinction can be made between strategic (simplified) models, business models with additional information, and technical models for describing executable workflows.

Avoiding Complexity
In particular, business models should avoid complex details. Unnecessary details (e.g., "turn on screen," "unplug cable") should be omitted unless they are of particular impor-

tance to the process. On the technical level (workflow), however, precise specifications are required, as the models may serve as the basis for process control.

Presenting the Process Flow Clearly

Well-designed BPMN diagrams are modeled so that the control flow, i.e., the sequence of activities, is depicted from left to right. Complex activities are represented and refined in separate diagrams. Control flows and other edges should not overlap or cross each other.

Use Consistent Symbols and Labels

It is important for the organization to define which symbols should and should not be used. Labeling rules should also be established:

- Activity: "Object and verb in present tense (e.g., 'Post invoice')
- Event: "Object and verb in past tense (e.g., 'Invoice has been posted')

This also includes, as far as possible, avoiding abbreviations that are not generally understood, as these may not be clear to new employees, for example.

Evaluation of the BPMN Method

Compared to the eEPK method, the BPMN method is often praised for its greater clarity, as the simple basic symbols and the use of pools and lanes make the process understandable even for inexperienced users (see Krems 2016). A disadvantage, however, is the significantly higher learning curve required to use the full notation compared to other methods.

The arguments are summarized in Table 5.6.

Tab. 5.6 Evaluation of BPMN Modeling

Advantages	Disadvantages
High level of global recognition, as the method is standardized	Extensive training required, as the notation and rules are very complex when used in full
Has been gaining traction in the IT sector for years; BPMN is often regarded as the "standard"	Modeling tools are essential, as the language covers not only business but also technical modeling
The basic notation builds on the swimlane method, meaning the method can also be used for business modeling with a limited set of symbols	Complex processes require a lot of space

[Table footer—please overwrite]

5.9   Process Simulation

5.9.1   Objectives of Process Simulation

Process simulation is considered a central tool in process management for quantitatively analyzing processes and identifying potential improvements (see the comprehensive literature review by Rosenthal et al. 2021). Simulation, that is, the reproduction of reality in a model for the purpose of experimentation, pursues three objectives: verifying the formal correctness of process models, assessing their fidelity to reality, and evaluating alternative process models.

1st Objective: Verification of Executability of Process Models
The first objective concerns the verification of process models with respect to formal correctness and consistency. To achieve this, it is necessary to use the prescribed modeling syntax, adhere to the underlying semantics, and create an executable workflow model. The executability of a workflow model can be checked using a simulation tool. Achieving this objective does not yet provide any information about the content of the verified workflow models, but only answers the question of whether the examined workflow model is executable and can serve as a basis for execution by a WFMS.

2nd Objective: Validation of the Fidelity of Process Models to Reality
An important prerequisite for the application of simulation is that the simulation model represents reality in such a way that the relevant aspects of reality are sufficiently reflected for the simulation objectives (see Klügl 2006, p. 412). The second objective concerns the clarification of the substantive and technical correctness, i.e., answering the question of to what extent a process model adequately represents reality. One way to validate a process model is to compare the results of simulation experiments based on an as-is model—such as average throughput times, average resource utilization, etc.—with various observations from reality. Therefore, validating an as-is model requires having relevant real-world data that can be compared to the simulation results of the as-is model.

3rd Objective: Evaluation of Alternative Process Models
The third objective is to provide information for qualitative process improvement. This involves clarifying to what extent alternative to-be models are suitable for improving the achievement of process objectives, such as throughput times, resource utilization, or process costs.

Figure 5.65 illustrates the relationship between reality, model types (as-is model, to-be model), and simulation objectives. Starting from reality, an as-is model is created by mapping it. First, the formal correctness and consistency of this model must be verified (1st objective) by checking the executability of the as-is model. Once formal correctness is established, the fidelity of the as-is model to reality can be validated (2nd

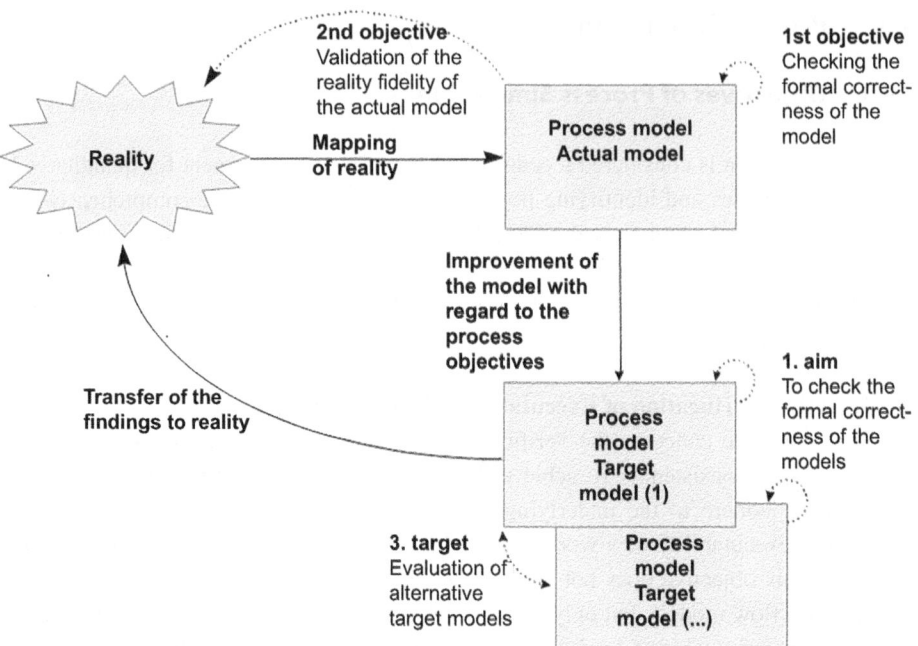

Fig. 5.65 Objectives of Process Simulation

objective). For this purpose, simulation experiments can be conducted with the as-is model, and the results compared with observable real-world values. The as-is model can then be improved by creating several alternative to-be models, which are again first checked for executability (1st objective). Subsequently, the to-be models are evaluated with respect to the achievement of process objectives.

5.9.2   Analysis Metrics

Figure 5.66 shows a structuring of analysis metrics for process simulation, which serve to answer the questions outlined above. Accordingly, a distinction is made between process-related and resource-related analysis metrics, which can in turn be subdivided into time-, value-, and quantity-oriented metrics.

With the help of process-related analysis metrics, instances generated during a simulation run can be evaluated with respect to their process behavior. The throughput time of an instance describes the duration from the start of instantiating the simulated instance to the completion of the last process step. Throughput time is often longer than execution time because, for example, waiting times may occur due to insufficient resources. Assessing process execution with cost rates for the temporal use of resources yields the process costs for executing the instance.

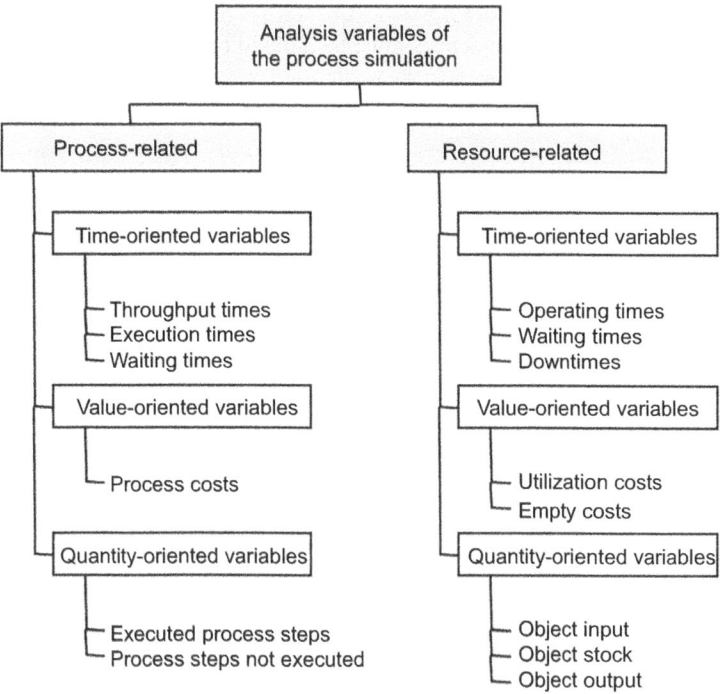

Fig. 5.66 Analysis Metrics of Process Simulation

Resource-related analysis metrics consider the instances generated during the simulation from the perspective of the required resources, i.e., primarily the human actors (processors), but also the computer resources (programs) used. Utilization times and waiting times provide information about resource utilization, which, when assessed with process cost rates, result in productive or idle costs. Downtimes arise from unplanned non-availability of resources (e.g., illness, hindrance) and must be included in idle costs. The objects processed or yet to be processed by the resources used are described by object metrics. Object input refers to the instances generated for a simulation run, object output to the instances actually processed during the simulation. The objects still being processed at the end of the simulation represent the remaining unprocessed workload of a resource.

5.9.3 Conducting a Simulation Study

The process of a simulation study can be carried out in seven steps, which are described below using the example of production planning.

STEP 1: DEFINING OBJECTIVES

Before starting the study, the objectives must be defined quantitatively. A suitable objective, for example, is to minimize lead times in engine assembly by using simulation to select appropriate priority rules for processing shop orders.

STEP 2: INFORMATION GATHERING

This step involves collecting the relevant basic data, including a plausibility and completeness check. In addition to processing and assembly times, output quantities, and the capacities of processing and assembly stations, it is also necessary to record disruptive factors such as downtimes or employee absences. The data must be classified and consolidated in such a way that they can be assigned to processing and assembly stations.

STEP 3: MODEL FORMULATION

To conduct the experimental series, information is needed on how the data should be used. In this context, these are the processing sequences of the processing and assembly stations as well as the priority rules to be examined.

STEP 4: IMPLEMENTATION

This refers to the concrete representation of the model in the simulator, i.e., entering the model data into the computer. The level of detail depends on the defined objectives.

STEP 5: VALIDATION

The model must be checked to ensure that it still corresponds to the reality it is intended to represent. Preliminary simulation runs can be used for this purpose, which are compared with already known results.

STEP 6: EXPERIMENTATION (SIMULATION)

This step constitutes the actual simulation phase. The user systematically runs various experimental series with varying parameters. The experimental parameters and results must be documented. For example, several simulation runs can be performed with different planning periods, capacities, or buffer sizes.

STEP 7: ANALYSIS AND EVALUATION OF RESULTS

Simulation software often provides only numerical results, which must be further processed graphically for analysis. The evaluation may lead to changes in the model and to new experimental series.

It is important that, for each simulation run, not more than one parameter (e.g., simulation duration and capacity data) is changed at the same time. Otherwise, it is not possible to attribute the causes of parameter changes to the effects observed in the simulation results.

5.10   Principles of Proper Modeling

Model content must not only be error-free but also tailored to the target audience. For this purpose, the "Principles of Proper Modeling (GoM)" were developed, a term modeled after the "Generally Accepted Accounting Principles (GoB)" in accounting (see Becker, Rosemann, and Schütte 1995 and Scheer 1998, pp. 198 ff.). The GoM comprise rules in the form of principles to ensure the creation of high-quality and error-free models: the principle of correctness, the principle of relevance, the principle of efficiency, the principle of clarity, the principle of comparability, and the principle of systematic structure (Scheer 1998, pp. 198 ff.).

Principle of Correctness
A model is **correct** if it is syntactically and semantically accurate, i.e., the notation is applied correctly and the model faithfully represents the behavior of reality.

Principle of Relevance
A model is **relevant** if it represents only those aspects of reality that are necessary for the model's objectives.

Principle of Efficiency
A model is **efficient** if the effort required to create it is commensurate with the expected benefit. In practice, elaborate and complex as-is models often violate this principle when too many unnecessary details and variants are included that cannot be used for the target design or quickly become outdated.

Example of Inefficient Process Modeling

An international corporation models all as-is processes from the top-level process at the group level down to the elementary level in all subsidiaries. However, the models are used only for documentation and not for optimization. In addition, the currency of the models cannot be ensured, which means that just a few months after the as-is data is collected, reality looks completely different from the modeled processes. ◄

Principle of Clarity
A model is **clear** if it is understandable to its intended audience. In addition, models should be appropriately structured into submodels to maintain clarity. A distinction should be made between overview models for management, detailed models for clerical staff, and technical models for workflow developers.

Principle of Comparability
A model is **comparable** if the modeling languages used (eEPK, BPMN, etc.) can be traced back to comparable metamodels, i.e., have the same structure.

An "XOR" connector in eEPK is comparable to the "XOR" connector in BPMN. Conversely, however, there are some notation elements in BPMN that are missing in eEPK (e.g., message flow). Therefore, models created with eEPK or BPMN are only partially comparable. ◀

Principle of Systematic Structure
A model is **systematically** structured if different perspectives (e.g., data view, organizational view) can be integrated into an overall view (e.g., process view) and are modeled consistently.

5.11   Selected Modeling Methods in Comparison

In practice, predominantly simple, non-formalized flowcharts (63%), the BPMN 2.0 method (49%), as well as the classic eEPK (47%), and to a lesser extent the IT-oriented UML (20%) are used (Minonne et al. 2011, p. 30). The term flowchart encompasses all non-formalized methods composed of arbitrary diagram elements (circles, rectangles, text, arrows, etc.). They are often used in conjunction with graphics programs. Their widespread use can be explained by the low effort required and the simplicity of their application.

For ad hoc situations in discussions, these methods are quite useful for quickly visualizing relationships. For professional process management, however, the other mentioned methods are usually employed in later project phases, once it becomes apparent that multiple people, distributed across time and location, need to access the process diagrams and the effort required for changes becomes too high.

The variety of notations presented in this book is illustrated in Fig. 5.67. The value chain diagram (WKD) is the simplest method, offering only rudimentary representation options. Compared to the WKD method, the swimlane method essentially adds notation elements for representing organizational aspects (departments = lanes) and, to a certain extent, process-related elements (yes/no decisions). The eEPK method is capable of additionally integrating data structures and information systems. The complex BPMN (here only in its basic notation) provides the most comprehensive notation, as it covers both business modeling and IT implementation (workflow). UML occupies a special position, as it was designed for software development and is therefore focused on the detailed modeling of processes as a specification for programming. It is more a tool for software architects than for process modelers. For this reason, UML is not depicted here; interested readers can refer to van Randen et al. (2016) for more information.

When the methods are compared in terms of target audience, modeling depth, standardization and dissemination, tool availability, method complexity, and required training effort, the picture shown in Fig. 5.68 emerges. The potential areas of application are

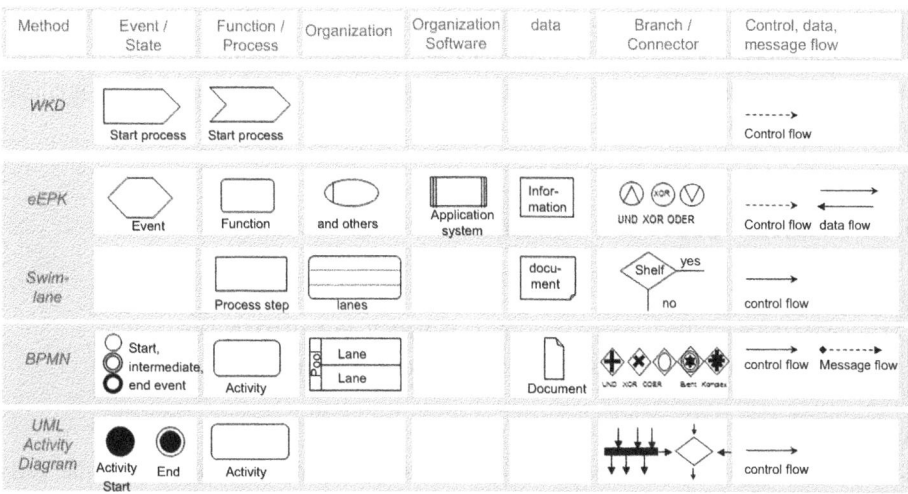

Fig. 5.67 Modeling methods in comparison—notation

Method	Main target group	Modeling depth	Standardi-zation	Dissemina-tion	Tools	Complexity	Training needs
WKD	Management	Rough models	no	international	yes	Very low	minimal
eEPK	IT/ specialist department	Detailed models	no	DACH countries	yes	high	high
Swim-lane	IT/ specialist department	Rough models	no	international	yes	Very low	minimal
BPMN	IT/ specialist department	Detailed models	OMG	international	yes	Very low	Very low
UML Activity Diagram	IT	Detailed models	OMG	international	yes	high	medium

Fig. 5.68 Modeling methods in comparison—characteristics

determined by the complexity. Simple methods, such as WKD, are more targeted at management and business departments, while complex methods are more suited to IT departments. The training effort correlates with the complexity of the method, i.e., the number of modeling elements.

WKD, eEPK, and Swimlane are not standardized. This is particularly surprising for the eEPK method, as it was developed as early as 1992. However, a standardization initiative launched in 2016 has apparently "come to nothing" (see Laue et al. 2021, p. 75). This complicates their use in companies, as a modeling manual must first be created to define the conventions. Incidentally, eEPK is considered more of a "German method" and is mainly used in German-speaking countries.

5.12   Review Questions and Answers

Questions
1. Compare the modeling approaches of the **"eEPK" and "BPMN"** methods.
2. Explain the concept of the **principles of proper modeling**.

Answers
1. The **"eEPK"** was developed for the **business modeling of processes** in the early 1990s and has been successfully used in practice for decades. Its advantage is its simple syntax, which can be learned quickly. "BPMN" was significantly expanded from around 2010 and has since established itself in practice as the most widely used method for **business and technical modeling**. It is considerably more complex, but also more powerful.
2. The **principles of proper modeling** were developed based on the principles of proper accounting, in order to **improve the quality of modeling** and enable person-independent standards. They address, among other things, the clarity and accuracy of process models and help ensure that process models are designed in practice so that they can be used by the relevant stakeholders.

References

Allweyer, T.: BPMN—Business Process Modeling Notation: Einführung in den Standard für die Geschäftsprozessmodellierung, Norderstedt, 3. edn (2015)

Becker, J., Rosemann, M., Schütte, R.: Grundsätze ordnungsgemäßer Modellierung. In: Wirtschaftsinformatik, **37**(5), 435–445 (1995)

Binner, H. F.: Prozessorientierte TQM-Umsetzung. Reihe: Organisationsmanagement und Fertigungsautomatisierung, München (2000)

eCH (eds.): E-Government Standards. http://www.ech.ch/vechweb/page (2011). Accessed 10. Nov. 2016

Fischermanns, G.: Praxishandbuch Prozessmanagement, 11. edn Gießen (2013)

Freie Universität Berlin (eds.): Prozesssteckbrief „Neue Studiengänge einrichten". http://www.fu-berlin.de/sites/prozessmanagement/index.html (2015). Accessed 2 Dec 2015

Gehring, H.: Betriebliche Anwendungssysteme, Kurseinheit 2. Fern-Universität Hagen, Hagen, Prozessorientierte Gestaltung von Informationssystemen (1998)

GI (eds.): Gesellschaft für Informatik e. V. „Layout von BPMN Prozessmodellen". http://www.gi-ev.de/fileadmin/redaktion/Informatiktage/studwett/prozessmodelle.pdf (2010). Accessed 23 Nov 2010

Hoffmann, W., Kirsch, J., Scheer, A.-W.: Modellierung mit Ereignis-gesteuerten Prozessketten, **101.** Universität des Saarlandes, Institut für Wirtschaftsinformatik (1992)

Jannaber, S., Karhof, A., Riehle, D.M., Thomas, O., Delfmann, P.: Invigorating event-driven process chains—towards an integrated meta model for EPC standardization. In: Oberweis, A., Reussner, R. (eds.) Modellierung 2016, Lecture Notes in Informatics (LNI), Gesellschaft für Informatik, S. 13–22. Bonn. https://dl.gi.de/bitstream/handle/20.500.12116/847/13.pdf?sequence=1&isAllowed=y (2016). Accessed 8 Sept 2021

Keller, G., Nüttgens, M., Scheer, A.-W.: Semantische Prozessmodellierung auf der Grundlage Ereignisgesteuerter Prozessketten (EPK). In: Scheer, A.-W. (eds.) Veröffentlichungen des Instituts für Wirtschaftsinformatik, **89,** Saarbrücken (1992)

Keller, G., Teufel, T.: SAP R/3 Prozessorientiert anwenden. Iteratives Prozess-Prototyping zur Bildung von Wertschöpfungsketten, Bonn (1997)

Kirchmer, M.: Geschäftsprozessorientierte Einführung von Standardsoftware, Wiesbaden (1996) Diss, zugl. Univ., Saarbrücken (1995)

Klügl, F.: Multiagentensimulation. In: Informatik Spektrum, **29**(6), 412–415 (2006)

Komus, A., Gadatsch, A., Kuberg, M.: 3. IT-Radar für BPM und ERP, Ergebnisbericht mit Zusatzauswertungen für Studienteilnehmer, Koblenz und Sankt Augustin, 1 Quartal. http://www.process-and-project.net/ (2016)

Krems, B.: Business Process Model and Notation (BPMN), Online-Verwaltungslexikon, Version 1.2. http://www.olev.de/b/bpmn.htm (2016). Accessed 6 Dec 2016

Kurbel, K., Nenoglu, G., Schwarz, C.: Von der Geschäftsprozessmodellierung zur Workflowspezifikation—Zur Kompatibilität von Modellen und Werkzeugen. In: HMD Theorie und Praxis der Wirtschaftsinformatik, **198,** 66–82 (1997)

Laue, R., Koschmider, A., Fahland, D. (eds.): Prozessmanagement und Process-Mining, Berlin/Boston (2021)

Lukas, T.: Business Model Canvas—Geschäftsmodellentwicklung im digitalen Zeitalter. In: Grote, S., Goyk, R. (eds.) Führungsinstrumente aus dem Silicon Valley. Springer Gabler, Berlin, Heidelberg (2018). https://doi.org/10.1007/978-3-662-54885-1_9

Maisch, B., Valdés, C.A.P.: Kundenzentrierte digitale Geschäftsmodelle. In: Fend, L., Hofmann, J. (eds.) Digitalisierung in Industrie-, Handels- und Dienstleistungsunternehmen. Springer Gabler, Wiesbaden (2022)

Meyer, A., Smirnov, S., Weske, M.: Data in business processes. In: EMISA-Forum, **31**(3), 5–29 (2011)

Minonne, C., Colicchio, C., Litzke, M., Keller, T.: Business process management 2011,—Status quo und Zukunft, Eine empirische Studie im deutschsprachigen Europa, Zürich (2011)

Neifer, T., Schmidt, A., Bossauer, P., Gadatsch, A.: Data science canvas: ein instrument zur operationalisierung von daten. In: Marion, S., Timo, K. (eds.) Big Data. Anwendung und Nutzungspotenziale in der Produktion, pp. 37–57. Stuttgart, Kohlhammer (2020)

OMG: Business process model and notation. http://www.omg.org/spec/BPMN/2.0 (2011). Accessed 6 Dec 2016

Österle, H.: Business engineering. Prozess- und Systementwicklung, Band 1, Entwurfstechniken, Berlin (1995)

Osterwalder, A., Pigneur, Y.: Business Model Generation. Wiley, Hoboken, New Jersey (2010)

Randen, v. H.J., Bercker, C., Fieml, J.: Einführung in UML: Analyse und Entwurf von Software, Wiesbaden (2016)

Riehle, D.M., Jannaber, S., Karhof, A., Thomas, O., Delfmann, P., Becker, J.: On the de-facto standard of event-driven process chains: how epc is defined in literature. In: Oberweis,A., Reussner, R. (eds.) Modellierung 2016, Lecture Notes in Informatics (LNI), Gesellschaft für Informatik, S. 61–76. Bonn. https://dl.gi.de/bitstream/handle/20.500.12116/830/61. pdf?sequence=1&isAllowed=y (2016). Accessed 8. Sept 2021

Rosenthal, K., Ternes, B., Strecker, S.: Business process simulation on procedural graphical process models. Bus. Inf. Syst. Eng. (2021). https://doi.org/10.1007/s12599-021-00690-3

Rump, F. J.: Geschäftsprozessmanagement auf der Basis ereignisgesteuerter Prozessketten, Stuttgart und Leipzig (1999)

Scheer, A.W.: ARIS—Vom Geschäftsprozess zum Anwendungssystem, 3. edn Berlin (1998)

Seidlmeier, H.: Prozessmodellierung mit ARIS®, 4. edn Wiesbaden (2015)

Seidlmeier, H.: Prozessmodellierung mit ARIS®. Eine beispielorientierte Einführung für Studium und Praxis, Braunschweig und Wiesbaden (2002)

Sharp, A., McDermott, P.: Workflow modeling: tools for process improvement and application development, Norwood (2002)

Spath, D., Weisbecker, A., Drawehn, J.: Business process modeling 2010. Modellierung von ausführbaren Geschäftsprozessen mit der Business Process Modeling Notation, Stuttgart (2010)

Wagner, K. W., Lindner, A.: WPM—Wertstromorientiertes Prozessmanagement, 3. edn Hanser, München (2022)

White, S. A.: Introduction to BPMN. http://www.bpmn.org/Documents/Introduction_to_BPMN. pdf (2010). Accessed 18 Febr 2010

IT Support for Process Management

6

Processes and IT belong together

Abstract

Process management is often associated with IT tools. Fundamentally, process management is a method for better understanding and continuously improving work within an organization. However, due to the complexity and diverse interrelationships, IT tools are necessary to document processes and support them in operational practice. This article provides a comprehensive overview of potential IT support and presents the tools commonly used in practice for process modeling and analysis, workflow management systems, enterprise resource planning systems, and more. Finally, the article addresses current topics such as digitalization, big data, cloud computing, and Industry 4.0 with regard to their points of intersection with process management. Review questions and a case study support the learning process.

6.1 Tools for Modeling, Analysis, and Design of Processes (BPM Tools)

6.1.1 Objectives and Terminology

For years, the software market for tools that provide fundamental support for business process management has been characterized by a large number of vendors and a wide variety of products. In general, the tasks of visualization, modeling, simulation, process execution (workflow management), and system development (Computer Aided Software

A. Gadatsch, *Business Process Management*,
https://doi.org/10.1007/978-3-658-49339-4_6

Engineering) can be distinguished, each of which is covered by different product categories (Fig. 6.1). Tools with this functionality are also referred to as "BPM tools."

▶ **BPM Tool** A BPM tool is a software system that supports the modeling, analysis, and documentation, and, if applicable, the simulation of processes. It is used on standardized hardware (in particular laptops, desktops, and in some cases tablet computers) utilizing file or database systems to store model data. Powerful BPM tools offer, in addition to modeling, features for checking models (syntax and consistency).

The graphical representation and documentation of processes are provided by many tools in various forms and levels of quality. The range extends from simple "drawing programs" to database-supported modeling tools that support a wide variety of methods.

The modeling and simulation of processes is the domain of specialized products. The automation of processes is carried out by workflow management systems, which are often also referred to as "Business Process Management Systems" or "BPMS."

So-called CASE tools (CASE stands for Computer Aided Software Engineering) support the development and testing of information systems, i.e., the process of providing information systems. For many of the product categories mentioned, free products are available that can be used, at least for teaching and learning purposes and, with some limitations, also in practical process management.

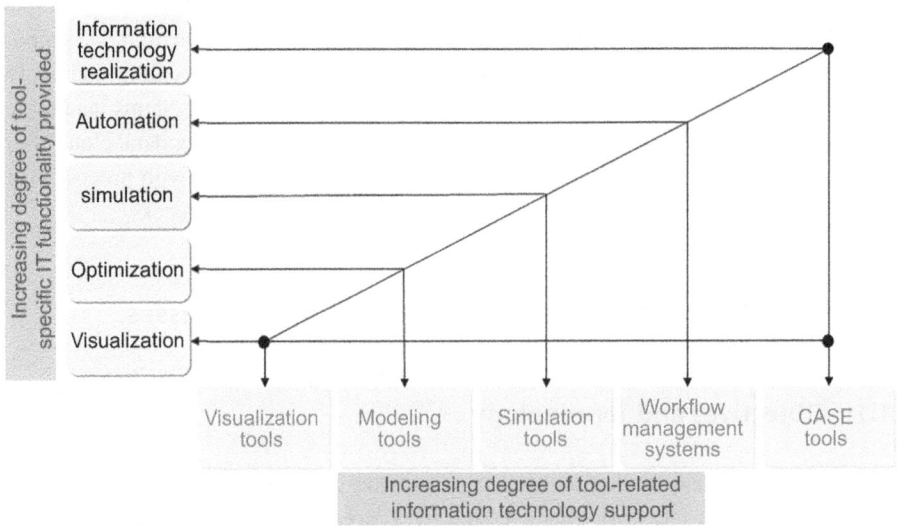

Fig. 6.1 Types of tool support (Nägele and Schreiner 2002)

The selection of an appropriate tool can be made in two steps based on company-specific criteria. The first step is to determine whether a pure documentation tool is needed or whether support for process execution is required.

Criteria for Documentation Tools

In the case of documentation, the tools must provide functions for modeling and representing processes. In particular, the two most well-known modeling standards, BPMN and eEPC, are important here. In addition, attention should be paid to the ability to import and export model data. Usability, that is, the simplest and most intuitive operation of the tools possible, is also a generally important criterion.

Criteria for Process Execution

BPM tools with an execution component compete as process-supporting systems with enterprise resource management systems. Therefore, it is important to select products that support high stability of IT operations and, at the same time, are flexible enough to adapt to process changes without requiring program modifications.

6.1.2 Selected Modeling Tools

The market for modeling tools is very extensive. The number of products available worldwide is likely in the low hundreds, as the website www.bpmn.org alone lists numerous tools that support the BPMN notation (see Allweyer 2014, p. 19). In addition to the traditional on-premise installation of purchased licenses on in-house hardware, a wide range of cloud-based usage models are now available. These range from public cloud solutions to self-managed clouds within the company (on-premise cloud in the company's own data center). For initial "trial runs" with modeling tools, public cloud solutions are usually sufficient, but they are often not suitable for productive use. However, vendors typically offer paid versions with more extensive functionality. In this context, aspects such as data protection, operational security, and administrative effort also play a significant role.

Table 6.1 provides a brief overview and description of some selected tools for process modeling.

Tab. 6.1 Overview of selected tools for business process management

Tool	Vendor	Description
Adonis Community Edition	BOC	Modeling with BPMN and other notations such as process maps. Limited free version
ARIS Business Architect	Software AG, formerly IDS Scheer	Database-supported modeling with a very large number (> 100) of notations such as eEPK, BPMN, process maps, as well as data modeling, function modeling, and other concepts
ARIS Express	Software AG, formerly IDS Scheer	File-based modeling with a limited selection of notations such as eEPK, BPMN, process maps, as well as data modeling
BIC Design	GBTEC	Modeling with various notations such as eEPK, BPMN
Bizagi Modeler	Bizagi	Part of the Bizagi suite, which also supports process execution (Bizagi Studio and Engine)
Blueworks Life	IBM	Modeling tool of the workflow management system "IBM Business Process Management"
iGrafx	iGrafx	Modeling with BPMN and other flowcharts (including the relatively rare IDEF0 diagrams)
Innovator	MID	Modeling with BPMN and other notations (including the relatively rare IDEF0 diagrams)
Signavio Process Editor	Signavio	Tool developed specifically for BPMN, which also supports EPK and value chain diagrams
TIBCO Business Studio	TIBCO	Modeling component of TIBCO's workflow system

6.2   Tools for the Control, Automation, and Machine-Based Analysis of Processes

6.2.1   Workflow Management Systems (WFMS)

Process management is more than just the graphical modeling of processes. This aspect is often overlooked in practice. Processes must also be executed and controlled in day-to-day operations. This requires technical support that goes far beyond the graphical modeling and representation of processes. Workflow management systems (WFMS) play a key role here. They support the modeling, simulation, and, above all, the execution and monitoring of business processes at the workflow level of detail.

Necessity of WFMS

The use of WFMS is not appropriate for all business processes. The process to be supported by a WFMS must be at least partially automatable and should occur regularly. A typical example is order processing in the insurance industry. One-off processes are not suitable for support by WFMS. The higher the proportion of repetitive activities, the more appropriate WFMS become. The complexity (structure) of the processes, on the other hand, can vary. In general, WFMS are more suitable for highly structured processes, as they describe and document process logic in the form of workflow models. However, even simple, less complex processes that run several times a day are suitable for support by WFMS. Application processing, for example, is a suitable use case. Simple processes that are only executed once or twice a month are less likely to be considered.

In more recent literature, WFMS are also referred to as process management systems (PMS) or business process management systems (BPMS). Dadam et al. (2011, p. 364) distinguish in this context between form-based, document-based, and service-oriented process management systems (PMS).

Form-based PMS are used to display the contents of database tables. Document-based PMS support the display and editing of documents, such as incoming invoices. Service-oriented PMS can execute any services per process step, which, in addition to the aforementioned tasks, also includes calling external applications (e.g., an ERP system).

▶ **Definition: Workflow Management System** A workflow management system is an application-independent software system, classified as middleware, that supports the modeling, execution, and monitoring of workflows, as well as, where applicable, additional functions such as simulation and analysis of workflows. In particular, it is capable of interpreting (semi-)formal workflow specifications, initiating the execution of process steps by the designated activity performers—employees or application programs—and, where necessary, providing required work instructions, tools, application programs, information, and documents (Gehring 1998).

The basic functionality of a workflow management system is illustrated in Fig. 6.2. A workflow consisting of several workflow steps (here, "Order Processing") is supported partly by different individuals and partly by various applications. The diagram shows partially automated workflow steps with human intervention, as well as a fully automated workflow step. The applications are supported in some cases by traditional office products, but also by ERP systems or custom-developed database solutions.

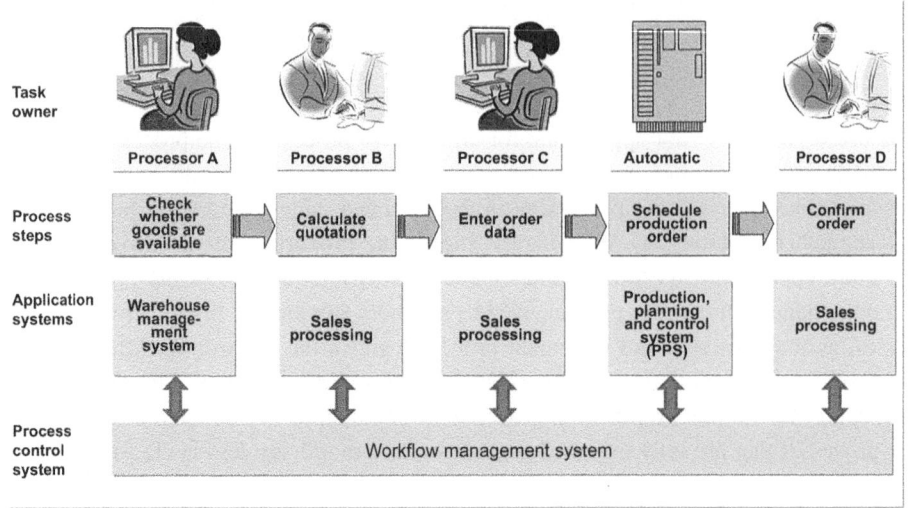

Fig. 6.2 Principle diagram of a workflow management system

Areas of Application

WFMS can, in principle, be used for any type of workflow. Currently, their primary area of application is in commercial and administrative business processes or office processes, whereas, for example, manufacturing processes are supported by production planning and control systems and manufacturing control centers. However, there are several approaches that, due to the similarities between WFMS and PPS systems, aim to integrate these previously separate system areas in order to provide seamless IT support for both administrative and manufacturing processes (see Loos 1997 or Lassen and Lücke 2003). The high degree of similarity in the core functionality of workflow management and production planning and control systems makes it possible to adopt established PPS methods—such as capacity planning and balancing, lead time scheduling, or load-oriented role resolution—for workflow management. In their study, Lassen and Lücke conclude that integrating PPS systems with WFMS leads to improved planning and control of business processes, as integration deficits in order processing can be reduced (see Lassen and Lücke 2003, p. 20, extended).

Selected WFMS

The market for workflow management systems and BPM suites is as extensive as that for pure modeling tools. The study published by Adam et al. (2014) from the Fraunhofer Institute for Experimental Software Engineering (IESE) in Kaiserslautern presents the key findings of a comprehensive market analysis. As part of the study, 20 BPM suites were analyzed and evaluated. The aim of the study was to compare a market selection of relevant tools in terms of their capabilities and user-friendliness from the perspective of

Tab. 6.2 BPM suites in the Fraunhofer market analysis (Adams et al. 2014)

Tool	Vendor	Description
AgilePoint iBPMS	AgilePoint Inc	Owner-managed US company, strong integration with Microsoft products
agito BPM	Agito GmbH	Small Berlin-based company, on the market since 2011
Appian	Appian Software GmbH	Owner-managed US company, product has received multiple awards
Appway Platform	Appway ǀ Numcom Software AG	Swiss company, product has received multiple awards
Axon.ivy BPM Suite	AXON IVY AG	Swiss company, spin-off from Landis+Gyr and ETH Zurich, product has received multiple awards, several times in the highest categories
Bizagi Suite	Bizagi Ltd	Company founded in Colombia, now headquartered in the UK, recognized multiple times as a BPM "Finalist" in 2014
DHC Vision	DHC Business Solutions GmbH & Co. KG	Company based in Saarbrücken, focus on process support and regulatory requirements
@enterprise	Groiss Informatics GmbH	Austrian company, received an award from Swiss Railways in 2013
HCM VDoc Process	HCM Customer Management GmbH	Stuttgart-based company, on the market since 2000, product received the "Best of Industrial IT" award in 2014
IBM BPM	IBM Deutschland GmbH	International IT corporation, product has received multiple international awards from analysts
BPM inspire	Inspire Technologies GmbH	German company, on the market since 2008, recipient of the SME award and TÜV certification for the product
JobRouter	JobRouter AG	Company based in Mannheim, on the market since 1993, focus on providing a development platform, SME Innovation Award
K2 blackpearl	K2 Northern Europe GmbH	South African company with several thousand customers worldwide, numerous international awards
Metasonic® Suite	Metasonic GmbH	German company based in Pfaffenhofen, on the market since 2004
ORACLE BPM Suite	ORACLE Deutschland B. V. & Co. KG	International IT corporation, comprehensive platform for BPM based on various standards (BPMN, BPEL, etc.)
FireStart	PROLOGICS IT GmbH	Austrian company, on the market since 2006, look and feel of Microsoft applications

(continued)

Tab. 6.2   (continued)

Tool	Vendor	Description
X4 BPM Suite	SoftProject GmbH	Software company based in Ettlingen, on the market since 2000, numerous adapters for third-party software integration
T!M – Task !n Motion 4.0	T!M Solutions GmbH	Company based in Freising, on the market since 2007, several recent awards for the product

BPM experts and BPM users. The evaluation was based on the weighted degree of fulfillment with respect to a standardized, previously developed requirements catalog, the power of the software in terms of customization options with standard tools, and the convenience of the provided functionalities (Adam et al. 2014, p. 6).

Table 6.2 lists the products analyzed in the referenced study. Overall, it is noted that all products exhibit a high level of functionality. With regard to usability, the study found that only very few products offer high usability across all individual aspects, with a significantly greater variance observed. The product from Bizagi received the best overall rating. It also achieved the highest usability score among all tools examined. The product from SoftProject received the highest rating for functionality (Adam et al. 2014, pp. 124–125).

Workflow management can be distinguished from workgroup computing as a special case, a concept that goes back to Krcmar (1993). Workgroup computing, or more recently "social workflow," aims to replace internal email communication and to support internal corporate communication with social web functionality (similar to "Facebook"). The functionality includes, among others, the following processes:

- Collaborative editing of documents and projects
- Chat, audio/video conferencing, webinars, newsfeeds,
- Tagging/liking/following files and people,
- Commenting on messages,
- Wikis, group calendars, surveys.

Current typical products and their core functionalities include, among others:

- Jira (workflows, tickets),
- Trello (Kanban board, project management for smaller teams),
- Asana (similar to Trello, but for larger teams and with more functionality)
- MS Teams (collaboration platform).

6.2.2 Robotic Process Automation (RPA)

The automated processing of process steps is the subject of many information technologies that have been in use for a long time. Many organizations are under enormous cost pressure and need to optimize their processes. The focus is often on repetitive, long-established processes that incur high personnel costs due to manual work and data entry in conjunction with legacy information systems. The current shortage of skilled workers further intensifies this effect.

As a possible tool for accelerating processes, software robots (Robotic Process Automation, or "RPA," also referred to as "bots") can be used to automatically perform the tasks of the involved personnel. Human input on the application's graphical user interface (GUI) is simulated by a program (i.e., a virtual employee), but is not altered in content or any other way. In the research literature, Robotic Process Automation is currently regarded as "The newest technological 'star' on the firmament of BPM research" (Reijers 2021, p. 4).

If the application provides an "Application Programming Interface" (API), it can also be controlled directly by a workflow engine. However, it is more common for the robot to access the application via the standard user interface, just as a "real" employee would.

▶ **Definition "RPA"** RPA is a technology that replaces humans in the execution of simple, repetitive IT tasks without changing the technologies in use. RPA programs access the same interfaces as human operators.

RPA programs are "rule-based software robots" for repetitive tasks, with typical use cases such as automated data entry, integration of systems without programmed interfaces, and process control (ensuring target process = actual process) (see van der Aalst et al. 2018). The widespread adoption of RPA applications demonstrates the enormous potential and interest in this technology. In 2020, 60% of companies in the DACH region planned to have between ten and twenty-five business processes handled by so-called software robots (see Freund 2019).

▶ **Definition "bot"** A bot is a virtual operator or virtual worker that executes strictly defined and routinely performed business processes. It simulates human input on the graphical user interface (GUI) of an application.

Typical RPA processes frequently encountered in practice include travel expense accounting, processing of terminations, onboarding of new employees, invoice processing, order processing, or vacation request handling. Interactive processes are also conceivable, such as conducting conversations with customers via voice input and output (Czarnecki et al. 2019, p. 797).

RPA tools can perform the same operations on the desktop as a human user, such as mouse movements and actions, entering characters, copying or modifying displayed values, clicking buttons, and logging in and out. They can also receive and send emails (Schiklang et al. 2019, p. 4). The interaction between RPA software and an application is illustrated in Fig. 6.3. Steps 1–4 simulate the human operator. If information is missing during the process, the RPA software notifies a predefined user group (e.g., by email).

An example of a process supported by RPA technology is shown in Fig. 6.4. After logging into various systems, the employee copies the necessary information, switches to the target application window, and pastes the information into the "invoice item" form. This part of the process is repeated for each invoice item. After the bot is started, it logs into the various systems and reads out the data required for all invoice items. The bot then switches to the target application window and enters all the information into the "invoice item" form for all items.

The cost savings achievable through the use of RPA technologies are enormous. If the cost of a full-time employee in Germany is set at 100%, a comparable employee in a low-wage country would cost 35%. The cost share of a bot using RPA technology is only 10% (see Hermann et al., p. 30).

Prerequisites for RPA

Not all processes are suitable for the use of RPA technologies. Important prerequisites that a process or subprocess must meet are (see Deloitte 2017):

- Rule-based execution of process steps,
- Processing of structured input data,
- Repeated execution of the process,
- Medium to high transaction volume,
- Stable process flow, low need for changes.

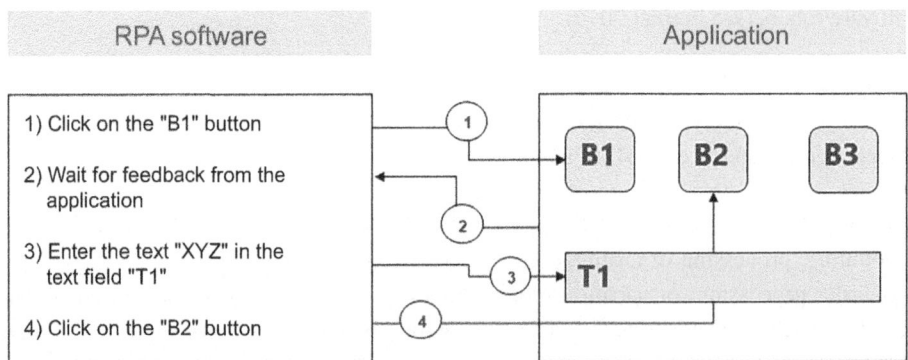

Fig. 6.3 Interaction between RPA software and application (adapted from Häuser and Schmidt 2018)

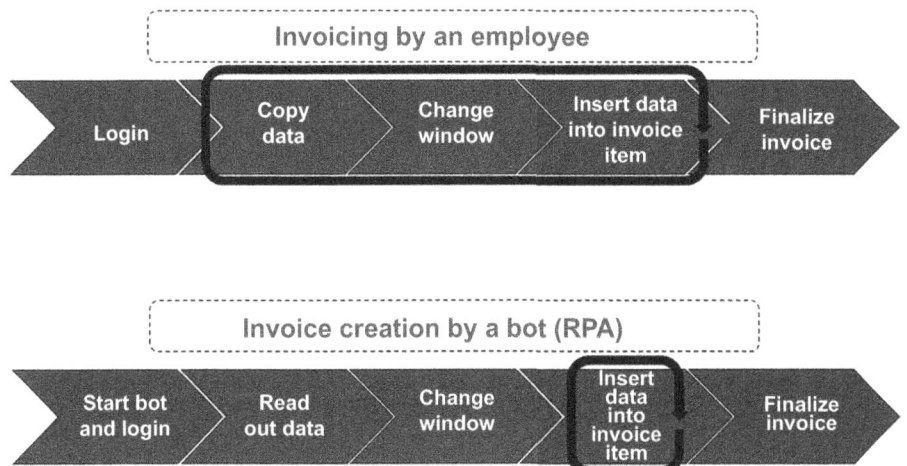

Fig. 6.4   RPA example process: invoice processing (adapted from Baumbach et al. 2016)

Potential Risks

The use of RPA software does not require process redesign, which creates the risk of "cementing existing processes." Instead of redesigning processes (business reengineering), they are automated by the robot and thus continue to be used for years to come. RPA can easily be deployed in business departments as "shadow IT," similar to Excel macros and comparable tools. As a result, information and process management lacks control over implementation. These tools are often criticized for lacking flexibility and being prone to errors. Exceptions in workflows and changes in the user interface can lead to errors during process execution.

RPA and BPM

Table 6.3 highlights the key differences between an RPA solution and Business Process Management (BPM) (cf. Williams 2017).

The increasing adoption of RPA technology raises a number of issues that need to be addressed. For example, it must be clarified who is responsible for selecting RPA-relevant processes, and who develops, tests, and operates the RPA programs. In addition, tasks such as error analysis and quality improvement must be defined. Such questions have led to calls for "RPA governance" (cf. Petersen and Schröder 2020), which is intended to regulate these aspects. This requires the definition of specific roles depending on the company's requirements, such as "RPA Program Owner" or "RPA Developer" (cf. Petersen and Schröder 2020).

Tab. 6.3 Comparison of RPA and BPM

Robotic Process Automation (RPA)	Business Process Management (BPM)
RPA executes processes in place of an employee	BPM is a methodology for process optimization
The focus is on replacing human labor with robot software	The focus is on process improvement (in terms of content, time, and cost) through restructuring
RPA does not change the process itself, only the interface at the top level (human-machine) is modified	BPM changes the process; RPA can be used as a partial solution for individual process steps
RPA is a software technology	BPM is a management approach
RPA is a fast and cost-effective interim solution that can be used instead of BPM ("quick wins")	BPM enables fundamental changes to processes, but is more complex and resource-intensive
Frequent changes in the process hinder RPA	Frequent changes in the process are implemented through BPM

[Table footer – please overwrite]

6.2.3   Process Mining

The term process mining originates from the work of Will van der Aalst (cf. e.g. van der Aalst 2011) and represents a further development of process analysis techniques from the late 1990s to the early 2000s (cf. Chapela-Campa and Dumas 2023). It refers to a technology that enables process analysis based on real process data and presents the results using visualization techniques. Figure 6.5 illustrates the overlap between "Process Science," i.e., the analysis and modeling of processes, and "Data Science," the application of statistical methods to data, which is referred to as "process mining."

A "process miner" analyzes the data generated by processes (such as newly created customer master records, newly entered customer orders, modified master data or orders, etc.) and assigns them to processes. This makes it possible to compare target process models with actual models that reflect reality. Data sources include, for example, log data from ERP systems, workflow management systems, or other databases that are populated by processes (e.g., order data, customer data in an order process). Deviations in actual processes can be compared with target processes to investigate the reasons why processes in reality differ from those planned (or modeled).

Possible reasons for deviations between actual and target processes include the following causes:

- Repetition of process steps,
- Unplanned rework,

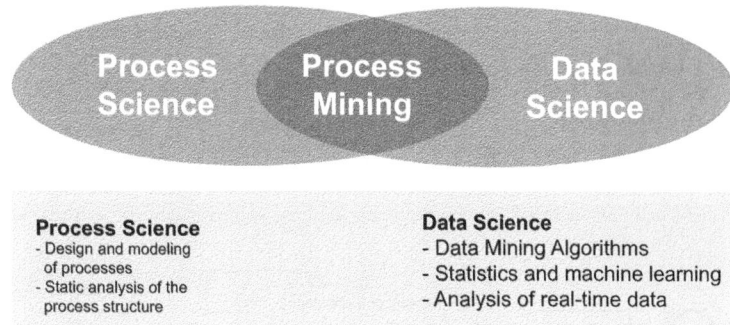

Process Science
- Design and modeling
  of processes
- Static analysis of the
  process structure

Data Science
- Data Mining Algorithms
- Statistics and machine learning
- Analysis of real-time data

Fig. 6.5 Process mining as the intersection of process science and data science

- Detours in the process flow (e.g., unnecessary process steps that do not add value to the process outcome),
- Delays in process steps.
- Lost items (e.g., a customer inquiry is not processed and "gets lost"),
- Ping pong (the process flow bounces back and forth between different departments without generating added value)
- Loops (repeated processing, e.g., an order is entered, checked, and then modified again),
- Fraud (e.g., unauthorized creation of a customer account and posting of an invoice to this account, which is then automatically paid),
- Lack of results (e.g., an inquiry is not processed through to completion).

Situation in Practice A study by FH Münster showed that the level of adoption in practice is still very heterogeneous: only 5% of companies use process mining, and 7% are in the testing or implementation phase (cf. IPD 2021). Interestingly, the study found that 39% of companies consider process mining to be an interesting topic, but do not pursue it for various reasons (cf. IPD 2021).

Figure 6.6 illustrates the basic concept of process mining. The target process modeled in the upper section is often not followed in practice. Employees may skip individual process steps, require more time, incur higher costs than planned, or add additional process steps, for example, by using shadow IT (such as Excel macros).

Case Study Figure 6.7 presents an example with a small process model and fictitious log data from the ERP system. It contains the process data of four orders (100, 101, 102, 103), each following the process in a different way.

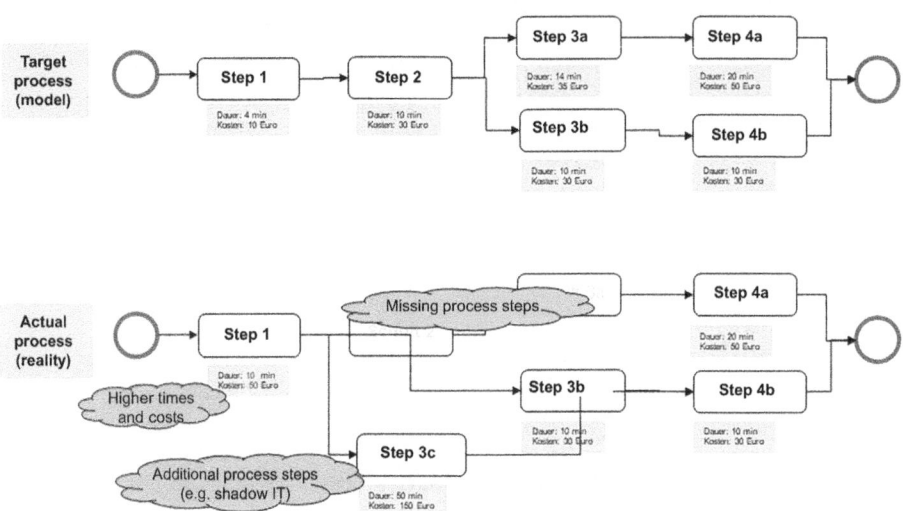

Fig. 6.6 Process Mining – Discrepancies between Target and Actual Processes

Process model   Log data

ORDER ID	Order ID	Customer ID	Process ID	Process name
1	100	10	P1	Check creditworthiness
2	100	10	P2a	Create order
3	100	10	P3	Send goods
4	101	20	P1	Check creditworthiness
5	101	20	P2b	Reject order
6	102	30	P1	Check creditworthiness
7	102	30	P2b	Reject order
8	102	30	P3	Send goods
9	103	10	P1	Check creditworthiness
10	103	10	P2a	Create order
11	103	10	P3	Dispatch goods
...				

Fig. 6.7 Case Study: Process Model with Log Data

Figure 6.8 shows the process flows for orders 100, 101, and 102. For order 100, the customer's creditworthiness is checked, the order is created, and the goods are shipped. For order 101, the customer does not have sufficient creditworthiness, so the order is rejected and the process ends. For order 102, the order is rejected after the credit check, but the goods are still shipped, which should not have happened according to the process model. Although this issue is apparent from the log data, it is not easy to detect.

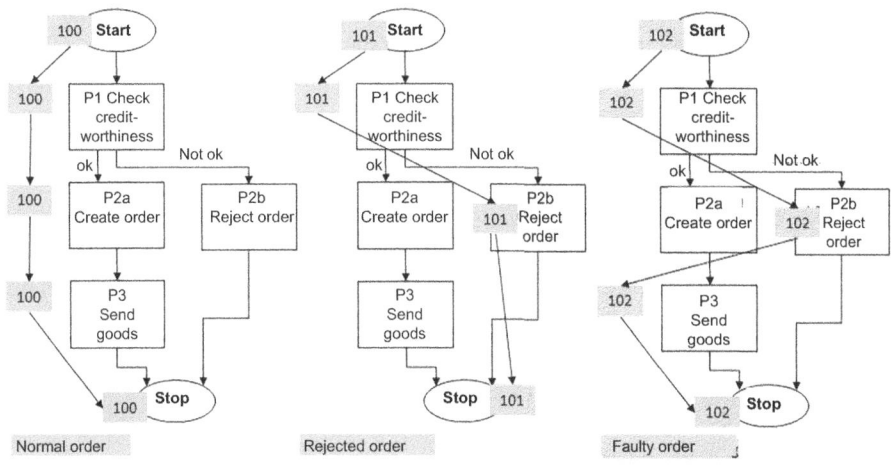

Fig. 6.8   Case Study: Visualized Process Flows Based on Log Data

In practice, this can have various causes, such as processing errors, fraudulent intent, or software bugs. The process flow for order 103 (a standard order) is the same as for order 100, so it is not visualized here.

Application Areas   The range of applications for process mining is broad. For example, auditors are increasingly using this technology to conduct automated analyses of entire business processes. This allows them to identify and assess anomalies in transactions (see Bruckner 2019, p. 6).

There are now a number of commercial software tools that have adopted van der Aalst's ideas and turned them into products. Below is an alphabetical selection of current tools (see also the interactive product overview by the consulting firm Gartner, Gartner 2021).

- ARIS Process Mining SaaS, Software AG,
- Celonis Process Mining, Celonis,
- Fluxicon Disco, Fluxicon,
- Signavio Process Intelligence, Signavio,
- UiPath Process Mining, UiPath (formerly Process Gold).

Process Mining in Small and Medium-Sized Enterprises
Bonn-Rhein-Sieg University of Applied Sciences, together with the Cologne-based consulting firm BPM&O GmbH, conducted a survey among several small and medium-sized enterprises (SMEs) to analyze the current state of process mining adoption in

SMEs (see Tsingeni et al. 2022). Three companies were surveyed: a bank, a toy manufacturer, and a company in the food industry (see Tsingeni et al. 2022).

The study found that many SMEs are interested in process mining, but have not yet
been able to launch a corresponding project for various reasons (e.g., lack of resources).
Key prerequisites for the successful introduction of process mining are:

- A process culture with an understanding of process management (thinking and acting
  in terms of processes, assigning responsibility for processes),
- Selection of suitable processes (end-to-end processes are often distributed across multiple systems, making it difficult to obtain clear process identification),
  Definition of objectives to be achieved with process mining (e.g., identifying and
  eliminating process weaknesses) (see Tsingeni et al. 2022).

Conclusion from a Process Management Perspective
Process mining can support process management by detecting both intentional and unin-
tentional errors in processes and identifying weaknesses in implementation. It represents
a bottom-up approach, which, in contrast to the traditional top-down approach of process
management, is based on real data. For controllers, auditors, and compliance officers,
process mining offers a way to support process controlling and actual-state analysis.

Current developments also leverage artificial intelligence techniques to achieve autonomously operating process optimizations, referred to as "Augmented Process Execution
Systems" (see Chapela-Campa and Dumas 2023).

6.3   Tools for Business Process Support

6.3.1   Standard Software versus Custom Software

A core question in business informatics is the procurement of application software
required to support business processes. For process management, it is important to determine whether pre-built standard software developed for many companies is used, or
whether software specifically tailored to the company is implemented.

Trend Toward Standard Software
In light of current trends such as cloud computing, the use of standard software is
becoming increasingly important. The traditional in-house development of software by
a company's own employees, possibly supported by specialized consultants, is becoming
less and less common. However, it still dominates in certain sectors (insurance, banking)
where the range of available standard software is relatively limited. The classic purchase
of standard software followed by implementation by in-house staff and consultants has
been on the rise for years in sectors with a wide range of software offerings (e.g., manufacturing, mechanical engineering, retail).

In-House Development as a Domain of Medium-Sized Enterprises

Traditional in-house development by an external software company (third-party development) is typically found in medium-sized enterprises, which usually have only limited development resources, but it is also used in larger companies for specialized applications. Since standard software requires comparatively high investments in personnel, hardware, and other resources, the rental model for standard software has become increasingly widespread in recent years. In this model, the purchase of standard software is eliminated, as this is handled by a specialized provider. The provider possesses the expertise for implementation and support, while the user pays for the use of the software.

Case Study: Insurance Industry

In the insurance industry, the proportion of self-developed software is still relatively high compared to the use of standard software. In a panel discussion with IT managers, the owner of a software company that primarily develops custom software expressed the following opinion: "One of our clients in the private health insurance sector developed their own software solution for risk assessment. The input for this software consists of the applicant's pre-existing conditions as well as other data such as place of residence, occupation, etc. The program outputs a probability of loss and, if necessary, a risk surcharge or, in extreme cases, a recommendation to decline the application. Decades of experience have been incorporated into this system, which is highly tailored to the company. We cannot imagine that such tasks will be solvable by standard software in the foreseeable future."

A representative of a major standard software provider, who was also present, disagreed. His response was: "The industrial use of standard software is not limited to accounting and inventory management. About 25–30 years ago, proponents of custom development argued that the core business of an industrial company was so specialized that it would hardly be possible to create production planning and control software for the mass market. Today, you will find software from the market leader or a competitor in virtually every company in the manufacturing and production sector. In this case, insurers can benefit from this development. Even for the insurance scenario described, I can imagine that standard software providers will offer framework-based solutions for the core business of insurance companies, which can be supplemented with custom modules for specific requirements. Such a module could be, for example, pricing or risk assessment."

There are similar examples in the manufacturing industry, as previously mentioned, in the area of set optimization. Standard software providers offer their customers the ability to integrate their own modules for set optimization at defined interfaces. ◀

Use of Custom Software for Process Support

- **Tailored Solution**

  The development and use of custom software offer the advantage of a tailored solution that may not require any organizational adjustments. In custom development, the user specifies the desired requirements, which are then implemented as a technical solution. No organizational changes are necessary, as the solution is adapted to the user's needs. Depending on the company's situation, this can be seen as an advantage. However, a problematic aspect is that the "integration" of custom developments can lead to complex application architectures. Older and newer generations of software systems are interconnected, making future maintenance more difficult. It is important to note that the use of standard software can "force" or at least induce long-overdue organizational changes. As a result, overdue organizational changes can be postponed more easily through the use of custom software than with standard software.

- **Independence**

  Developing software in-house has the advantage that no dependency on a software vendor is created, a relationship that typically lasts for many years, often decades. This dependency is much stronger than, for example, the dependency on a hardware manufacturer, since replacing software is far more complex than replacing hardware.

- **Strategic Aspects**

  Companies need strategic unique selling points to remain competitive in the long term and to ensure customer loyalty. They want to present themselves individually to the outside world in order to differentiate themselves from competitors. For many companies, the homogeneous support of business processes through standard software is a reason to develop custom software. With this approach, they can create targeted competitive advantages in selected process areas. Suitable areas include product- or market-oriented processes with an innovative character (e.g., product development) or externally visible systems such as sales or systems for designing the company's online presence. In traditional business administration areas, which mainly cover internal business processes—such as financial accounting, cost accounting, controlling, human resources, as well as logistics and materials management—the range of functionality and the quality of available standard software packages are now so high that custom development is rarely considered.

- **Costs Difficult to Predict**

  The development of custom software requires significant financial investment and is highly risky due to the many unknown influencing factors. In practice, it is often observed that, despite modern development methods—and frequently due to time constraints—the documentation of delivered programs is insufficient or, in some cases, not available at all.

- **Dependence on Employees**

  The independence from software vendors achieved through custom development is traded for a dependence on key employees in software development. It is not uncommon for IT departments to experience reduced performance during the absence of certain employees due to vacation or illness. The use of modern software engineering and quality assurance methods can increasingly mitigate this disadvantage, but it cannot be completely eliminated. Ultimately, dependence on individual IT staff is a particularly risky issue for smaller companies.

Use of Standard Software for Process Support

- **Acquisition of Know-how**

  For many companies, the use of standard application software (in short: standard software) is an alternative for providing modern support to their business processes. By purchasing standard software, they are not only acquiring software, but also predefined business processes, which, however, still need to be adapted to the specific needs of their company. Alternatively, the company's organizational structure and workflows must be changed if the software "does not fit the processes." The latter is often the case in practice.

- **Cost Advantages**

  The acquisition costs are lower compared to the costs of custom software development, as the manufacturer's development costs are spread across a larger customer base. However, it should be noted that acquisition costs are not the dominant cost factor when implementing standard software. The introduction of standard software often incurs additional costs for hardware upgrades. In some cases, it is also necessary to procure additional software, such as a specific database management system or faster end devices.

- **Up-to-date Software**

  Competition among standard software vendors ensures that products are continuously improved and generally reflect the latest business expertise in the form of software programs. Customers of standard software providers therefore benefit from the ongoing development of the software and can usually take advantage of current market standards. A recent example is the enhancement of business standard software with internet functionalities.

- **High Functionality**

  Today, business standard software offers a very comprehensive range of functions compared to previous years, typically covering all standard requirements of a functional area (e.g., finance). It is not uncommon for some features to go unused during the initial implementation due to the abundance of available functions, but to be utilized at a later stage. Standard software is often used internationally. Modern software packages support all major world languages, including Japanese, Chinese, Arabic, and Russian scripts. This enables global teams to work with the same standard software and on the same data sets. Each employee can use the system in their preferred language.

  Business standard software is available independently of hardware and software platforms for various industries. Early generations of standard software offered little or no customization options for customers. Current software products can be adapted to user requirements within the scope of the available functionality through so-called customizing. The number of "adjustment levers," i.e., possible parameterizations, is so complex that no general statements can be made. In principle, such standard software products can be extensively adapted to the requirements of the respective company, although organizational and business process adjustments are still to be expected.

- **Organizational Changes**
  The use of standard software is often justified by strategic considerations. The decision to use standard software, often from a specific vendor, is usually made at the highest management level. This can be quite sensible if there is appropriate motivation, for example, when the software implementation project is intended to justify and enforce necessary organizational changes. This situation is frequently encountered in practice, as custom software development often uses the current organizational structure and business processes as the basis for target concepts. In such cases, the use of standard software can prompt a desirable "reconsideration" of the advantages of the current organizational structure and business processes. Such projects then take on the character of business reengineering projects, with standard software serving as a tool, i.e., as an enabler for revising business processes. In addition, the responsible employees from the business units are involved in the project at a relatively early stage, since a functional software system is already available and adapting it to operational requirements becomes primarily a business management task. This ensures that the future software solution is more likely to meet requirements than is often the case with in-house developments, where business unit staff are less involved during the development phase.

- **Low Subsequent Effort**
  The main strategic advantage of using standard software lies in the lower ongoing effort required for expanding the installed system. Extending the functionality of custom-built applications often exceeds the effort of the original implementation project and frequently results in full-scale (maintenance) projects. With standard software, functional extensions can be made at any time by activating the required features and configuring them (customizing). However, this only applies as long as the functional extensions remain within the standard scope of the software. If requirements go beyond this, additional developments (so-called add-ons) or even changes to the source code (so-called modifications) are necessary, which are essentially custom developments.

- **Strategic Aspects**
  Nevertheless, strategic aspects are not always decisive or applicable. The use of business standard software is less critical in the area of internal administrative business processes with a cross-sectional character, such as accounting and human resources. Greater care is required when selecting software for core business processes that provide significant value to the company. In these cases, it is often not possible to realize competitive differentiators with standard software. The decision for a particular vendor and product inevitably leads to a certain, sometimes high, degree of depend-

ency, as there is usually only limited influence—often only indirectly via user groups, etc.—on product policy and further development. This dependency is even more significant when standard software is used for strategically relevant process areas. In contrast, process areas with a high degree of standardization, such as finance or office communication (word processing, email, etc.), are less critical. The practice of modifying the source code, which was common in earlier software generations, is often technically impossible (as the source code is not provided by the vendor) or too costly in the long term. The latter is increasingly the case, as source code changes can no longer be implemented with reasonable effort when there are multiple releases per year.

- **Training**
  The introduction and operation of standard software requires significant training and, in most cases, consulting effort from the vendor or specialized consulting firms, both once during the initial implementation and on an ongoing basis during operation.

- **Expensive Specialized Personnel**
  The required specialized personnel are generally expensive and difficult to recruit. This disadvantage can be mitigated through early involvement and training of employees who will later serve as coaches within the company, provided that project management is appropriate.

- **Changed Requirements for Personnel**
  It should also be noted that, in practice, the use of standard software leads to medium- and long-term changes in the personnel structure of the IT department, making a switch from standard software back to custom development more difficult. The reason for this is a significant reduction in personnel capacity for application development, as these resources are only needed for the development and adaptation of extensions (add-ons). Instead, personnel resources with business and organizational skills are built up, meaning that the introduction of standard software is associated with a shift in the IT department from development to internal business consulting.

6.3.2 Enterprise Resource Planning Systems (ERP Systems)

Objectives and Definition
ERP systems (ERP = Enterprise Resource Planning) have played a major role in the development of process management and remain a central component in process implementation today. Prior to their development and introduction in the 1980s, dedicated systems were predominantly used for individual business functions. As a result, companies sometimes operated systems for inventory management, sales, accounting, human resources, etc., on their own hardware, each managing its own data. This led to high data redundancy and resulted in a multitude of interface programs to ensure mutual data exchange, which often became unmanageable.

▶ **Definition of ERP System** An ERP system is a modular software system in which multiple standard business applications are integrated through a shared data base. Typical business applications include finance and controlling, production planning and control, procurement and logistics, sales and shipping, as well as human resources. Each business application is represented by a module consisting of several individual programs. The primary focus of an ERP system is to support processes within a company, rather than to facilitate inter-company business processes with suppliers and upstream vendors. Customization allows adaptation to individual requirements.

Characteristics of ERP Systems

ERP systems are distinguished primarily by the following characteristics: data integration, process integration, operational functionality, unified development concept, layered architecture, and transaction orientation (see Table 6.4).

Data Integration A key feature of integrated standard software is the shared use of data. Sales data, for example, can illustrate this. Customer master records are typically created by sales staff. This involves tasks such as assigning a customer number, entering the customer name, address, sales data, and so on. The accounts receivable accountant can access this information available in the ERP system and supplement it with accounting-specific details (e.g., credit limit, reconciliation account, payment terms). Both employees access the same data sets. Data integration is particularly evident in the "posting through" of business transactions across all activated components of the standard software. For instance, if a company uses an integrated application system with the sub-functions logistics/materials management, production planning, and accounting, then posting the receipt of goods for raw materials required for production control triggers the following activities:

- Updating inventory quantities in logistics and materials management,
- Triggering a production order that is waiting for this material,
- Increasing inventory values in accounting.

Process Integration A key issue in business process management is the continuity of process support, i.e., the avoidance of changes between employees, departments, or software systems. Only a seamless connection of multiple application modules into a business process allows for the elimination of interfaces to a large extent and ensures that data is captured only once, at its point of origin, and subsequently processed in all components. Integrated databases require plausibility checks for all data already at the point of entry into the system. For example, even when recording goods receipts in terms of quantity, all accounting-relevant data fields must be entered and validated. It must be verified, for instance, whether a cost center to be charged with the goods receipt actually

Tab. 6.4 Characteristics of ERP Systems

Characteristic	Brief Description	Example
Data Integration	The system's software modules share data	A sales and an accounting module both use customer master data
Process Integration	Cross-departmental business processes are jointly supported by multiple software modules	Order processing is supported from receipt of the customer inquiry, through production, to delivery and payment using several software modules (sales processing, production planning, shipping, finance)
Operational Functionality	Support for a company's operational tasks in handling business transactions	Order processing, production planning, customer accounting, accounts payable processing, payroll
Unified Development Concept	Software modules use a shared repository and are based on uniform development standards	Consistent screen layouts, standardized error messages
Layered Architecture	Software architecture supporting processing distributed across multiple departments, locations, and potentially countries	Client/server architecture enabling decentralized access to data and functions
Transaction Orientation	Online processing of business transactions and storage of data in databases	Creating a customer order, posting an incoming invoice
Multi-tenancy	Separation of the logical view (company, division) from the technical view	Multiple legally independent companies can be managed on a single SAP® system. Users and data are completely separated

Characterization of ERP Systems

exists. In such application scenarios, the data from the business transaction must also be passed on to all affected application modules, i.e., "posted through."

It is only the seamless, interface-free connection of individual functions—such as logistics, accounting, or sales—into a complete system that constitutes integrated standard software. All system components access commonly used databases. In contrast, "integration" of different modules via batch interfaces merely supplies data to individual components and cannot be considered true integration. "Batch programs" run without user intervention. Another, somewhat outdated, term for this is "batch processing." In contrast, dialog programs require user interaction, such as entering customer data on the screen. Data needed by non-integrated programs for different purposes is exchanged via interface programs. When data volumes are high, this is often implemented using batch programs. This is the case, for example, when transferring customer master records from a sales system to a financial accounting system.

The decisive factor is whether process chains can be mapped across all modules of the standard software. For example, order processing must be implemented in the standard software system in accordance with the actual processing flow through sales, logistics, production, and shipping functions, and must be executed seamlessly without media discontinuities. In the background, administrative functions such as accounting and controlling must be supplied with the necessary information.

The process overview of the primary procurement process in Fig. 6.9 illustrates how, starting from purchase requisitions (BANF) in logistics, commitment data is updated in controlling (e.g., on an order or a cost center). Purchase requisitions are requests to procurement to acquire specific materials or services. They can be created, for example, by the originator of the requirement (e.g., the head of a cost center) in the materials management module. A commitment refers to obligations arising from contracts or planning decisions that have not yet been recorded in accounting. A purchase commitment is triggered by the purchase order in procurement. The goods receipt results in preliminary actual values in controlling reports, which are later replaced by the "actuals" upon invoice receipt. The goods receipt is posted to material accounts in the general ledger as part of the secondary finance process. The invoice receipt is posted via the invoice verification function of the materials management module to the accounts payable subledger and, using simultaneous posting, to the general ledger.

Figure 6.10 shows the core sales process, which acts as a data provider for the involved cross-functional processes. Order entry in the sales module triggers the credit limit check in accounts receivable. At the same time, the relevant controlling objects (e.g., order) are updated and included in forecast analyses in the sales controlling module. Posting the goods issue in sales, in turn, triggers invoicing. When integrated business standard software is used, this also triggers the posting of the invoice, which is updated

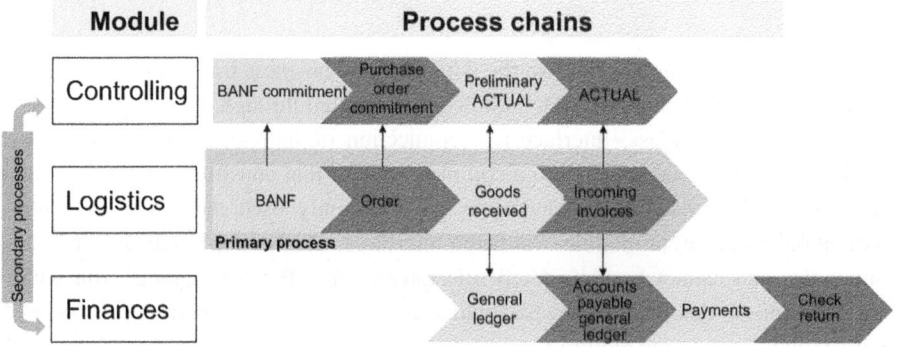

Fig. 6.9 Process integration using the example of procurement logistics

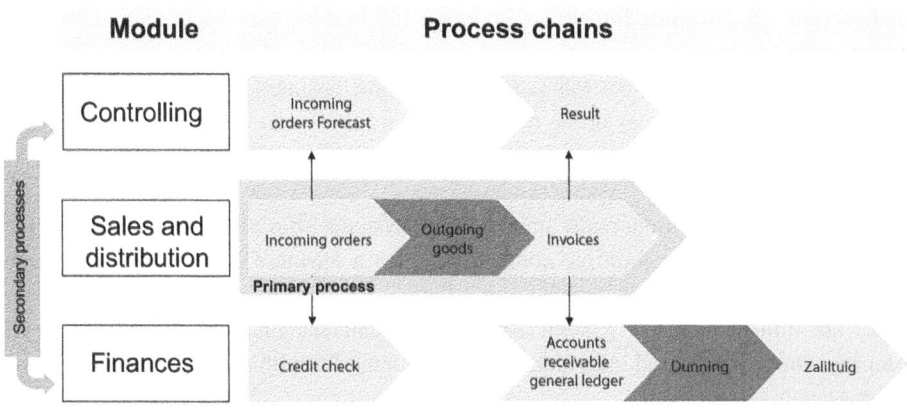

Fig. 6.10 Process integration using the example of sales logistics

in the accounts receivable subledger and, via simultaneous posting, in the general ledger. Depending on customer behavior, dunning or payment processing in finance follows. For simplicity, the process overview omits consideration of payment-relevant transactions as part of financial disposition (treasury).

Operational Functionality ERP systems support functions necessary for the operational processing of a company's routine business transactions. Examples include recording orders, processing sales orders, payroll, and so on. This distinguishes them from management information systems, which are used to support data analysis, such as customer sales analyses.

Unified Development Concept Individual sub-functions designed independently of one another cannot be integrated into a complete system that meets the above requirements. Integrated standard software systems are therefore based on a unified development concept. In the form of a layered model, a base system is designed at a lower level with overarching "services" required by all sub-functions. In addition, integrated systems employ uniform standards, such as a consistent screen and print output layout, the database systems or database interfaces used, and the use of open interfaces (e.g., TCP/IP).

Layered Architecture ERP systems are not single-user systems, such as a word processing program that is fully installed and used on a single workstation. They support business functions that are typically required by multiple employees in different departments and at various locations. For this reason, a layered architecture is necessary, usually implemented in the form of the client/server principle, with a separation of presentation, processing, and data storage.

Transaction Orientation Supporting operational business transactions requires the modification of data using online transactions. ERP systems are transaction-oriented, meaning they provide a set of transactions to support business processes (e.g., transactions for creating a customer order, recording a purchase order, modifying an employee master record, etc.).

Multi-Tenancy In addition, many standard ERP systems offer multi-tenancy. This refers to the ability to manage multiple companies, from a business perspective, completely independently within a single technical installation. Basic settings that apply to all companies are limited to a few general aspects (e.g., calendar entries). Beyond this, each company can be configured individually and accounted for within the installation.

Selection Criteria for ERP Systems
An ERP system is generally a standard software product developed by the software vendor for a wide range of potential customers, possibly limited to specific industries. The selection of an ERP system is typically a multi-stage and complex preliminary project before the software is implemented (see Section 6.4). It is therefore important to define criteria during the selection process that can be used to narrow down the possible systems.

Table 6.5 lists some possible selection criteria that may be relevant in the context of system selection.

6.3.3   Cost-effectiveness of Standard Software

The introduction of standard software is often associated with expectations that it will maintain and secure the company's competitiveness. In addition, it is generally assumed that costs will be lower than with custom software. However, apart from the acquisition costs of the standard software, other types of costs become significantly more important during the implementation of standard software.

Cost-effectiveness of Standard Software Using the Example of SAP ERP® (see Buxmann and König 2000)

Due to the high demand for product-specific expertise, the implementation of SAP® systems is usually associated with the use of external consultants. Consultants are typically involved in all project phases, especially in the business process reengineering that often accompanies SAP® implementation, but above all in system customization, user training, the realization of extensions (particularly in-house developments), and very often over extended periods in supporting the productive system after go-live. As a result, as the above empirical study shows, consulting costs are the primary cost category associated with the implementation of SAP® systems.

Tab. 6.5   Selection criteria for ERP systems (adapted from Scopevisio AG 2025)

Vendor reliability	The vendor should be familiar with the customer's requirements and be able to provide references. This may differ between large corporations and medium-sized enterprises.
Functionality	The ERP system must be able to support the company's processes. This can be challenging with legacy systems that have been in use for a long time, especially if there are many individual processes or process variants that are not common in the industry. The degree of coverage should be as high as possible.
Scalability	If the company grows, the software must be able to "grow" as well. This means accommodating more users (licenses), data, and processes or process variants. The system should also be able to cover affiliated companies both domestically and internationally.
Flexibility and interfaces	ERP systems require and generate data. This necessitates direct communication with other systems. This should be possible via standard interfaces with little (or no) programming effort. Changes in the company's processes should also be reflected in the ERP system with minimal effort.
User-friendliness and mobility	Today, users expect modern, intuitive user interfaces. Ease of use is a key success factor for the long-term use and acceptance of the system within the company. This also includes the integration of mobile devices into processes (especially smartphones and tablets).
Support services	ERP systems require ongoing support from the vendor, as processes are constantly evolving. 24/7 hotlines, training, and consulting services must complement the software product.

[Table footer – please overwrite]

- Costs for external consultants,
- Costs for the acquisition or expansion of hardware and system software,
- Costs for assigning internal staff to the implementation project,
- Acquisition and maintenance costs for the standard software,
- Costs for training measures.

Despite the considerable costs, the success of the SAP® system demonstrates that the effort is offset by significant potential benefits that can justify its use. The main benefit categories are:

- Improved planning, management, and control of business processes,
- A unified and consistent data base,
- Enhanced flexibility in adapting information systems and business processes to changing requirements,

- Shorter lead times for business processes,
- Qualitative improvement of business processes. ◀

Martin et al. (2002) distinguish four categories of benefits from the use of ERP systems:

- Process efficiency (business processes),
- Market efficiency (customer and market orientation),
- Resource efficiency (productivity and cost-effectiveness), and
- Delegation efficiency (efficiency of information acquisition).

They define process efficiency as a company's ability to improve business processes in terms of cost, quality, and time. Examples include reducing order lead times or increasing on-time delivery performance. Market efficiency refers to the improved exploitation of opportunities in sales and procurement markets through coordinated interaction with customers and suppliers. On the procurement side, this can be achieved, for example, by bundling demand, or on the sales side by offering improved products and services. Resource efficiency is the improvement of productivity and cost-effectiveness, i.e., the optimized use of resources such as personnel, equipment, machinery, and capital. Examples include improved capacity utilization, reduced inventory levels, or a reduction in the number of employees required. Delegation efficiency measures the increased utilization of the problem-solving potential of higher-level organizational units. Examples include faster and higher-quality information processing through IT-supported reports and analyses. Access to a single, unified database often enables worldwide analyses for an entire group without the need to merge and consolidate different data sets.

6.4   Implementation Processes for Standard Software

6.4.1   Process Management in the Context of Standard Software Implementation

Projects involving the implementation or update of standard software also impact process management, as workflows must be adapted, may be eliminated, or newly introduced. The implementation or update of standard software often places unfamiliar demands on employees within the affected organizations. In addition to technical and business-related issues, new requirements arise for collaboration among employees both within and between the relevant departments, since integrated software systems do not recognize departmental boundaries. The introduction of business standard software, especially ERP systems, constitutes a major intervention in an organizational system, which cannot be accomplished without conflicts (Maucher 2001, p. 23).

The use of standard software therefore changes the processes within a company. For this reason, the software implementation phase must be planned with particular care, as these changes take effect within a short period of time. Ideally, the company adopts 100% of the software's standard processes, which generally requires significant adaptation by the organization and is rarely achieved in practice (see Fig. 6.11).

However, the typical scenario for ERP system implementation often looks quite different (see Fig. 6.11). Since standard software vendors cannot cover all process variants, there are regularly processes that are not available in the standard software or are represented in the system in a form that is completely different from what the customer desires. Some processes, on the other hand, can at least be supported by the system in a modified form while achieving the same result.

Processes in the standard system that are not currently needed are less critical. They can potentially be used at a later stage. However, the software customer still pays for this functionality without making use of it (see Fig. 6.12).

As a result, for processes that cannot be mapped in the standard system, satisfactory solutions are often not possible, leading to individual extensions, workarounds, or modifications of the standard system (see Fig. 6.13).

According to Heilmann et al. (2003, p. 283), there are three basic scenarios for the introduction of new information systems:

- *Complete replacement of the legacy system* by new application software: In this case, some elements may be standardized, but the new software is predominantly custom-developed.
- *Complete replacement of the legacy system* by standard software: Here, the old system is fully replaced, with no significant proportion of custom development (e.g., full implementation of an ERP system).
- *Porting of the legacy system* to a new technical platform (1:1 migration): In this scenario, no changes to the functional capabilities are intended; rather, the existing application continues to operate in a new system environment. This is therefore a purely technological change (e.g., migrating a system to a private cloud).

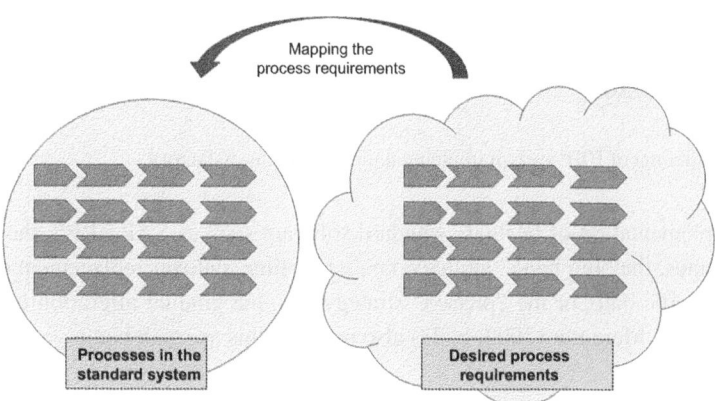

Fig. 6.11 Ideal scenario for the implementation of an ERP system

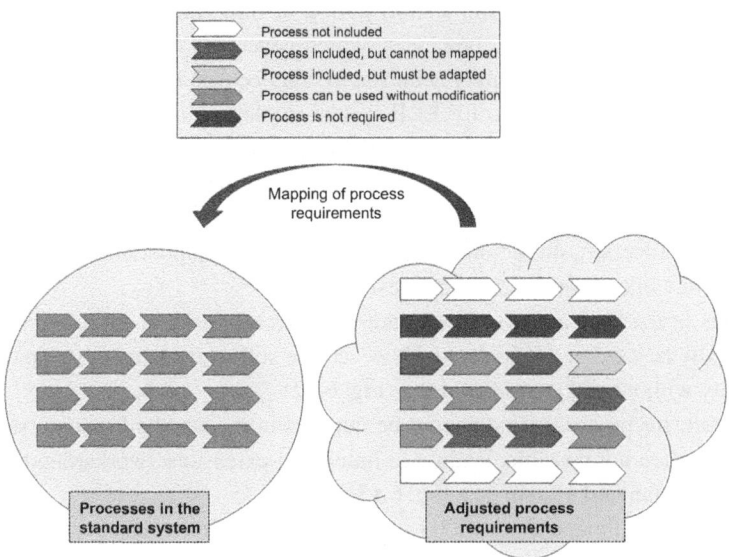

Fig. 6.12 Typical scenario for ERP system implementation

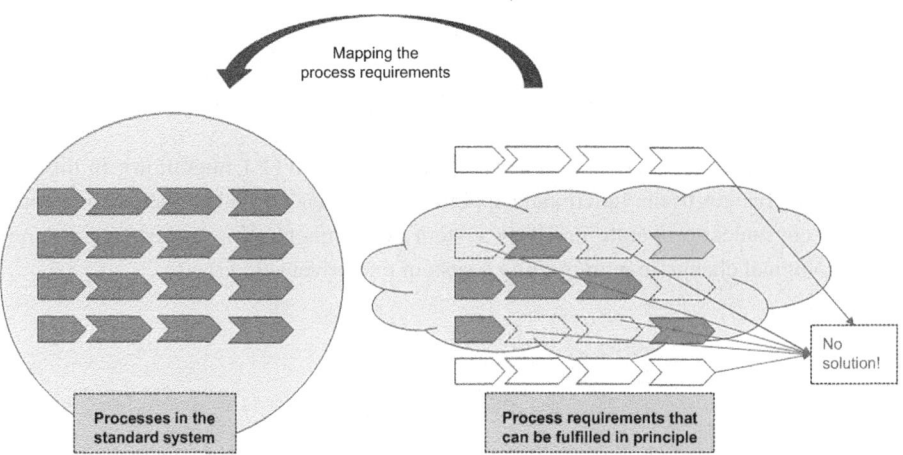

Fig. 6.13 Outcome of ERP system implementation often unsatisfactory

For the implementation of business standard software such as SAP ERP®, there are two basic strategies: the "big bang" strategy, i.e., a one-time, cutover replacement of the system on a specific date, or the "phased" strategy, i.e., the gradual migration of processes to a new system. Mauterer (2002, p. 23) also refers to this as small bangs.

6.4.2   Big Bang

With the big bang approach, it is possible to carry this out for the entire company or, in the case of a decentralized organizational structure, to implement it successively for decentralized units (e.g., countries or regional branches) as a so-called roll-out after defining a master system. For the phased strategy, criteria must be established to define the sequence of steps; typically, a distinction is made between department-based or function-oriented migration and market-oriented or process-based migration of the system.

The big bang strategy is theoretically the optimal solution, as no interface problems arise and an integrated software solution covering the entire process is available from the outset. There are also no transitional issues with duplicate work in the old and new systems, and there is no risk of data inconsistencies, since a strict distinction can be made between old data before the cutover date and new data after the cutover date.

The greatest disadvantage is the extremely high project risk, which, in the event of a total failure of the new system, can threaten the very existence of the company. Practical experience shows that this can indeed occur. To minimize project risks, extensive testing and fallback scenarios are necessary. A big bang places very high demands on project management and requires a concentrated deployment of personnel resources (both business and IT departments, and usually also external consultants) within a very tightly defined timeframe.

6.4.3   Roll-Out

To mitigate the disadvantages of the big bang approach, companies with a decentralized organization (e.g., regionally structured branches, locations in multiple countries) have the option of a roll-out. In this approach, a central master system with common processes is first defined and then gradually rolled out, i.e., distributed to the regional units. If necessary, the rolled-out systems are locally adapted before being put into productive use.

Pursuing a roll-out strategy results in significantly lower risks, as the experiences from the initial projects can be leveraged for subsequent projects, and in the event of problems, only parts of the company (e.g., a single branch) are affected. Resource deployment can also be spread out over time much more effectively.

Unfortunately, a roll-out is not always possible. It requires a decentralized organization with a manageable level of complexity. If the local organizations are so large that even a local big bang cannot be carried out, the stepwise strategy must be adopted instead. Additional disadvantages include the fact that an integrated system is only available after the entire roll-out has been completed, which, depending on the size of the company, can take several years.

6.4.4   Stepwise Function-Oriented Implementation

In many companies, terms such as "accounting system," "warehouse management system," or "sales system" are well known. These terms refer to a functional division of labor and document the function-supporting systems developed for this purpose. In such an architecture, it is quite common to proceed in a "function-oriented" manner during a system change, i.e., the "old" warehouse management system is replaced by a new warehouse management system.

The function-oriented approach gradually replaces individual functions or functional areas (accounting, inventory management, etc.) from the legacy system, for example, with new software, and temporarily connects the two "worlds" via interfaces. For a transitional period, processes are thus supported in parallel by both the "old software" and the "new software." Compared to big bang strategies, the advantage is the shorter duration of individual projects, as the overall project can be divided into several independent subprojects. The subprojects are easier to manage, thereby reducing the overall project risk.

On the other hand, disadvantages arise due to the interface problem. The effort required to implement the interfaces is enormous. For the transition period, which can last several years, there is no integrated overall system available. Where interfaces are not (or cannot be) implemented, affected employees face a high manual workload. There is also a risk of inconsistencies due to data redundancies, since both the "old world" and the new ERP system need to be supplied with data.

6.4.5   Stepwise Process-Oriented Implementation

Since the 1990s, process orientation has established itself as a paradigm for organizational design and has become standard practice in many companies. As an alternative to the traditional function-based approach to implementing standard software, a strategy aligned with this paradigm can be adopted. The individual steps of the migration are carried out based on market-oriented considerations. This means that individual process chains are completely separated from the legacy system and immediately supported end-to-end by the new ERP system. Typically, primary processes are converted step by step, while cross-functional processes (accounting/payroll) are planned en bloc at the beginning or end of the project. A prerequisite for this approach is that the individual processes can also be organizationally separated and operated independently.

In principle, this approach offers the same advantages as the function-oriented implementation of standard software. However, the project risk is significantly lower, as the subprocesses are autonomous and the sequence of subprojects can be managed according to the risk for the company. For example, less critical processes can be converted first. Later, once experience has been gained and the project team is "up to speed," other processes can follow. As a rule, it is advisable to first convert the replacement business and then the new business. This ensures that experience is gained not with the core business—selling new products—but with the downstream spare parts business.

The effort required for project execution is also lower, as fewer interfaces need to be maintained due to the end-to-end process support. Typically, interfaces to cross-functional processes such as accounting and payroll, and possibly shared master data (e.g., material master, customer master), still arise. In addition, the interfaces remain more stable during the system transition than in the function-oriented approach.

The disadvantages of the function-oriented transition generally also apply here. Beyond that, there are no further negative aspects, except for some redundancies in master data management that may have to be accepted.

6.4.6 Strategic Portfolio

The strategic portfolio in Fig. 6.14 classifies the presented courses of action according to the particularly important decision criteria "project risk" and "effort" in a portfolio representation. Here, the effort required for the implementation and dismantling of interfaces is emphasized, as it represents the most significant distinguishing feature.

When the key aspects are compared, there are many advantages in favor of the stepwise process-oriented approach, with hardly any disadvantages that are significant for the company's existence. In principle, a case-by-case assessment of the decision basis is required, as a variety of prerequisites must be met and exogenous decision parameters, such as time pressure, corporate policy requirements, and others, must also be taken into account.

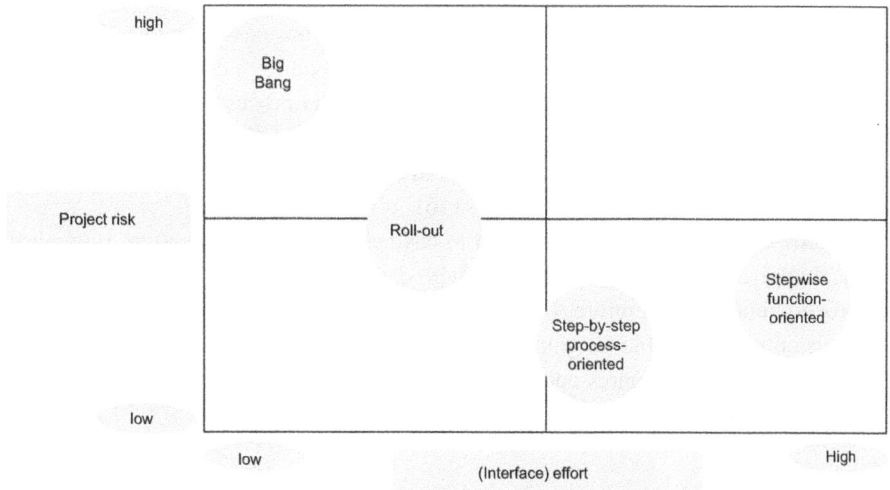

Fig. 6.14 Strategies for the Implementation of Standard Software

6.4.7   Practical Example: SAP S/4 HANA

The provider of ERP systems for medium-sized and large enterprises, SAP SE, offers its product "SAP S/4 HANA" in three operating models (see Brugger et al. 2021, p. 107):

- On-Premise Version: (installation at the customer's site, maximum range of functions, source code customization possible),
- Cloud Version: (installation, operation, and maintenance in SAP's public cloud, reduced range of functions, standard processes only),
- Hybrid Version: (installation on a private cloud with dedicated hardware, infrastructure as a service provided by SAP).

With the on-premise version, the customer acquires a software license and operates the software on the company's own hardware under its own responsibility. Maintenance and administration are carried out and managed by the company's own staff (see Brugger et al. 2021, p. 108). The customer retains full control over the type and extent of use of data, applications, and processes. In the cloud version, only standard processes can be configured and used, and release cycles are scheduled periodically (see Brugger et al. 2021, p. 109). While the customer can focus on using the software, they must accept a reduced range of functions and have less freedom in decision-making compared to the on-premise version. The advantage of the hybrid version for the customer is that, unlike the cloud version, they do not have to share hardware resources with other companies and have greater control over usage.

For implementation, a radical approach (greenfield) or a moderate, step-by-step approach (brownfield) is recommended, depending on the company's interests (see Brugger et al. 2021, pp. 114–116 for details).

The radical greenfield approach can be described as business reengineering, involving a complete reimplementation of the system, which requires a comprehensive requirements and process analysis. The company must align its processes with SAP standard processes. This is also a prerequisite for using the public cloud version to fully leverage the capabilities of SAP S/4 HANA. Existing structures and processes usually need to be changed (see Brugger et al. 2021, pp. 114–116).

The brownfield approach is more akin to business process optimization. It involves a technical upgrade of existing components with database migration, requiring only selective process analysis. Therefore, only partial adaptation of business processes is necessary. This option is suitable for companies that do not wish to use a cloud-based version. As a result, existing structures and processes can largely be retained (see Brugger et al. 2021, pp. 114–116).

6.5   Impact of Current Technologies on Process Management

6.5.1   Digitalization

Currently, the term "digitalization"—that is, the electronic planning, control, and execution of business processes—is the subject of numerous discussions. However, the term cannot be considered in isolation from trends such as "Big Data," "Cloud Computing," "Industry 4.0" or "Internet of Things," and the "Social Web," as these topics are highly interconnected (see Fig. 6.15).

Digitalization and the associated technologies offer significant growth potential if management is willing to invest in innovative new business models and processes (see Gadatsch 2016, p. 63). The long-standing trend of process digitalization continues to accelerate and is reaching application areas that were previously unimaginable. For example, Werth, Greff, and Scheer outline a digitalized consulting process under the label "Consulting 4.0," which, unlike today—where digitalization in many consulting firms ends with the contact form—encompasses the entire consulting process from problem identification, analysis, and problem-solving to implementation (see Werth et al. 2016).

Homo Digitalis
Digitalization affects not only workflows within companies but also people themselves. The futurist Markowetz refers to the "Homo Digitalis," a new generation of people who can no longer manage their daily lives without digital connectivity (see Markowetz 2015, p. 15). They are permanently connected to the internet and base their actions on the rec-

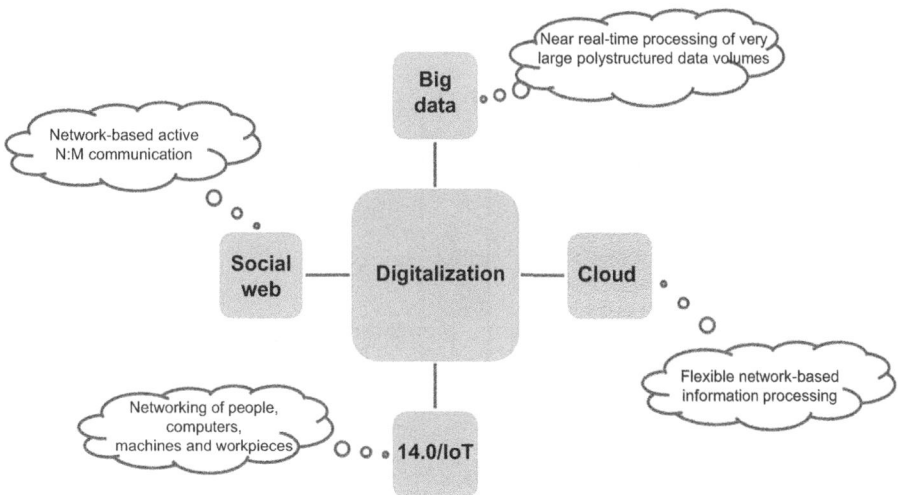

Fig. 6.15 IT Megatrends

ommendations of digital assistants. This aspect will have a lasting impact on the business processes of the future.

Impacts on Human Labor

The adoption of new technologies coincides with a drastic paradigm shift in the world of work (see Fig. 6.16). Many companies no longer view profit maximization as their sole corporate purpose, but instead seek more sustainable corporate visions. Hierarchies as a management tool have, in many cases, already become obsolete and are being replaced by network-oriented structures that emphasize teamwork. Mutual knowledge transfer is replacing centralized, control-oriented leadership behavior. The previously mentioned agile methods are supplanting planning-oriented management approaches and subordinate levels (such as process management). Transparency is replacing discretion, aiming to overcome the long-standing silo mentality within organizations, as discussed here.

Digitalization is leading to a changed set of requirements for the workforce (see Fig. 6.16). The demand for highly qualified employees is rising, while those with lower qualifications need to be upskilled. This also applies to professions that are not generally considered low-skilled, but are largely rule-based. Digital tools make it possible to replicate and automate rule-based work and the associated processes (see Fig. 6.17).

Impacts on Selected Professions (Case Study: Tax Advisors, Auditors)

Many tax advisory and auditing firms are likely unprepared for this scenario: The (future) world's largest provider of auditing and tax advisory services may not own any offices, employ any tax advisors or auditors, and may operate exclusively digitally on a platform-based model similar to those of Uber, Airbnb, or Facebook.

For tax advisors, activities such as "bookkeeping," "preparing financial statements and annual accounts," and "preparing and reviewing tax returns" are likely to be among the losers, meaning these tasks will be carried out more or less digitally by robotic soft-

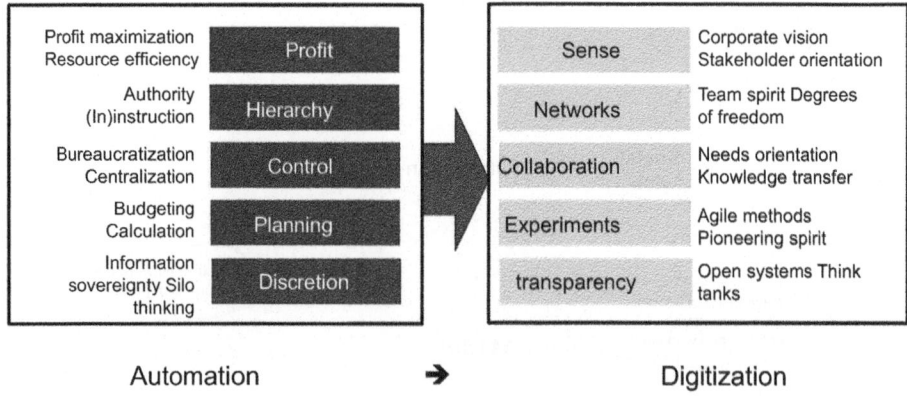

Fig. 6.16 Paradigm shift in the world of work

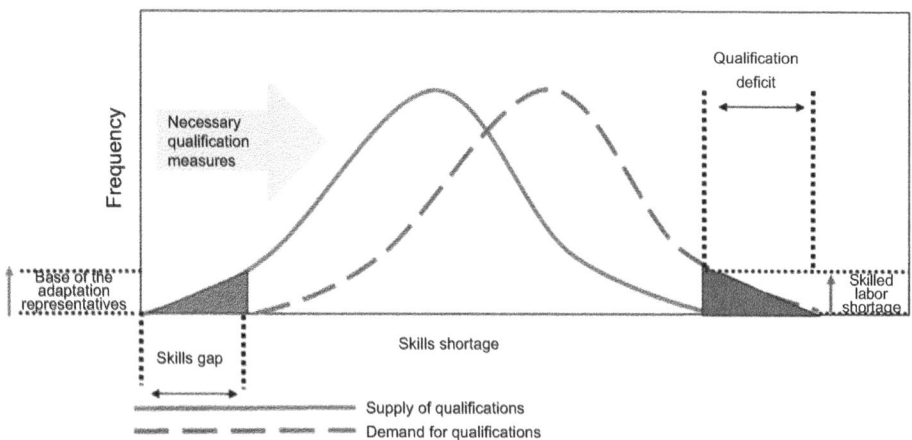

Fig. 6.17 Impacts of digitalization on human labor

ware. Activities such as tax declaration consulting and tax planning consulting are less rule-based and therefore less affected by digitalization (see Fig. 6.18).

The situation is similar for auditors, though it is not as critical. The proportion of consulting activities is higher here than in tax advisory professions, making them less susceptible to replacement by robots and similar technologies. Nevertheless, a number of rule-based tasks, such as traditional audit procedures, are threatened by digitalization (see Fig. 6.19). Consulting and expert activities, as well as fiduciary management, can be supported by systems but will not disappear.

Impacts on Selected Processes (Here: Controlling Processes)
In simple terms, controlling means planning, management, and monitoring. This activity requires comprehensive methodological expertise. Below are some exemplary cases from

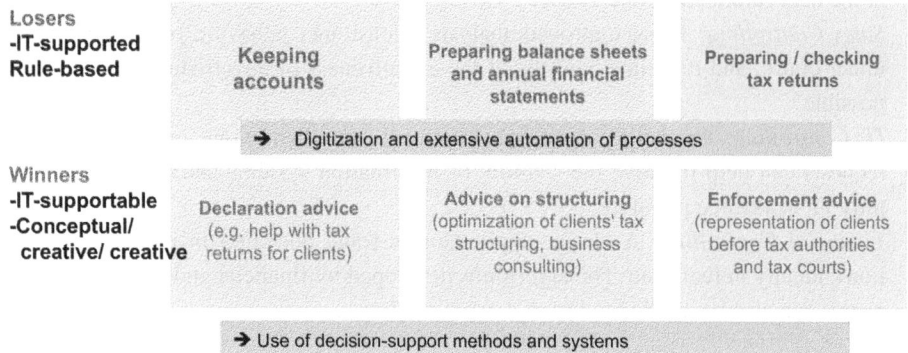

Fig. 6.18 Impacts of new technologies on the profession of "tax advisor"

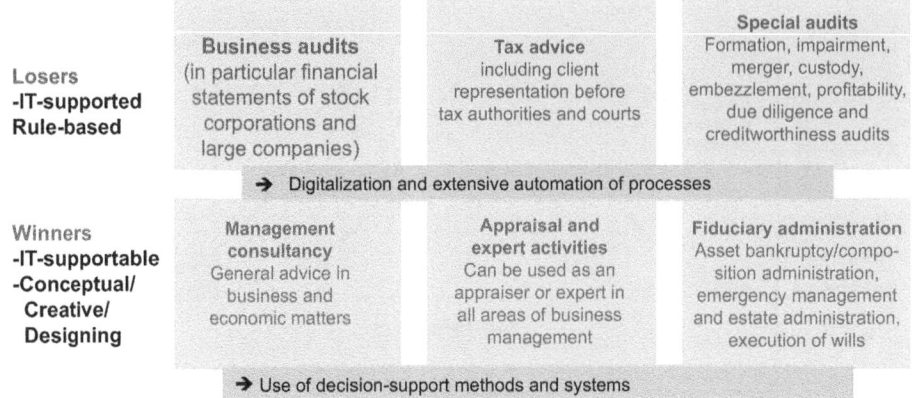

Fig. 6.19 Impacts of new technologies on the profession of "auditor"

the field of controlling, illustrating that there is still potential to leverage new technologies for support (taken and adapted from Gadatsch 2016, p. 65).

- *Public Financial Controlling:* The US state of North Carolina was able to use Big Data to combat billing fraud and identify suspicious claims amounting to 200 million US dollars.
- *Public Customer Controlling:* In France, a city analyzes social media posts to identify and prioritize the needs of its citizens.
- *Production Controlling:* The analysis of machine components during ongoing operations enables the creation of dynamic preventive maintenance plans.
- *Production Controlling:* Numerous solutions have already been implemented in practice in this sector. The software provider "Blue Yonder" reports on a predictive maintenance solution. Their software can use systematically analyzed machine data to detect early on which systems worldwide are likely to experience technical problems in the near future (see Blue Yonder 2015).
- *Sales Controlling:* Here, improved analysis of customer behavior, prediction of customer churn, and real-time analysis of the effectiveness of advertising campaigns are possible.
- *IT Controlling:* Predicting operational failures and disruptions or surges in user requests can help improve the stability of information systems and, as a result, simplify IT workforce planning.
- *Financial Controlling:* A classic application is fraud detection in payment transactions, ideally in real time. The algorithms developed by financial and credit card companies can also be applied to internal payment flows.

- *HR Controlling:* The shortage of well-trained specialists can be mitigated by early detection of employees who are considering leaving, provided that timely counter-measures can be taken.

6.5.2   Big Data

Interest in Big Data is steadily increasing (see Google Trends 2015). Initially, the focus was primarily on technical aspects such as storage technologies (e.g., *in-memory*) and database types (e.g., *NoSQL databases*). In the meantime, business use cases such as the development of new strategies and business models as well as the optimization of business processes are being discussed.

Origin of the Term
The origin of the term cannot be clearly determined (see Klein et al. 2013). In principle, Big Data can be seen as a natural evolution in the analysis and use of data. Over the past 30 years, terms such as "Decision Support," "Executive Support," "Online Analytical Processing," and "Business Intelligence and Analytics" have been used for this purpose. Since around 2010, the term Big Data has been increasingly adopted. The so-called "three Vs"—volume, velocity, and variety—coined by the analyst and consulting firm Gartner, are often referenced to describe it. Big Data is characterized by high data volume, enormous processing speeds (data velocity), and the diversity of data types that can be processed (data variety). These characteristics were later expanded to include value and validity (see Bachmann et al. 2014, p. 23). Other authors have also added the aspect of veracity (see Beyer and Laney 2012).

Definition of Big Data
One of the earliest definitions comes from Doug Laney, who defined Big Data in 2001 as "data sets that are larger than what you are used to" (see Beyer and Laney 2012). The approach of using polystructured data makes it clear that not only structured data from ERP systems and other sources are used, but also semi-structured or unstructured data such as videos, images, or free text (see Fig. 6.20).

A practical and management-oriented definition comes from BITKOM: "Big Data is the economically meaningful extraction and use of decision-relevant insights from qualitatively diverse and differently structured information that is subject to rapid change and arises in previously unknown volumes" (BITKOM 2012, p. 7). This explanation highlights not only the technical background but also focuses on the business aspect underlying Big Data. The aim is to use new tools for both strategic and operational business. Big Data provides tools that support business-critical applications such as sales management or production monitoring and enable the development of new business models based on available data. Since not all data can be analyzed, it is important for controlling to focus

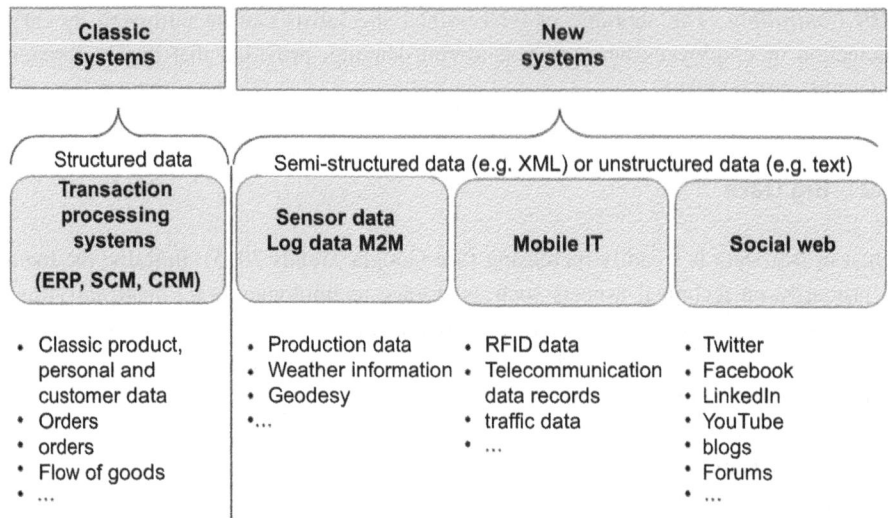

Fig. 6.20 Big Data Data Sources

on the most relevant information. Visualization tools have created new possibilities in this area.

Many companies primarily use Big Data technologies to accelerate established business processes such as reporting, customer analysis, or behavioral analysis. However, Big Data offers significantly greater growth potential if management is willing to invest in innovative new business models and processes.

6.5.3 Cloud Computing

Definition of Terms

One of the more recent terms in IT practice is cloud computing. Even among professionals, cloud computing is often associated with the offerings of major "hyperscalers" such as Amazon Web Services (AWS) or Google. Unfortunately, the various forms of cloud computing are often presented in a highly simplified manner, so that one might superficially say that cloud computing is the use of IT resources via the Internet.

At its core, cloud computing refers to different "sourcing options" for the use or procurement of IT services (see Brassel and Gadatsch 2019 for a detailed discussion). Cloud computing stands for the use of virtualized hardware.

Figure 6.21 shows five levels of possible options for the provision of IT services. In practice, there is also a wide variety of other variants. The following variants can therefore be distinguished.

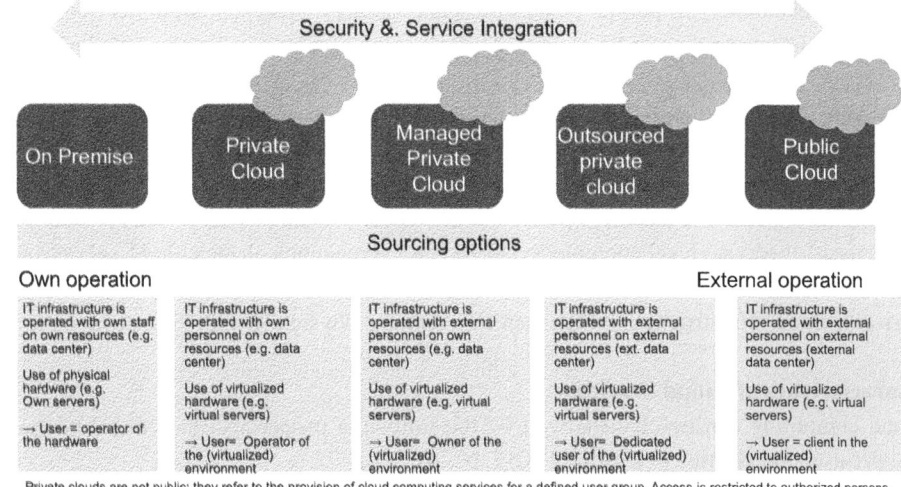

Private clouds are not public; they refer to the provision of cloud computing services for a defined user group. Access is restricted to authorized persons and usually takes place via an intranet or VPN. Managed Private Cloud' is operated by a service provider on the customer's premises on the basis of SLAs. With the outsourced private cloud, the service provider builds or takes over a cloud infrastructure which then remains physically with them.

Fig. 6.21 Cloud sourcing options (adapted from Münzl et al. 2009 and Brassel and Gadatsch 2019)

- **On Premise:** The IT infrastructure is operated with *internal* staff on *internal* resources (e.g., in a data center). Usage is based on dedicated physical hardware (e.g., servers). The software user is also the operator of the hardware.
- **Private Cloud:** The IT infrastructure is (also) operated with *internal* staff on *internal* resources (e.g., in a data center). However, "virtualized" hardware (e.g., servers) is used. The software user is also the operator of the (virtualized) hardware.
- **Managed Private Cloud:** The IT infrastructure is operated with *external* staff on internal resources (e.g., in a data center). As with the private cloud, only "virtualized" hardware (e.g., servers) is used. The software user is now only the owner of the (virtualized) hardware, but no longer the operator. The managed private cloud is therefore a private cloud operated externally.
- **Outsourced Private Cloud:** The IT infrastructure is operated with *external* staff on *external* resources (e.g., in a data center). Again, only "virtualized" hardware (e.g., servers) is used. The software user is now neither the owner nor the operator of the (virtualized) hardware. They are "merely" a dedicated user of a virtualized environment.
- **Public Cloud:** The IT infrastructure is operated with *external* staff on *external* resources (e.g., in a data center). Again, only "virtualized" hardware (e.g., servers) is used. The software user is now a "tenant" in a (virtualized) highly standardized environment.

Typical examples of public cloud offerings include "Amazon Web Services" or Microsoft's Office services (Office 365). The following aspects can also be added:

- **Private clouds** are not public; they refer to the provision of cloud computing services for a defined user group. Access is restricted to authorized individuals and is usually provided via an intranet or VPN.
- **'Managed Private Cloud'** is operated at the customer's site by a service provider on the basis of service level agreements (SLAs, i.e., agreements on specific IT services).
- In the case of the **'Outsourced Private Cloud'**, the service provider builds or takes over a cloud infrastructure, which then also remains physically with the provider.

Characteristics of Cloud Services

Cloud computing can be characterized by the following properties: on-demand access, pay-per-use, and elasticity (see Biebl 2012, p. 24).

- **On-demand access:** The user can automatically "book and cancel" IT resources. Provisioning and termination of services occur without direct interaction and within a very short time.
- **Pay-per-use:** IT services are billed according to usage. There are generally no fixed costs, or only comparatively low ones. Common billing units include, for example, data transfer volume or data storage volume. The user can independently verify the basis for billing.
- **Elasticity:** The user can access seemingly unlimited resources. Services are provisioned in the shortest possible time. This is of interest in the case of short-term demand spikes, when large volumes of data need to be analyzed in a short period.

Cloud computing thus differs from traditional outsourcing models, which are characterized by static arrangements. Traditional outsourcing models require lengthy contract negotiations, have longer durations, and are difficult for companies to reverse, often resulting in an undesirable dependency on the IT service provider.

Technical Perspective

Cloud computing is typically considered on four hierarchical levels: "Human as a Service," "Software as a Service," "Platform as a Service," and "Infrastructure as a Service."

The lowest level, **"Infrastructure as a Service"**, provides access to virtual hardware. Typical examples include Amazon's services for provisioning virtual servers ("Elastic Compute Cloud") or Google's provision of mass storage ("Cloud Storage"). These services relieve customers from operating their own data centers with the necessary security infrastructure.

The next layer up is primarily aimed at software developers. **"Platform as a Service"** provides developers with complete development environments. An example of this is Microsoft's "Azure," a platform for building cloud applications.

The layer most familiar to end users is **"Software as a Service"**. This refers to applications primarily targeted at end users, whether private or business. The number of possible examples is extremely large. Typical applications include email services (web.de), search engines (Google), office solutions (Microsoft 365), or comprehensive enterprise resource planning systems (SAP Business ByDesign).

The top layer, **"Human as a Service"**, is less well known from the user's perspective and represents a crowdsourcing approach. It uses cloud solutions to delegate tasks to human resources. A typical example is Amazon's "Mechanical Turk" service, which allows microtasks to be distributed to and monitored by a large number of "crowdworkers." More recent examples include "transportation services with private cars" and "food and beverage deliveries by bicycle couriers."

Simplified Organizational Forms

As mentioned above, the organization of cloud services is usually described in simplified terms using the categories "Private Cloud," "Community Cloud," "Public Cloud," and "Hybrid Cloud" (see Fig. 6.22).

In a "Private Cloud," the provider (e.g., internal IT department) and the users (business units within the company) belong to the same user organization (in the example in Figure 2, to the "user organization"). The main motivation for this concept is security: control over the data remains entirely with the user. However, a private cloud requires extremely high investments in hardware, software, and personnel.

The "Community Cloud" enables the provision of standardized services for user organizations with similar requirements regarding security, compliance, or functionality. Operation can be handled by one or more user organizations, an external organization,

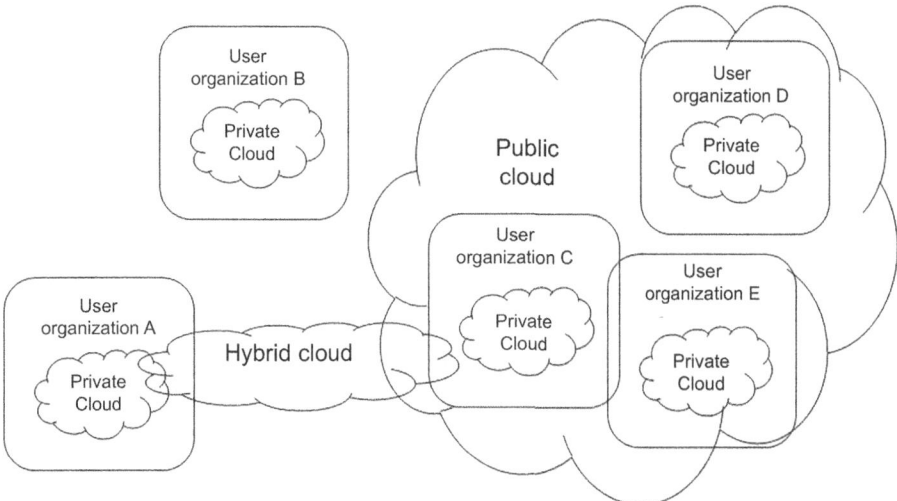

Fig. 6.22 Cloud organization (adapted from Baun et al. 2010, p. 26)

or any combination thereof. Such a solution may be of particular interest to highly regulated industries such as financial services or healthcare, but also to the public sector.

The "Public Cloud" is the standard case for cloud computing. Providers and users belong to different user organizations. Access to the cloud is often via an internet-based portal. Usage requires a contract between the parties, which is often concluded easily online.

Hybrid clouds refer to any combination of these forms. A typical use case is the provision of resources for peak loads by a provider from the external public cloud. In business intelligence (BI), for example, reporting content is sourced from both internal ("Private Cloud") and external ("Public Cloud") sources and made at least partially accessible to external users (Seufert and Bernhardt 2010).

The increasing use of cloud services has consequences for companies that are difficult to assess, since any employee can become active without involving the IT department, provided they have internet access and, for paid services, the necessary funds. The proportion of companies that have outsourced at least significant parts of their applications to the "cloud" has risen dramatically (see Chow et al. 2009).

This trend toward "shadow IT" has already led to changes. Whereas the CIO was previously primarily responsible for supporting users, their role is shifting toward advisory, strategic, and regulatory activities, collectively referred to as IT governance (see Bremmer 2014).

Cloud Portfolio for Decision Makers

Companies are often faced with the question of finding an appropriate solution for a given use case. The portfolio shown in Fig. 6.23 can be used for this purpose. Relevant processes can be classified according to the criteria "requirements for service integration" and "requirements for data autonomy." Requirements for service integration include aspects such as flexibility, on-demand access, pay-as-you-use models, and elasticity or scalability. Requirements for data autonomy concern issues such as the ability to access one's own IT staff and, above all, control over who does what with the data and when. Accordingly, the five sourcing options from Fig. 6.21 can be classified (see Fig. 6.23). An important aspect of outsourcing or cloud computing is that activities shift from internal to external, and increased attention must be paid to managing interfaces with the provider. Otherwise, there is a risk of greater vulnerability in the process chain (Kühl 2015, p. 116).

6.5.4   Industry 4.0/Internet of Things

The term "Industry 4.0" is closely linked to the "Internet of Things." This refers to networked resources (machines, devices, buildings, etc.), people, and intelligent objects that are aware of their status, usage, and history. In a smart factory, all objects are merged

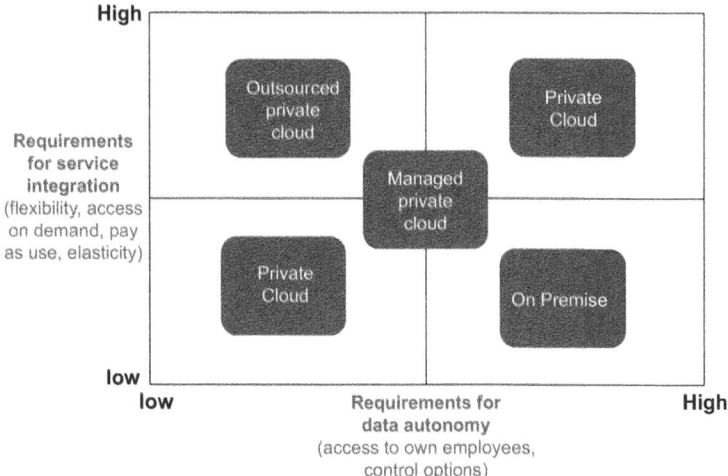

Fig. 6.23 Cloud portfolio for decision makers

into cyber-physical systems (CPS), which execute production processes flexibly (see Arbeitskreis Industrie 4.0 2013).

The trending topic of "Industry 4.0" or "Internet of Things" is driving extensive activities not only in industry but also at the governmental level, with the German federal government taking supportive measures to strengthen Germany as a business location. The Federal Ministry for Economic Affairs and Energy has commissioned studies by external specialists to explore the potential of Industry 4.0 applications for small and medium-sized enterprises (SMEs) and is establishing "SME 4.0 Competence Centers" to support SMEs in the adoption and use of Industry 4.0. The task of these centers is to translate actionable knowledge about the application of Industry 4.0 in business processes "into the language of SMEs." The aim is to encourage SME management, which is often family-run, to initiate transformation within their companies.

Despite the current intense discussion, the maturity level of Industry 4.0 remains rather modest. The technologies discussed in the context of Industry 4.0, such as augmented reality, machine-to-machine communication, virtual reality, and enterprise 3D printing, will in some cases only reach the necessary level of maturity for productive use in regular operations in about 10 years (see Siepmann and Roth 2016, p. 251).

6.5.5   Artificial Intelligence (AI)

The use of artificial intelligence (AI) has dominated discussions in nearly all areas of society for several years. In the context of process management, it can be stated that the use of AI will become the standard in the coming years, as companies that leverage AI for process management will have an advantage over those that do not.

Defining the term AI is not straightforward, as there are numerous definitions. Legg and Hunter (2007) list more than 70 different definitions of AI.

▶ **Definition "Artificial Intelligence"**

One possible definition is: "Artificial intelligence refers to the ability of a machine to perform cognitive tasks that we associate with the human mind. This includes capabilities such as perception, as well as the ability to reason, to learn independently, and thus to autonomously find solutions to problems." (Löchner 2024).

Accordingly, three types of evaluations can generally be used: description (depiction of the "as-is"), prediction (forecast of the "will be"), and prescription (recommendation of the "what"). Overall, the use of AI represents an interdisciplinary interplay of numerous formal and mathematical-statistical methods (Köhler 2021). There are now a large number of possible applications for AI in process management, some of which are outlined in Table 6.6.

In the context of applied research, initial prototypes have been developed for the use of chatbots to create BPMN models (Ziche 2024).

Some modeling tool vendors already offer tools for language-based modeling. For example, the company GBTEC in Vienna has introduced its "Arty Tool" as part of its modeling suite, which generates a BPMN model based on text (e.g., from an interview). The automatically generated model is intended to represent a "60% use case" that still requires manual refinement (Pommerin 2024).

Tab. 6.6 Application areas for AI in process management

Application Area	Technology	Examples
Process Documentation	Process Mining Speech Mining	Creation of as-is process models from log files or conversation transcripts Creation of accessible documents (translation of BPMN diagrams into readable text)
Process Analysis	Process Mining	Bottleneck analysis or benchmarking of processes
Process Redesign	Generative AI Speech Mining	Generation of proposals for target processes as a starting point for further refinement
Process Execution	RPA Bot	Rule-based processing of routine processes, error handling in processes
Process Controlling	Generative AI	Deviation analysis and development of counter-measures

[Table footer – please overwrite]

6.6   Review Questions and Exercises

6.6.1   Questions and Answers

Questions
1. Explain the **difference between graphics programs and specialized modeling tools**
2. What are key considerations to keep in mind when **selecting a modeling tool**?
3. Describe the **core functionality of a workflow management system**
4. Explain the **concept of an ERP system** and name some areas within a company that are typically supported by ERP systems.
5. Justify the necessity of **using reference process models** for the implementation of standard software.
6. How do **new trends,** such as digitalization or the use of AI, impact process management?

Answers
1. **Graphics programs** provide options for graphical modeling of processes, which are stored statically in files. Automated analysis or simulation is not possible. **Modeling tools** offer, in some cases, powerful features for modeling and analyzing processes. Cloud-based databases support collaborative work with extensive features that can be utilized within process management.
2. When **selecting a modeling tool**, the supported modeling methods (e.g., BPMN) are of primary importance. Additionally, questions of usability (cloud usage, collaborative work, versioning, and more) as well as licensing (group license, single license, etc.) need to be addressed.
3. A **workflow management system** controls business processes across departmental and information system boundaries. Processes are implemented as mostly graphical process models and are operationally managed by a workflow engine. Most systems offer **real-time process monitoring** and numerous options for **analyzing executed processes retrospectively.**
4. **ERP systems** are used to **support the core processes of a company.** They have a long tradition, dating back more than 40 years. In principle, they support processes in finance and accounting, controlling, human resources, as well as core processes in sales, production, warehousing, and shipping. Their implementation generally requires little to no programming effort. Adaptation to specific requirements is carried out through system customizing.
5. **Reference process models** graphically represent the **standard processes of the system.** They serve as a "blueprint" for adapting to the needs of the company during customizing. Process steps can thus be omitted, modified, or extended within the capabilities of the software.

6. **Process management** encompasses **people** and **systems.Digitalization** and the **use of AI** are aspects that are increasingly being considered in process design. Many processes today are already partially or fully digitalized. Purely manual processes play hardly any role in business life. This trend will continue. Rapidly evolving AI tools will find their way into nearly all areas of process management, from strategy development to process documentation and analysis, as well as to the target design and implementation of processes.

6.6.2   Case Study

The case study examines a plant engineering company with approximately 1,400 employees. About 75% of them work at the company headquarters in Germany. The remaining staff are employed worldwide in regional warehouses, sales offices, and branches. The annual turnover amounts to EUR 640 million.

SITUATION DESCRIPTION

The central Organization and IT department is responsible for organizational and IT planning, the data center, application development, and PC user support, and reports to the CFO.

PC user support is provided by an external service provider. For the implementation of the company's largest current IT project, "Introduction of a Standard Business Software," a major software company with relevant experience in such projects was commissioned. The company is introducing a complex standard business software solution.

The project budget, excluding the cost of new hardware, is approximately EUR 2 million. Up to now, the company has used largely self-developed software, which no longer meets its growing requirements.

The legacy system has seen little further development in recent years due to cost considerations. The aim of the project is the complete replacement of the legacy system and the most comprehensive possible use of the standard software. A software company was commissioned to carry out the implementation project, as the company itself lacks the necessary expertise. As part of the project, in-house staff are to be trained so that they can independently maintain and further develop the standard software in the future. The project was divided into five functionally defined subprojects, aligned with the company's organizational responsibilities: accounting, human resources, logistics and production, sales, and a cross-sectional subproject for technology. The project manager is a member of the IT department with a background in business administration and many years of experience. He reports to the Head of Organization and IT, who also chairs the steering committee. The steering committee includes the heads of the organizational units for accounting, human resources, etc.

After only a few months, the responsible CFO receives serious indications from staff regarding the project's progress, which are briefly outlined in the following sections.

Project Status

The functional specifications for the accounting and human resources subprojects have been largely completed, as the responsible managers were able to agree on the extensive use of the software's standard functions. Due to the high level of integration of the standard software modules, several cross-departmental tasks relating to the logistics and production subproject as well as the sales subproject still need to be addressed. For example, the procurement process passes sequentially through the purchasing, goods receipt, invoice verification, accounts payable, and general ledger departments. Since the overall process must be coordinated, regulations must be established in several functional specifications. The specifications for the logistics and production as well as sales subprojects are incomplete. Key business processes are still under discussion. The reason is that current workflows in these areas differ significantly from the reference processes of the standard software, and no agreement has yet been reached on process restructuring. The heads of the specialist departments insist, in discussions with the software company's consultants, on transferring historically developed workflows into the standard software and, in particular, on maintaining existing organizational responsibilities. The software consultants argue that the company's processes could be addressed within the capabilities of the standard software if there were greater willingness for business reengineering. However, they are not always able to prevail in discussions with the responsible staff of the specialist departments. The technology subproject covers technical tasks in the narrower sense (setup and commissioning of hardware, networking, etc.) as well as the development of an authorization concept. This involves the organizational and technical definition of responsibilities for processes (e.g., Who is authorized to execute the accounts payable payment run? Who may create and modify supplier and customer master records?) and objects (access to individual cost centers, materials, personnel data, etc.) and their technical implementation in system tables. Due to the still incomplete description of the functional concepts, not all authorizations have been defined and implemented so far.

Project Organization

The members of the project team are distributed across several locations. Project meetings are held weekly in various meeting rooms that must be rented individually. There is no central project office. Short-notice meetings with more than four participants are often not feasible due to a lack of suitable meeting rooms. Many staff members from the specialist departments are not released from their regular duties. In the past, this has repeatedly led to scheduling conflicts, with the result that day-to-day business has often taken precedence over project activities. Some consultants from the software company are also involved in other projects for different clients. In particular, in the logistics and production subproject, complaints from specialist department staff about the unavailability of certain consultants are increasing. Some subproject leaders from the specialist departments are not authorized to make binding decisions for the project, as their respective managers have reserved important decisions for themselves. This regularly leads to delays in project work on difficult issues, such as when business processes and organizational rules need to be changed, since the software consultants must convince several staff members from the specialist departments.

TASK DEFINITION

The CFO wishes to obtain an independent assessment of the project situation and commissions an external consultant to develop proposals for improving the situation.

PROPOSED SOLUTION

A fundamental problem of the project is the disregard for the relationship between business reengineering and the use of information technology. The introduction of standard software is generally only successful if the company adapts its processes to the capabilities provided by the standard software. Insisting on traditional solutions increases implementation costs and future maintenance efforts, for example, during a release upgrade.

Modern standard business software typically requires a process-oriented organization, which is clearly not present in this case. The management board should halt the project and initiate a restructuring phase, during which a reorganization aligned with the reference processes of the selected standard software is considered. If the standard software does not cover the core business objectives of the company (production, logistics, and sales), the selection decision may also need to be reconsidered. The functional structure of the project encourages departmental thinking and silo mentalities. This also affects the chosen project organization, which mirrors the company's organizational structure.

Once a concept for process organization is in place (see above), the project organization should be structured not by functional tasks, but by comprehensive process chains (e.g., subprojects for order processing, spare parts business, etc.). Project members must be delegated decision-making authority by the responsible managers (process owners). For the duration of the project, the core team must be provided with a central project office with conference and work rooms. The consultants from the commissioned software company must be available continuously for the duration of the project. The project manager should report to the entire management board, as this is a business-critical project. The steering committee should be reconstituted, depending on the future process organization.

References

Adam, S., Koch, S., Neffgen, F., Riegel, N., Weidenbach, J.: Business Process Management – Marktanalyse 2014, BPM Suites im Test, Fraunhofer IESE, Kaiserslautern (2014)
Allweyer, T.: BPMN-Prozessmodelle und Unternehmensarchitekturen. Untersuchung von Ansätzen zur Methodenintegration und ihrer Umsetzung in aktuellen Modellierungstools, Forschungsbericht, Hochschule Kaiserslautern (2014)

Arbeitskreis Industrie 4.0: Deutschlands Zukunft als Produktionsstandort sichern Umsetzungsempfehlungen für das Zukunftsprojekt Industrie 4.0 Abschlussbericht des Arbeitskreises Industrie 4.0, Frankfurt. http://www.plattform-i40.de (2013). Accessed 26 Febr 2016

Bachmann, R., Kemper, G., Gerzer, T.: Big Data – Fluch oder Segen? Unternehmen im Spiegel gesellschaftlichen Wandels, Heidelberg (2014)

Baumbach, T., Dürr, R., Thieme, J., obach, P., Schuber, I., Hayes, E.: Robotic Process Automation – Robots conquer business processes in back offices, A2016 study conducted by Capgemini Consulting and Capgemini Business Services, S. 13. https://www.capgemini.com/consulting-de/wp-content/uploads/sites/32/2017/08/robotic-process-automation-study.pdf (2016). Accessed 23 June 2019

Baun, C., Kunze, M., Nimis, J., Tai, S.: Cloud-Computing, Berlin (2010)

Beyer, M.A., Laney, D.: The importance of big data. A definition. Stamford, CT. (2012)

Biebl, J.: Wofür steht Cloud-Computing eigentlich? Wirtschaftsinformatik und Management **01**, 22–29 (2012)

BITKOM (eds.): Big Data im Praxiseinsatz – Szenarien, Beispiele, Effekte, Berlin (2012)

Blue Yonder: White Paper Vorausschauende Wartung, Karlsruhe (o. J.)

Brassel, S., Gadatsch, A.: Software-Lizenzmanagement kompakt, Wiesbaden (2019)

Bremmer, M.: BT-Umfrage: Schatten-IT verändert die Rolle des CIO, in: CIO-Magazin, 31.12.2014.   http://www.cio.de/a/schatten-it-veraendert-die-rolle-des-cio,2979274?utm_source=twitterfeed&utm_medium=twitter (2014). Accessed 2 Jan 2015

Bruckner, A.: Digitalisierung: Nur wer Risiken beherrscht, kann Chancen erfolgreich nutzen, in: Zeitschrift für Internationale Rechnungslegung (IRZ), **1,** 5–6 (2019)

Brugger, T., Czeslik, M., Hager, A., Uebel, M.: Business Transformation mit S/4 HANA, Wiesbaden (2021)

Buxmann, P., König, W.: Zwischenbetriebliche Kooperationen auf Basis von SAP-Systemen, Berlin (2000)

Chapela-Campa, D., Dumas, M.: From process mining to augmented process execution. In: Software and Systems Modeling (2023) https://doi.org/10.1007/s10270-023-01132-2

Chow, R., Golle, P., Jakobsson, M., Shi, E., Steddon, J., Masuoka, R., Molina, J.: Controlling data in the cloud: outsourcing computation without outsourcing control. In: Proceedings CCSW '09 Proceedings of the 2009 ACM workshop on Cloud computing security, S. 85–90, ACM New York, NY, USA ©2009 (2015) https://doi.org/10.1145/1655008.1655020

Czarnecki, C., Bensberg, F., Auth, G.: Die Rolle von Softwarerobotern für die zukünftige Arbeitswelt, in: Praxis der Wirtschaftsinformatik, HMD, **56**, 795–808 (2019) https://doi.org/10.1365/s40702-019-00548-z

Dadam, P., Reichert, M., Rinderle-Ma, S.: Prozessmanagementsysteme, Nur ein wenig Flexibilität wird nicht reichen. In: Informatik Spektrum, **34**(4), 365–376 (2011)

Deloitte (eds.): Die Roboter kommen, Die unsichtbare Revolution im Einkauf (01.03.2017). https://www2.deloitte.com/content/dam/Deloitte/de/Documents/operations/Deloitte_Operations_Robotics_Die-Roboter-kommen_03-2017.pdf (2017). Accessed 28 Mar 2019

Freund, J.: Klartext: „RPA entwickelt sich immer häufiger zu einem süßen Gift" – Warum RPA die Transformation behindert. https://www.it-finanzmagazin.de/klartext-rpa-gift-transformation-85578/ (2019). Accessed 22 Febr 2019

Gadatsch, A.: Die Möglichkeiten von Big Data voll ausschöpfen. Controll. Manage. Rev. Sonderheft **1**, 62–66 (2016)

Gartner (eds.): Process-Mining Reviews and Ratings. https://www.gartner.com/reviews/market/process-mining (2021). Accessed 28 Nov 2021

Gehring, H.: Betriebliche Anwendungssysteme, Kurseinheit 2. FernUniversität Hagen, Hagen, Prozessorientierte Gestaltung von Informationssystemen (1998)

Google Trends: Schlagwortsuche „Big Data". https://www.google.de/trends (2015). Accessed 2. Nov. 2015

Häuser, M., Schmidt, A.: Robotic Process Automation (RPA). Comput. Recht. **34**(4), 266–276 (2018). https://doi.org/10.9785/cr-2018-340412

Heilmann, H., Etzel, H.-J., Richter, R.: IT-Projektmanagement – Fallstricke und Erfolgsfaktoren. Erfahrungsberichte aus der Praxis, 2. überarbeitete und erweiterte Auflage, Heidelberg (2003)

IPD: Institut für Informations- und Prozessmanagement (IPD). FH Münster, IPD-Praxisimpuls, Prozessmanagement ist tot, lang lebe Prozessmanagement **08**(06), 2021 (2021)

Klein, D., Tran-Gia, P., Hartmann, M.: Big Data. In: Informatik-Spektrum, **36**(3), 319–323 (2013)

Koehler, J.: Zum Begriff der Künstlichen Intelligenz, t in: Handbuch Künstliche Intelligenz und die Künste, eds. von Stephanie Catani und Jasmin Pfeiffer, Reihe „De Gruyter Reference", De Gruyter Verlag Berlin (2021)

Krcmar, H. (1993). Computerunterstützung für die Gruppenarbeit — Computer Aided Team (CATeam). In: Kurbel, K. (Hrsg) Wirtschaftsinformatik '93. Physica-Verlag HD. (1993). https://doi.org/10.1007/978-3-642-52400-4_31

Kühl, S.: Wenn die Affen den Zoo regieren, Frankfurt, 6. edn. (2015)

Lassen, S., Lücke, Th.: IT-Projektmanagement in der modernen Softwareentwicklung. In: Projektmanagement, **1**, 18–28 (2003)

Legg, S., Markus, H.: „A Collection of Definitions of Intelligence". Technical Report 07–07, IDSIA Lugano (2007)

Löchner, A.: Künstliche Intelligenz. In: Der andere Sport. Springer Gabler, Wiesbaden (2024) https://doi.org/10.1007/978-3-658-46873-6_3

Loos, P.: Dezentrale Planung und Steuerung in der Fertigung – quo vadis? In: Organisationsstrukturen und Informationssysteme auf dem Prüfstand. 18. Saarbrücker Arbeitstagung 1997 für Industrie, Dienstleistung und Verwaltung, pp. 83–99. Heidelberg (1997)

Markowetz, A.: Digitaler Burnout. Warum unsere permanente Smartphone-Nutzung gefährlich ist, München (2015)

Martin, R., Mauterer, H., Gemünden, H.-G.: Systematisierung des Nutzens von ERP-Systemen in der Fertigungsindustrie. In: Wirtschaftsinformatik, **44**(2), 109–116 (2002)

Maucher, I.: ERP-Einführung: Den komplexen Wandel bewältigen. In: Zeitschrift für industrielle Geschäftsprozessen, **4**, 23–26 (2001)

Mauterer, H.: Der Nutzen von ERP-Systemen, Eine Analyse am Beispiel von SAP R/3, Wiesbaden (2002)

Münzl, G., Reti, M., Schäfer, J., Sondermann, K., Weber, M.: Cloud Computing – Evolution in der Technik, Revolution im Business. https://pdfs.semanticscholar.org/e8cc/ea9f497fc4d7f715dbd-55c618e82b220d1c5.pdf (2009). Accessed 19 June 2019

Nägele, R., Schreiner, P.: Bewertung von Werkzeugen für das Management von Geschäftsprozessen. In: Zeitschrift für Organisation, **71**(4), 201–210 (2002)

Petersen, J., Schröder, H.: Entwicklung einer Robotic Process Automation (RPA)-Governance. In: HMD, **57**, 1130–1149 (2020). https://doi.org/10.1365/s40702-020-00659-y

Pommerin, S. (GBTEC): Synergien entfesseln zwischen BPM, EAM und KI, 22. PzM Summit (Vortragsunterlagen) Wien (2024)

Reijers, H.: Business Process Management: The evolution of a discipline. In: Computers in Industry, **126**, 10344. https://www.sciencedirect.com/science/article/pii/S0166361521000117 (2021). Accessed 29 Mar 2021

Schiklang, M., Förth, J., Kraus, S.: BARC Score Robotic Process Automation DACH, Publikation: 04. Juni 2019, https://barc.de/products/score-rpa (2019). Accessed 10 July 2019

Seufert, A., Bernhardt, N.: Business Intelligence und Cloud-Computing, HMD, **275**(47), 39 (2010)

Siepmann, D., Roth, A.: Industrie 4.0 Ausblick. In Roth, A. (eds.) Einführung und Umsetzung von Industrie 4.0, pp. 247–260. Berlin und Heidelberg (2016)

Skopevisio AG: Wie finde ich das passende ERP-System? White Paper, Bonn. www.scopevisio. com (2025). Accessed 27 Febr 2025

Tsingeni, V., Knuppertz, Th., Gadatsch, A.: Process Mining erfolgreich im Mittelstand anwenden, White Paper, Köln und Sankt Augustin (2022)

van der Aalst, W.M.P.: Process Mining, Berlin und Heidelberg (2011)

van der Aalst, W.M.P., Bichler, M., Heinzl, A.: Robotic Process Automation. Bus. Inf. Syst. Eng. **60**, 269 (2019)

Werth, D., Greff, T., Scheer, A.-W.: Consulting 4.0 – Die Digitalisierung der Unternehmensberatung, HMD, **53,** 55–70 (2016). https://doi.org/10.1365/s40702-015-0198-1

Williams, D.: How is RPA different from other enterprise automation tools such als BPM/ODM? (10.07.2017). https://www.ibm.com/blogs/insights-on-business/gbs-strategy/rpa-different-enterprise-automation-tools-bpmodm/ (2017). Accessed 28 Mar 2019

Ziche, C.: Leveraging Large Language Models for Process Modelling in Organizations – A Practical Examination. In: ERCIS Master Theses Series, Münster (2024). https://doi.org/10.17879/04968695630

Case Study: Process Management

7

7.1 Introduction to the Case Study "Bicycle Shop"

The case study "Bicycle Shop" describes a fictional company that sells, services, and rents bicycles, e-bikes, and home fitness equipment to both private and corporate customers on a larger scale. This section aims to illustrate, in a simplified manner, how the process management methods presented can be applied in practical situations.

7.1.1 Historical Development

The company operates from a large, conveniently located site that houses administration, salesrooms, workshop, a café for customers and staff, as well as the online shop and warehouse. Test rides can be conducted on the company's own premises. A large parking lot allows both customers and staff to park cars and bicycles.

Staff numbers fluctuate significantly throughout the year. In spring and summer, the core team is supplemented by seasonal temporary workers. In autumn and winter, the number of employees is lower, so that over the course of the year, approximately 90–160 people are employed.

Initially, the company only performed bicycle repairs. Later, it expanded into the sale of bicycles and e-bikes and gradually increased its retail space. This was accompanied by capacity expansions, especially in the workshop.

To compensate for seasonal fluctuations, the company invested in the new business area of "sales of fitness equipment" (treadmills, cross trainers, etc.).

Online retail was later added after it became clear that customers increasingly wanted to use this channel (especially for accessories, but also for bikes and clothing).

© The Author(s), under exclusive license to Springer Fachmedien Wiesbaden GmbH, part of Springer Nature 2026
A. Gadatsch, *Business Process Management*,
https://doi.org/10.1007/978-3-658-49339-4_7

Occasional customer events (e.g., lectures, guided bike tours) serve marketing and customer relations purposes.

7.1.2   Current Situation

In the beginning, the company was still very manageable. Staff knew each other personally, and the organizational structure was very flat. Processes were undocumented, apart from a few checklists for sales or the workshop. Due to the "corona effect," demand for bicycles increased sharply from 2020 onwards.

This led to an expansion of the business. The previous "workshop organization," with few departments and undocumented roles and processes, resulted in numerous disruptions to business operations. In particular, the need for coordination between departments and staff increased. As management plans to open additional locations, it wants to first put the company's organization "to the test" and optimize it. Meanwhile, the market for bicycles, e-bikes, and fitness equipment has cooled somewhat, threatening the company's profitability. Management aims to reduce internal costs and improve workflows for customers in order to differentiate itself from nearby competitors (both regional and online).

7.1.3   Project Progress—Approach Model

Management has decided to commission an external consulting firm to conduct a business and process analysis in order to restructure and improve them in terms of cost and performance.

For this purpose, the process management lifecycle will be used as the approach model, applying the most common methods. This is illustrated in Fig. 7.1.

In the first phase, the business model is defined, which can be described using the "Business Model Canvas" method. From this, a process map is then derived, describing the company's key processes (management, core, and support processes). This is followed by the as-is analysis and redesign of selected processes, which can be documented professionally using various methods (eEPK, Swimlane, BPMN). During implementation, technical modeling takes place, for example using the "BPMN" method or directly through customizing and/or programming in "Workflow Management Systems" (WFMS), Robotic Process Automation tools (RPA), or Enterprise Resource Planning systems (ERP). In the execution and controlling phase, processes are executed using the aforementioned systems. Process controlling can be performed using a "Process Scorecard" and supported by "Process Mining" tools. Additionally, process mining tools can already be used in the first phase for process documentation.

Fig. 7.1 Process management life cycle and possible use of methods and tools

7.2 Project Progress of the "Bicycle Shop" Case Study

7.2.1 Business Model

The consulting firm commissioned for the project first conducts several workshops with the management team and selected specialists from sales, the workshop, and administration in order to gain an overview of the business model.

To this end, an initial unsorted list of processes ("process list") is created, reflecting the company's key core activities, which are presented here in excerpted form only:

- Advising customers in the shop,
- Selling new products (bikes, fitness equipment, accessories),
- Selling used products (only bikes taken in as trade-ins),
- Repairing bikes,
- Sending fitness equipment to manufacturers for repair,
- Leasing company bikes through corporate clients,
- Operating an online shop,
- Shipping and receiving products via delivery service,
- Sending invoices to corporate customers, including reminders if necessary,
- Processing payments in the shop and online shop (cash, card, PayPal, Apple Pay, etc.),
- Creating staff deployment schedules,
- Carrying out logistics processes (procurement, storage, retrieval),

- Handling complaints,
- Processing thefts and damages from a legal and accounting perspective (e.g., police reports, insurance claims).

Based on intensive discussions, the method "Business Canvas Model (BMV)" introduced in Sect. 5.2 can be applied to create a clear business model, which is illustrated in Fig. 7.2.

7.2.2 Process Map

The previously created Business Model Canvas provides a solid foundation for developing a process map (see also the discussion in Sect. 5.3), which depicts the key processes of the bicycle shop. It is important to ensure that, based on the process list, not all detailed processes are included, but rather a balanced structure is chosen at the top level.

In practice, the process map is developed in the form of facilitated workshops, to which company representatives who are well acquainted with the current processes are invited. The group should, and indeed must, be cross-hierarchical to ensure the most accurate representation of the current situation. The purpose of the process map should be explained to participants in detail beforehand, so that processes and process steps are not confused with departments, functions, or responsibilities.

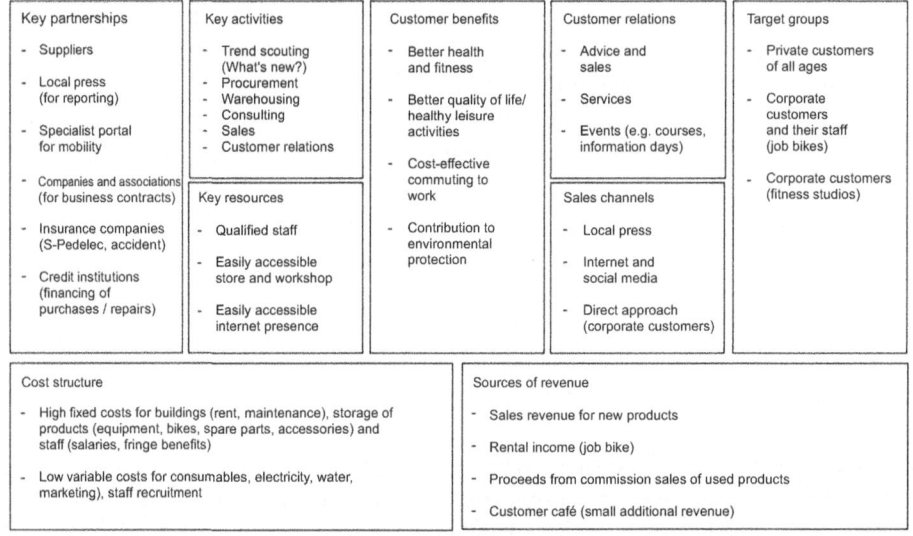

Fig. 7.2 Case Study: Bicycle Shop—Business Model Canvas

Figure 7.3 shows a process map that could have been developed in such a workshop. It displays the three core processes "Handling private sales," "Handling business customer processes," and "Handling service processes," each with more detailed business process steps. The management processes (top) and support processes (bottom) are shown only at the top level.

7.2.3   Process Scorecard

The process scorecard plays an important role in both strategic and operational process management. Objectives, key performance indicators, target values, and measures are typically developed using a top-down and bottom-up countercurrent approach. The management of the bicycle shop aims to reduce costs and improve process performance.

This should also be reflected in an appropriate process scorecard. Such a scorecard can be created for the entire company as well as for key processes, for example, the core processes.

Since it is generally unrealistic in practice to define key performance indicators for all processes, processes should be prioritized, for example, according to urgency. This can be done using a "heat map," where workshop participants mark the processes on the process map with points to indicate where the most significant problems are that need to be addressed.

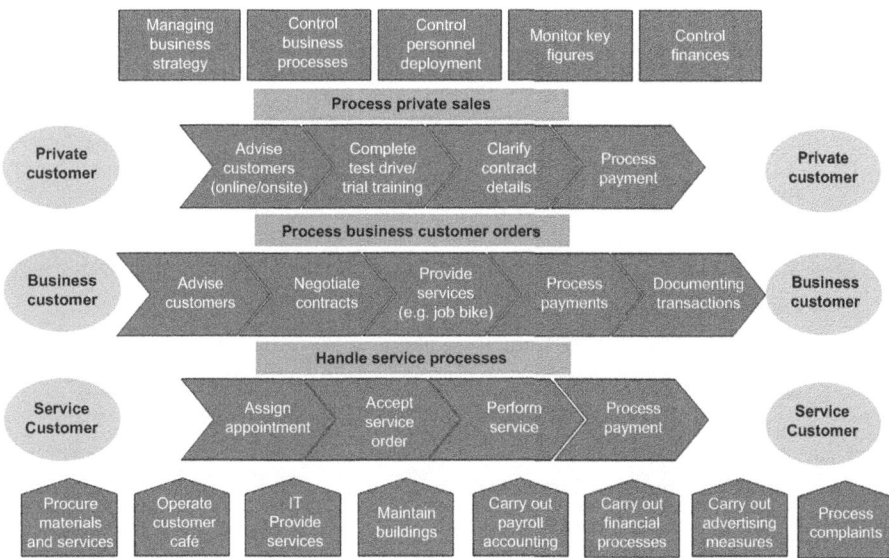

Fig. 7.3   Case Study: Process Map

In this case, we assume that the process "Handling Private Sales" is one of the highest-revenue processes, but it also records a comparatively high number of complaints (e.g., long waiting times at the checkout in the store, long waiting times for pickup in the warehouse, long waiting times for service appointments, long service times for repairs and inspections). Many customers have reported that these processes are handled more quickly at nearby competitors. Therefore, this process was selected, and objectives, key performance indicators, target values for the future, and the necessary measures were identified. The process scorecard in Fig. 7.4 documents these results.

7.2.4   Process Organization

Management has repeatedly received indications from various sources (e.g., staff, customers, suppliers) that the current organization of the company is not conducive to seamless, customer-oriented processes, as there are recurring inefficiencies. The project team first creates an organizational chart of the current situation (see Fig. 7.5) and conducts an analysis.

The company structure is primarily organized by function. Cross-departmental workflows (processes) are not documented, but have instead become embedded in the "minds" of the staff over time.

Process scorecard for the "Handle private sales" process

Customer					Process performance			
Target	Key figures	Target values	Measures		Target	Key figures	Target values	Measures
Achieve high customer satisfaction	Sales per customer	+2%	Survey customers after purchase Organize customer events		Perform sales / service faster than competition	Sales lead time	< 2 h	Carry out process analysis Benchmarking with competition
	Number of customer complaints	Percentage <1%	Handle complaints quickly			Processing time for services	<1 h	Support processes digitally

Resources/personnel					Financials			
Target	Key figures	Target values	Measures		Target	Key figures	Target values	Measures
Staff trained to meet requirements and ready for deployment	Number of training days/ employee	5 days per year	Compare requirements with training status Create training plan		Positive deca- sion contribution per sales or service order	DB%/ turnover per customer	DBk > 30%	Customer ABC analysis Product ABC analysis
	Keeping appointments with customers	Percentage >99%	Monitor customer appointments			DB%/per product	DBk > 30%	Align product prices with competition

Fig. 7.4   Process scorecard for the process "Handling Private Sales"

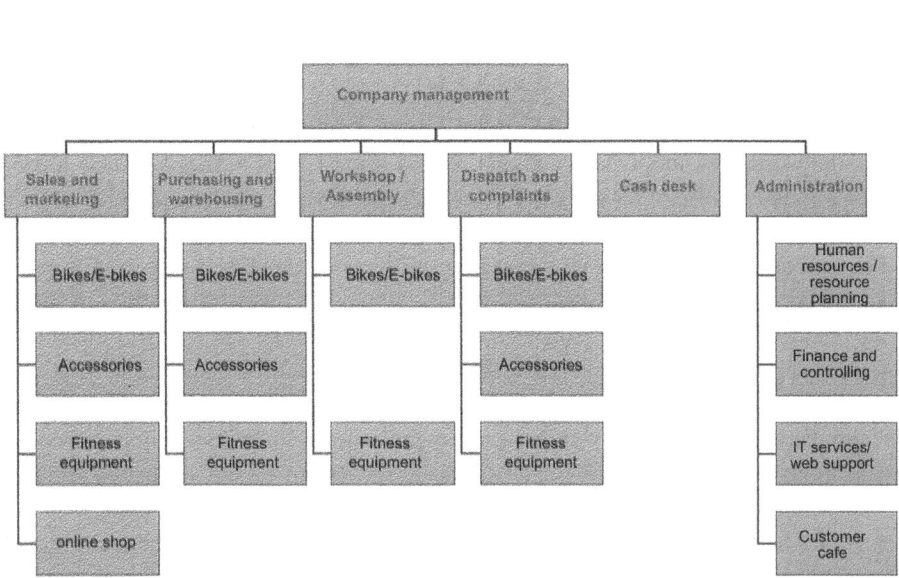

Fig. 7.5 Current organizational chart of the bicycle shop

There are departments for Sales and Marketing with substructures for the product groups "Bicycles / E-Bikes," "Accessories," "Fitness Equipment," and the "Online Shop," which offers all of the aforementioned products. The departments "Purchasing and Inventory Management" as well as "Shipping and Complaints" are organized in a similar way. The Cash Desk department is responsible for payment processes across the company, except for the café, which operates its own cash register. Administration is divided into several groups for HR, Finance, IT, and Facility Management. Tasks that are not assigned to a specific department are handled by company management.

The lack of documented or formalized processes leads to media discontinuities and coordination problems between the various departments. According to an initial analysis, the following situations are typical:

- During the sales process, no complimentary initial inspection appointment is scheduled for customers. As a result, when customers later request an appointment, they are often not prioritized to receive an inspection within the warranty period, leading to complaints about the resulting costs.
- Information transfer in the sales and complaints processes of the online shop is not integrated, but is sometimes handled manually using printouts, Excel spreadsheets, or similar solutions.

- In the sales process, accessories are sometimes offered that are not available at the time the assembled bicycle is handed over.
- Inventory levels are not always up to date, as withdrawals are sometimes not recorded. This leads to complications, especially in online sales, when products that are not in stock are displayed as "available."
- Processes are not reproducible, but instead depend on individual staff members. Process knowledge is not documented, but resides in the minds of the staff. Due to staff turnover and the use of many seasonal workers, processes are often carried out differently, which has already led to customer complaints and supplier grievances.
- Private customers who are also business customers cannot be viewed as a single entity. For example, a large medical practice leased job bikes for its staff. However, the practice owner was not recognized as a private individual and was prioritized for a service appointment for his private bike, which caused him frustration.

The company's project team is considering organizational alternatives. A pure process organization, i.e., structuring the organization entirely by processes, seems too complex for the company, as central resources such as inventory, workshop, shipping, or cash desk would have to be maintained multiple times. As a starting point, the team is considering introducing a staff organization with process owners who are professionally responsible for process integration. This would enable processes to be identified, documented, and monitored.

The process owners will be selected from the "Sales and Marketing" department, giving them a dual role in the sense of a matrix organization. However, the company is also aware that this solution may lead to conflicts. All cross-departmental activities will be consolidated in the shared service area "Central Services."

The revised organizational chart of the company is shown in Fig. 7.6.

7.2.5   Modeling and Analysis of a Selected Process

The next step involved modeling and analyzing selected processes. For this purpose, a workshop is held using the process map (see Fig. 7.3) to first select those processes that are particularly important for the company. Due to space constraints, the case study focuses on a single process: the immediate purchase of bicycles and e-bikes by private customers. This process (see the BPMN model in Fig. 7.7) generates high sales and contribution margins, but also exhibits a number of weaknesses.

The process is then examined for weaknesses. These are visualized in the BPMN diagram in Fig. 7.8. Virtually every process step shows potential for improvement.

No IT Support for Consultation
Customer consultations are conducted entirely without IT support, such as an app. With IT assistance, information such as inventory levels, prices for bikes or accessories, and

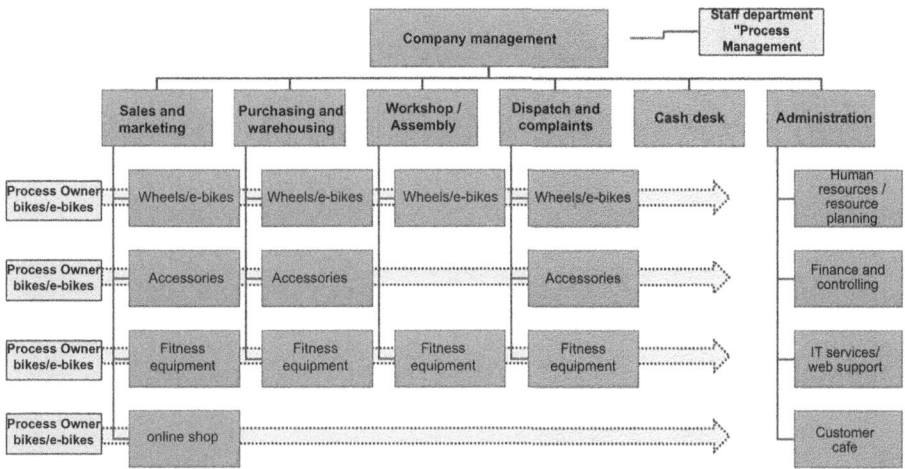

Fig. 7.6 Target organizational chart of the bicycle shop

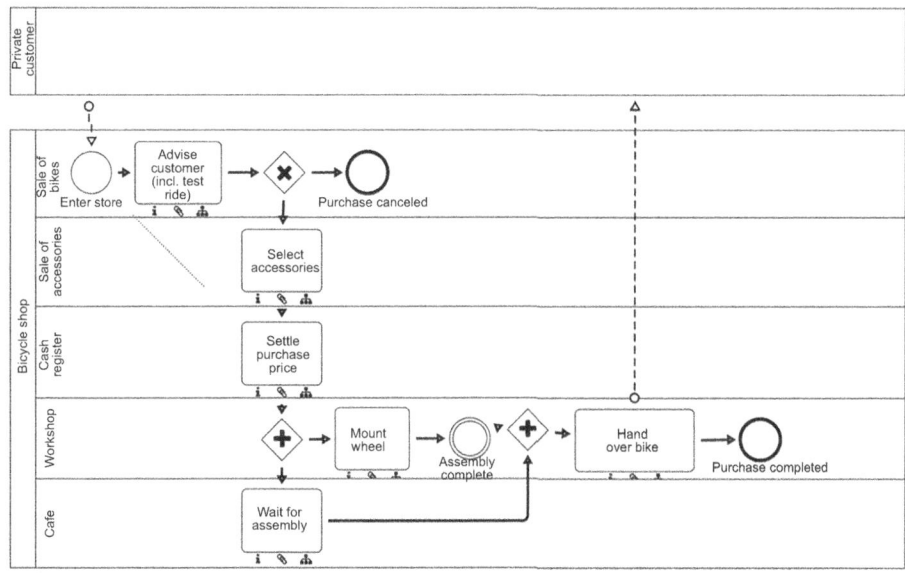

Fig. 7.7 Case Study: As-Is Process for Immediate Purchase of Bicycles and E-Bikes by Private Customers

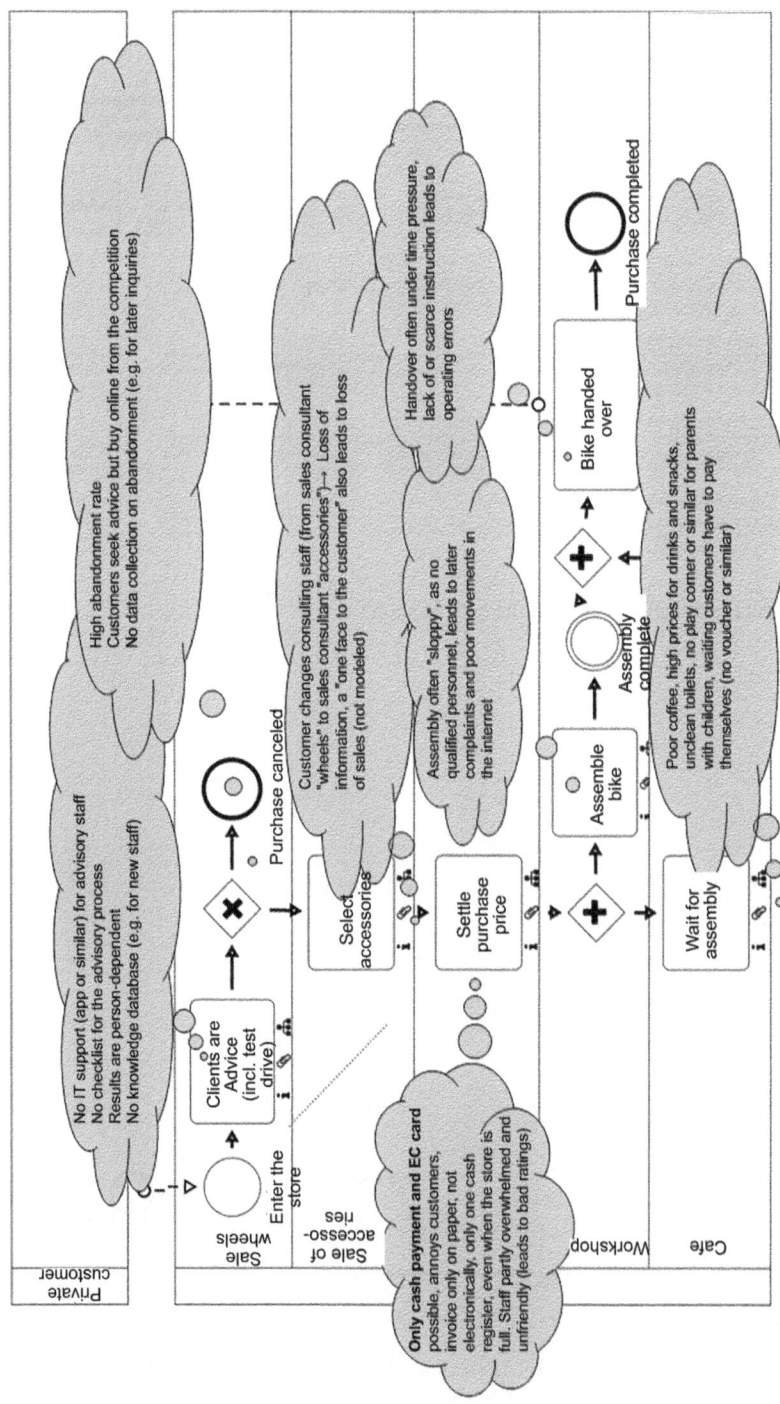

Fig. 7.8 Case Study: As-Is Process for Immediate Purchase of Bicycles by Private Customers with Visualization of Weaknesses

other data could be accessed. There is also no checklist for the consultation process, making the results highly dependent on the individual, as process knowledge varies greatly and is retained in the minds of the consulting staff.

A knowledge database (e.g., for new staff) is not available. As a result, newly hired employees cannot access the knowledge of existing staff without asking.

High Dropout Rate After Consultation

Overall, the dropout rate after consultations is very high. Many customers receive extensive advice but later make their purchases from competitors or online. Data from the consultation is not recorded, so there is no way to analyze it or to follow up with the customer at a later time.

It is not possible to schedule appointments for consultations. During periods of high customer traffic, this leads to insufficient staff on site and causes interested customers to leave the store prematurely in frustration.

Staff Change During the Purchase Process

Customers are handed over to different staff members when moving from the consultation to accessory selection, as the departments operate separately and are paid on commission. This results in loss of information and, in some cases, (not modeled) cancellations of the sales process.

Outdated Payment Process

The bike shop only accepts cash or debit card payments, which frustrates many customers. Receipts are only provided in paper form, not electronically. The store operates with only one checkout, even when it is crowded; staff are often overwhelmed and perceived as unfriendly. This leads to many negative online reviews.

Outdated Café Service

Customers spend an average of 30–90 minutes in the café waiting for their bike to be handed over. Poor coffee, high prices for drinks and snacks, unclean restrooms, and the lack of a play area for parents with children make the wait unpleasant for many customers. In addition, customers who have just spent several thousand euros on a bike must pay for their own drinks, as the sales staff do not provide vouchers.

Poor Assembly and Handover

The assembly of sold bikes is often "sloppy" because there is not enough qualified staff available. This leads to subsequent complaints and negative online reviews. The handover of the bikes often takes place under time pressure. Instructions on how to use the bike are sometimes incomplete or missing altogether. This results in user errors by customers and subsequent complaints.

Tab. 7.1 Optimization of the Immediate Purchase Process for Bicycles by Private Customers (model based on Bleicher 1991, modified)

No.	Concept	Explanation
1	Eliminate	Paper invoices should be omitted if customers prefer to receive an electronic invoice
2	Outsource	The in-house café should be operated by a professional service provider. This provider should be managed through performance targets to ensure a pleasant experience for waiting customers and potential clients
3	Combine	The steps "conduct consultation" and "select accessories" should be supported by the same person who provided the consultation
4	Parallelize	The consultation, sales, and payment process should be integrated via an app, allowing IT-savvy customers to be advised and accompanied by a single person through to contract completion. In parallel, assembly can be initiated online once it is clear that the contract will be concluded
5	Relocate	The assembly of bicycles ordered online should be prioritized. In addition, all common bicycle models should be pre-assembled and kept in stock so that handover can take place "immediately" after a brief quality check
6	Accelerate	Consultation appointments should be available spontaneously (possibly with waiting time) or prioritized through prior scheduling (online, by phone, or via app). Payment options should be expanded to include common modern methods (Apple Pay, PayPal, etc.)
7	Avoid loops	
8	Supplement	To prevent consultation errors, an app with standard procedures and checklists should be developed for the sales staff. The consultation can then be digitally supported by the app up to contract signing and payment To avoid complaints, assembly should be quality-assured by a second person. Staff must receive additional training regarding assembly work and bicycle handover. Checklists should also be developed for this purpose. The assembly and handover processes must be documented

Source: Own illustration based on Bleicher 1991

7.2.6   Optimization of the Selected Process

The optimization of the previously analyzed process will be carried out using the process optimization framework already introduced (see Table 7.1).

7.3   Lessons Learned

Process management is, first and foremost, about the overarching interaction of people and, secondly, a matter of technology. Often, process management is initially associated with digital technologies. While these are necessary, they are not sufficient for success.

This case study has demonstrated how common process management methods can be applied. However, it is important to experience it firsthand, as many aspects of a real project cannot be captured in an introductory textbook like this one. The practice of process management is significantly more complex than can be presented here.

Students interested in process management should therefore take every opportunity to deepen the knowledge acquired in this book or elsewhere through real-world projects. These may include practical projects or thesis work in a professional setting.

The manufacturer's authorised representative in the EU is Springer
Nature Customer Service Centre GmbH, Europaplatz 3, 69115 Heidelberg,
Germany. If you have any concerns regarding our products, please
contact ProductSafety@springernature.com

Printed and bound by CPI Group (UK) Ltd, Croydon, CR0 4YY

23/04/2026

02095592-0017